WMO

Tolley's
Managing Fixed-Term and
Part-Time Workers

A practical guide to employing temporary and
part-time staff

by

Lynda A C Macdonald MA FCIPD LCM

Tolley
LexisNexis™

Members of the LexisNexis Group worldwide

United Kingdom	LexisNexis Butterworths Tolley, a Division of Reed Elsevier (UK) Ltd, 2 Addiscombe Road, CROYDON CR9 5AF
Argentina	LexisNexis Argentina, BUENOS AIRES
Australia	LexisNexis Butterworths, CHATSWOOD, New South Wales
Austria	LexisNexis Verlag ARD Orac GmbH & Co KG, VIENNA
Canada	LexisNexis Butterworths, MARKHAM, Ontario
Chile	LexisNexis Chile Ltda, SANTIAGO DE CHILE
Czech Republic	Nakladatelství Orac sro, PRAGUE
France	Editions du Juris-Classeur SA, PARIS
Hong Kong	LexisNexis Butterworths, HONG KONG
Hungary	HVG-Orac, BUDAPEST
India	LexisNexis Butterworths, NEW DELHI
Ireland	Butterworths (Ireland) Ltd, DUBLIN
Italy	Giuffrè Editore, MILAN
Malaysia	Malayan Law Journal Sdn Bhd, KUALA LUMPUR
New Zealand	LexisNexis Butterworths, WELLINGTON
Poland	Wydawnictwo Prawnicze LexisNexis, WARSAW
Singapore	LexisNexis Butterworths, SINGAPORE
South Africa	Butterworths SA, DURBAN
Switzerland	Stämpfli Verlag AG, BERNE
USA	LexisNexis, DAYTON, Ohio

A CIP Catalogue record for this book is available from the British Library.

ISBN 0 75451 662-8

Typeset by Tradespools Ltd, Frome, Somerset
Printed and bound in Great Britain by Hobbs the Printers Ltd, Totton, Hampshire

Visit Butterworths LexisNexis *direct* at www.butterworths.com

Note About the Author

Lynda Macdonald is a self-employed, freelance employment law advisor, management trainer, and writer. For fifteen years, prior to setting up her own consultancy business, she gained substantial practical experience of employee relations, recruitment and selection, dismissal procedures, employment law and other aspects of human resource management through working in industry. With this solid background in human resource management, she successfully established, and currently runs, her own business in employment law and management training/consultancy. She is also appointed as a panel member of the Employment Tribunal service in Aberdeen, where she lives.

Lynda is a university graduate in language and a Fellow of the Chartered Institute of Personnel and Development. Additionally, she has an LLM degree in employment law.

She is the author of Tolley's Managing E-mail and Internet Use.

Others in this Series

Also in this series:

Managing Dismissals: Practical guidance on the art of dismissing fairly– 075451255X
Managing Business Transfers: TUPE and takeovers, mergers and outsourcing–
075451661X
**Managing E-mail and Internet Use: A practical guide to employers' obligations and
employees' rights**– 0754513947
**Managing Sickness and Maternity Pay: A comprehensive guide to payroll practice
and procedure**– 0754519899

Related books from Tolley:

Payroll Management Handbook, 16th edition– 0754517500
Employment Tribunals Handbook: Practice, procedure and strategies for success–
0754514889

Other books from IRS:

IRS Managing Employee Representatives– 0754519546
IRS Managing Diversity in the Workplace– 0754519554
IRS Managing Absence and Leave– 0754519538

Visit our website:

www.payrollalliance.com

For further information on Tolley books, please contact Customer Services on 020 8662
2000 (or by fax on 020 8662 2012). For further information on IRS books, please contact
the Marketing Department on 020 7354 6747.

Preface

Traditionally, the conventional model of working life has been the full-time, permanent (or open-ended) contract. The world of employment is, however, changing rapidly and in the last two decades employment relationships have diversified into an array of different patterns, many of which lie outside the mainstream of employment legislation. Employers may elect to engage workers on one of a range of different types of contract. Whilst the so-called 'permanent' employment contract is still the most common form of employment, atypical arrangements for engaging staff are becoming more common, and afford many advantages for employers and workers alike.

The scope of employment protection legislation

Employment protection legislation was originally devised primarily to protect individuals employed on full-time, permanent employment contracts with a single employer. Nowadays, however, many people choose to work part-time or on a casual basis, or for a variety of reasons seek and accept temporary contracts. The use of fixed-term contracts in particular has become very popular with employers. Other individuals choose to work for a range of employers through employment agencies or their own limited company. A rise in the cost of further education has led to a larger number of students seeking temporary or part-time work. This diversity of working relationships and patterns has created legal divides between 'employees', 'workers' and self-employed people, each of whom have different rights and entitlements in law.

UK employment law

The dilemma of different groups of workers having different employment rights has to an extent been recognised and addressed both in the UK and by the European Union. Thus employment law in the UK is heading steadily in the direction of equality of treatment for workers engaged on temporary and part-time contracts. Furthermore, it is likely that the distinction between employees and workers engaged on other forms of contract will be further reduced or even removed in the future for the purposes of statutory employment rights.

Back in 1998, the UK Government emphasised in its 'Fairness at Work' White Paper the importance of extending employment rights to those currently exempted from such entitlements because of their employment status as workers (as opposed to employees). Subsequently the *Employment Relations Act 1999* was enacted with a provision in *section 23* that authorises the Secretary of State to make Regulations to extend many existing employment rights to workers who are not engaged on a contract of employment. If such Regulations are introduced in the future, workers such as contract staff, casual workers, etc will become entitled to a range of employment rights from which they are currently exempted. At present, however, certain statutory employment protection rights (in particular the right to claim unfair dismissal, redundancy pay entitlement and maternity rights) are still unavailable to workers who are not engaged on a contract of employment.

A further barrier for many is that certain employment protection rights require a minimum qualifying period of continuous service with the result that many temporary workers and workers whose working patterns involve frequent gaps between periods of employment do not acquire sufficient continuous service to gain protection. Importantly, the right to claim unfair dismissal requires a minimum of one year's continuous service, whilst an employee must have worked for two years continuously in order to be eligible for statutory redundancy pay.

The influence of EC law

The European Union, having recognised that workers engaged on atypical contracts are often exploited by employers because they have limited employment protection rights has adopted measures to improve the entitlements of such atypical workers. Since 1983 there has been a series of draft Directives that have sought to provide atypical workers with equal benefits (on a pro-rata basis) to those available to full-time, permanent employees. As a result, the *Part-Time Workers (Prevention of Less Favourable treatment) Regulations 2000* were brought into force in the UK in July 2000, whilst the *Fixed-Term Employees (Prevention of Less Favourable treatment) Regulations* are set to be implemented in July 2002. Other measures to afford protection to agency workers and casual workers are underway.

Discrimination law

Another pertinent issue is that the majority of workers with non–standard patterns of employment or working arrangements are women. Examples are part–time working, casual working, temping through agencies and to some extent home-working. As a result, there is a comprehensive body of case law demonstrating that less favourable treatment of part-time workers in particular equates to indirect sex discrimination.

Conclusion

This book aims to address the management of temporary and part-time workers by exploring the many different types of contract, their implications and individuals' rights under each type of contract. The issues of employment status, continuity of employment and avoiding sex discrimination against temporary and part-time workers are also covered in depth.

Contents

Contents

Table of Cases

Table of Statutes

Table of Statutory Instruments

1. Employment Status and Statutory Rights

Introduction [1.1]

Many statutory employment rights are available only to employees, i.e. those engaged under a contract of employment (sometimes known as a 'contract of service'). By contrast, individuals engaged under a contract for services have limited statutory employment rights, although the trend in recent years has been for new legislation to cover all workers, whether employed directly or engaged indirectly.

A part-time, temporary or fixed-term worker may be employed under a contract of employment, or alternatively may be engaged under a contract for services. This chapter aims to explore the distinction between employees and workers, and the implications of this distinction.

A further potential hurdle for temporary and fixed-term workers is that certain statutory employment rights depend on a minimum period of service, for example the right to claim unfair dismissal (which is available only to employees and not other workers) requires a minimum qualifying period of service of one year. Continuity of service is dealt with fully in CHAPTER 6.

The Distinction Between Employees, Workers and the Self-Employed [1.2]

There are no universal definitions of 'employee' or 'worker'. Some help is at hand, however, by dint of *section 230(1)* of the *Employment Rights Act 1996* which defines an 'employee' as 'an individual who has entered into or works under a contract of employment'. Thus the existence of a contract of employment establishes the relationship of employer/employee between the parties.

By contrast, a contract for services implies the appointment of an independent contractor or someone working on a freelance basis. Such a person is usually referred to as a 'worker'. *Section 230(3)* of the *Employment Rights Act* defines a 'worker' as:

1

'An individual who has entered into or works under ... a contract of employment or any other contract ... whereby the individual undertakes to do or perform personally any work or services for another party to the contract whose status is not by virtue of the contract that of a client or customer of any profession or business undertaking carried on by the individual'.

Thus a worker is someone who provides their services personally to the organisation with whom they contract, even though they are not regarded as an employee. The definition means that a wide range of people (for example casual workers, freelance workers, agency staff and certain independent contractors) can be classed as workers, provided the other party to the contract is not their client or customer.

A third category outside the scope of the definitions of 'employee' and 'worker' is the self-employed entrepreneur whose relationship with the organisation for whom they work is that of client/service provider, i.e. the person is in business on their own account and the organisation for whom they provide their services is their client or customer. Although some self-employed people can be classed as 'workers' for the purposes of certain employment protection legislation, the genuinely self-employed entrepreneur cannot. Examples of self-employed individuals whose contracts are with clients as opposed to employers could be solicitors or barristers who represent their clients in legal proceedings, and joiners and electricians who personally perform skilled work for individual customers.

In *Byrne Brothers (Formwork) Ltd v Baird IRLR 683*, however, the EAT held that four carpenters who worked on assignments for a building contractor – purportedly on a self-employed basis – were 'workers'. This was because they provided their carpentry services personally and did not run their own individual businesses, as the company contended.

There is one exception to the general principle that self-employed people in business on their own account are not covered by employment protection legislation. All four anti-discrimination laws (the *Sex Discrimination Act 1975*, the *Equal Pay Act 1970*, the *Race Relations Act 1976* and the *Disability Discrimination Act 1995*) avoid the distinction between 'employee' and 'worker' and instead refer to 'employment'. 'Employment' is defined as employment 'under a contract of service or of apprenticeship or a contract personally to execute any work or labour'. This definition is to be found in *section 82(1)* of the *Sex Discrimination Act 1975, section 1(6)* of the *Equal Pay Act 1970* and *section 78(1)* of the *Race Relations Act 1976*. Very similar wording appears in *section 68(1)* of the *Disability Discrimination Act 1995*. Thus individuals who provide their services personally for a client or customer are protected against sex, race and disability discrimination, even though they cannot enjoy most other employment protection rights.

The Implications of the Distinction Between Employees and Workers [1.3]

Case law over many years has made it apparent that the distinction between a contract of employment and a contract for services can be blurred, and furthermore that an individual's employment status can be successfully challenged at an employment tribunal. Typically, an individual engaged on a contract for services (who is therefore not an employee) may challenge their status following termination of their contract, or some other dispute with the employing organisation. In that eventuality, an employment tribunal will not regard the label the employer has put on the contract as conclusive proof of the individual's employment status, but will instead examine the actual working relationship between the employer and the worker with a view to judging whether, in reality, it was akin to an employment contract. Although the stated intention of the parties is a relevant factor, it is not the sole determinant of employment status, as it is only one factor amongst many others (see **1.30** below). Clearly, if it were otherwise, it would be too easy for unscrupulous employers to contract out of employment protection legislation and deny a wide range of workers their statutory rights. Essentially, the interpretation of who is an employee and who is a worker will depend on all the circumstances of the particular case, and is based on a long line of case law.

What is clear is that where the evidence is such that the working arrangements and working relationship between employer and worker are in fact typical of an employment contract, the tribunal will decide that the individual is in fact an employee, rather than someone engaged on a contract for services. The status of a self-employed worker or someone working through their own personal service company may also be challenged by the Inland Revenue or the Department of Social Security given the different consequences under tax and social security law (see **CHAPTER 8** at **8.11**).

The Importance of the Distinction [1.4]

The key importance of the distinction between employees and workers is that employees enjoy the full range of statutory employment rights, whilst independent workers have considerably fewer employment protection rights. In particular, the provisions of the *Employment Rights Act 1996*, which include the right to claim unfair dismissal, the right to a statutory redundancy payment and maternity rights, are available only to employees and not other workers. This may be an important distinction to many employers and of course to many workers.

There are other reasons why the distinction between an employee and a worker is important:

- Employers must deduct income tax and national insurance contributions under the PAYE scheme for all their employees. A worker who is self-employed on the other hand can be paid a fee gross of income tax as they will have responsibility for their own taxation and national insurance contributions under Schedule D, which is generally regarded as more advantageous than the tax regime applicable to employees.

- Only employees are entitled to certain social security benefits, e.g. unemployment benefit.

- There are various implied duties imposed on employers in a contract of employment which do not necessarily apply to other workers. These include the duty of trust and confidence, the duty to provide a reasonably suitable working environment and the duty to afford employees the opportunity to obtain redress for any grievance they may have. Employees too have implied duties under a contract of employment, for example a duty to obey reasonable instructions and a duty of fidelity, obligations which are not imposed to the same extent on workers.

Possible Future Provisions   **[1.5]**

It is possible that the distinction between employees and workers engaged on other forms of contract will be removed in the future for the purpose of statutory employment rights. The *Employment Relations Act 1999, s 23* introduced authority for the Secretary of State to make Regulations to extend existing employment rights to workers who are not engaged on contracts of employment. If such Regulations are introduced in the future workers such as contract staff, homeworkers, agency temps, etc may become entitled to the full range of employment rights in the same way as employees. Such a step would have a major impact on many businesses. In the DTI's Explanatory Notes to the Act (para 232), it is stated that the Government is committed to ensuring that:

'all workers other than the genuinely self-employed enjoy the minimum standards of protection that the legislation is intended to provide, and that none are excluded simply because of technicalities relating to the type of contract or other arrangement under which they are engaged'.

Advantages and Disadvantages of Engaging Workers as Opposed to Employees [1.6]

There are various reasons why an employer may wish to engage individuals on a contractor or self-employed basis, rather than engaging them on contracts of employment. These include the following situations:

- Where the work is thought to be of an uncertain or limited duration.
- Where the work output involves seasonal or other peaks with periods of low demand at other times.
- Where the amount of work fluctuates such that no guarantee of a fixed pattern of days or hours can be given.
- Where the employer needs extra resources on an ad hoc or planned basis to cover periods of leave, such as annual holidays, long-term sickness absence, maternity leave and parental leave.
- Where the employer wants to be able to call on additional resources in order to cut down on overtime payments to employees.

The obvious advantage to the employer of engaging workers instead of employees is that workers have no unfair dismissal or redundancy pay rights.

There are, however disadvantages:

- Someone engaged as a worker is less likely than an employee to be committed to the business interests of the employer.
- A worker may not always be available at the times when the employer wishes to recruit extra staff.
- The worker may, in any event, be able to succeed in a challenge that their real status is that of employee.

Model Contractual Clause to Indicate that a Worker is not an Employee [1.7]

The following clauses can be used in contracts to indicate that the employer does not intend to enter into a contract of employment with a worker:

> 'These terms constitute a contract for services between the company and the worker and will not give rise to a contract of employment. There is no mutuality of obligation whatsoever between the company and the worker. The company is not obliged to offer the worker ongoing work, or any minimum amount of work, nor is the worker obliged to accept any offer of work made by the company.'

> 'Throughout the course of this contract, the worker has the right to advertise for, seek and undertake contracts to supply services to other parties.'

> 'The nature of the work covered by this contract is intermittent and of no fixed pattern. There is no obligation on the employer to offer you a minimum amount of work in any given week or month and no obligation on you to accept any minimum amount of work.'

> 'The Worker will be paid a fee of [£ – per hour/per day]. This will be paid monthly in arrears on production of a correct invoice [by cheque/ bank credit transfer] [after deduction of income tax and national insurance].'

> 'You will be paid at the hourly rate of [£—] for all hours worked. This will be paid gross and you will be expected to make your own arrangements as a self-employed person for the payment of income tax and national insurance. You are not an employee of the company.'

> 'It is a condition of the contract that the worker, as a self-employed person, takes out and maintains in force professional indemnity insurance in terms satisfactory to the company, and that the worker exhibits the policy to the company if requested.'

It should be remembered at all times that it is the reality of the working relationship and working arrangements that are important in the event of a challenge to an individual's employment status. Thus no contractual clauses will be capable of creating a contract for services if the actual working relationship is one of employer/employee (see next section).

Criteria for Determining Employment Status [1.8]

Determining whether an individual is employed under a contract of employment, or engaged on a contract for services can be a complex issue.

According to the Court of Appeal in *O'Kelly v Trust House Forte [1983] IRLR 286*, a tribunal tasked with establishing an individual's employment status must consider:

> 'all aspects of the relationship, no single feature being in itself decisive and each of which may vary in weight and direction, and having given such balance to the factors as seems appropriate to determine whether the person was carrying on business on his own account'.

Where an individual elects to challenge their employment status at an employment tribunal, the tribunal will generally hold a preliminary hearing to determine the matter. The tribunal will examine the wording of the contract, assess the intention of the parties, but most importantly analyse the actual working relationship between the parties in order to reach their decision. The wording of the contract is not, by any means, the only relevant factor and where the wording of the contract and the reality of the working arrangements appear to the tribunal to be at variance with each other, the reality of the working arrangements will usually prevail. This means that it is not open to an employer to avoid their responsibilities in employment law by simply issuing a contract that states the individual is not directly employed by the organisation. If the circumstances are otherwise, then the individual will be able to enforce statutory employment rights as an employee.

Thus, there are circumstances where an individual apparently working on a contract for services may be deemed by a tribunal to be an employee, irrespective of the structure or wording of the contract, or even the apparent original intention of the parties. In such a case the worker will in effect gain entitlement to the full range of statutory employment rights.

Tribunals' Approach to Employment Status [1.9]

Over the years, tribunals have developed 'tests' for determining an individual's employment status, where this is being challenged. The following represent the key issues that an employment tribunal will examine:

- Whether there is 'mutuality of obligation' between the parties, i.e. whether the employer is obliged to provide regular employment for

7

the worker, and whether the worker is obliged to accept work when it is offered (see **1.10** below).

- How long the individual has worked for the employer (see **1.10** below).

- Whether or not the individual retains freedom to work for other organisations, and whether they do so in practice (see **1.10** below).

- Whether the individual has an obligation to perform the work personally, or whether they are permitted to provide a substitute (see **1.11** below).

- To what extent the person's work is subject to close control and direction by the company (see **1.14** below).

- Whether the worker works mainly on the employer's premises or from their own workplace (for example from home) (see **1.14** below).

- Whether or not the worker is engaged to carry out work that is an integral part of the employer's business (see **1.15** below).

- The extent to which the individual stands to gain financially, or bears any financial risk as a result of their engagement (see **1.20** below).

- Whether the employer or the worker supplies any tools and equipment that the worker needs to perform the job (see **1.21** below).

- Whether the responsibility for hiring any helpers required to assist the worker in performing their duties lies with the employer or the individual (see **1.22** below).

- How the individual is paid (see **1.24** below).

- Whether tax and national insurance are deducted by the employer or paid directly by the individual (see **1.25** below).

- Whether the individual is registered for VAT (see **1.26** below).

- Whether the worker is required to take out and maintain professional indemnity insurance (see **1.27** below).

- Whether or not the individual receives company benefits like sick pay, medical insurance cover, etc (see **1.28** below).

- Whether the individual is subject to the company's normal disciplinary rules and procedures and grievance procedures (see **1.29** below).

● The intention of the parties (see **1.30** below).

These criteria are examined further below.

Mutuality of Obligation [1.10]

The question of whether there is a reasonable degree of mutuality of obligation between the parties has often been a key determining factor as regards the distinction between an employee and a worker. Essentially, a contract of employment cannot be said to exist unless there is an obligation on the employer to provide work and a corresponding obligation on the individual to perform the work. For example in the case of *Nethermere (St. Neots) Ltd v Taverna and Gardiner [1984] IRLR 240*, the Court of Appeal stated that a contract of employment could exist only if there was a minimum of obligations on both sides. The case centred around two women who worked from home sewing garments. Both workers had some say as regards the amount of work that they would accept (and the time in which they completed it), provided the amount of work was sufficient to justify a company driver making deliveries to their homes. Even though the Court of Appeal found that there was no obligation for the company to continue to provide work, or for the individuals to continue to accept the work, there was a 'well-founded expectation' that the work would continue. The Court commented further that there had been a regular 'giving and taking of work over periods of a year of more' and thus there was sufficient mutuality of obligation for a contract of employment to exist even if at times no work was taken in. They stated the view that, where well-founded expectations of continuing work existed, these expectations could develop into an enforceable contract of employment through a regular course of dealing.

Other factors that might be relevant in assessing the mutuality of obligation between the parties are:

● The freedom of the individual to provide a substitute (see **1.11** below).

● The length of time the individual has worked for the employer.

● Whether the individual has in practice worked for other organisations during that time.

● The existence of a notice period in the contract.

● Whether the working hours and patterns are set and regular.

The Freedom of the Individual to Provide a Substitute **[1.11]**

If an individual's contract permits them to provide a substitute worker, for example if they are unable to work on a particular day or week, then it is unlikely that the contract under which they work would be assessed as a contract of employment. However, if a contractual power to delegate is never used in practice and appears in the contract for the sole purpose of preventing the worker from gaining employee status, it is unlikely to be effective in achieving that aim.

In *Express and Echo Publications v Tanton [1999] IRLR 367*, the Court of Appeal held that if the contract allowed a worker to provide a substitute in the event of their unavailability, and if the worker did in fact allocate their work to another worker from time to time, the worker could not be defined as an employee. Thus where a worker can choose whether to perform the contract personally or pay someone else to do the work, this would be inconsistent with the existence of a contract of employment. The obligation to do the work in person constituted an 'irreducible minimum'. The Court relied in this case on the earlier decision in *Ready Mixed Concrete (South East) Ltd v Minister of Pensions and National Insurance, High Court (Queen's Bench Division) [1968] QB 497* in which it was held that, although the absence of an obligation to provide services personally was fatal to the existence of an employment contract, 'a limited or occasional power of delegation may not be'. This point was crucial in the recent case of *MacFarlane & anor v Glasgow City Council [2001] IRLR 7*, discussed below:

Key Case **[1.12]**

MacFarlane & anor v Glasgow City Council [2001] IRLR 7

Facts

Ms MacFarlane was a gymnastics instructor engaged by Glasgow City Council to teach specific sessions at set times at various sports centres. There was no written contract and Ms MacFarlane was paid an agreed rate on the basis of each individual teaching session she conducted. At the start of each term, the Council sent a letter containing terms and conditions to all its instructors. One of these terms provided that, if for any reason Ms MacFarlane was unable to teach a particular session, she should arrange for a replacement instructor selected from the Council's list of approved instructors who would then be paid directly by the Council. Occasionally the Council would take the initiative to hire a replacement, but this was not the usual practice.

Aspects of the contract that pointed towards self-employed status were that Ms MacFarlane was not entitled to holiday pay, sick pay or occupational pension benefits, and she was obliged to fund her own public liability insurance.

Other factors in the employment relationship, however, pointed towards employee status. Ms MacFarlane was required to wear the Council's uniform and use their premises and facilities for her gymnastics sessions. All the support staff were engaged by the Council.

After a number of years, the Council decided to regularise the arrangements with their instructors and issued Ms MacFarlane with a new agreement that purported to make her self-employed. Ms MacFarlane refused to accept the terms in the agreement, resigned and brought a claim for constructive dismissal to an employment tribunal. As a preliminary matter, the tribunal had to determine Ms MacFarlane's employment status, as only employees (and not other workers) are eligible to bring claims for constructive dismissal.

Findings

The employment tribunal held unanimously that Ms MacFarlane was self-employed but this decision was not upheld on appeal to the EAT, who remitted the case back to the tribunal.

In the EAT's judgement, although the absence of an obligation to provide services personally would often preclude a worker from being classed as an employee, it did not automatically follow that this was the case. They made an analogy with a school teacher who might be permitted, if they were unable to teach a particular class, to ask a colleague to cover the class. This type of arrangement, in the EAT's view, would not transform an employment contract into a contract for services. In the case in question, the authority for Ms MacFarlane to delegate her teaching sessions was limited to those on the Council's approved list and the Council could veto her suggested replacement. Furthermore, the facility for her to delegate her sessions only arose when she was 'unable' to do the work and did not include occasions when she was 'unwilling' to do so. In addition, there were many other aspects of the working relationship that were relevant to the question of employment status which the tribunal should have taken into account in assessing whether or not Ms MacFarlane was an employee.

The implications of the *MacFarlane* case (above) are that, although the ability for a worker to provide a substitute in the event of inability to do the work personally will often mean that the contract under which the person is working cannot be characterised as an employment contract, this principle is not an absolute one. This means that an occasional power to delegate the work to another individual will not necessarily mean that the individual is not an employee, especially if the power to delegate is limited or controlled by the employer. The key principles can be summed up as follows:

- There has to be some obligation to perform the work personally for a contract of employment to exist.

- A limited or occasional power of delegation will not necessarily change the fact that the working relationship is one of employer/ employee, but where an individual in practice exercises a right to provide a substitute, the contract under which they work will be classed as a contract for services, and not a contract of employment.

Casual and Seasonal Workers   [1.13]

The question of whether a mutual obligation exists to provide and accept work is one that often arises in relation to the employment status of casual workers and seasonal workers. Casual staff may work on either a regular or variable ad hoc basis, whilst seasonal workers may provide their services for specific periods of time with long gaps in between each period of 'employment'.

The absence of mutuality of obligation can be a barrier for casual workers who wish to establish that they are employees of the organisation for whom they perform services. In *O'Kelly and others v Trusthouse Forte plc [1983] IRLR 369*, the Court of Appeal upheld an employment tribunal's decision that a casual wine waiter who could be called upon to work as and when he was required was not an employee of the hotel where he worked even though he was regarded as a regular member of staff and given preference over other casual staff. The decision was based on the absence of any obligation on the employer to provide work and a similar absence on the part of Mr O'Kelly to accept work when it was offered.

The question of the employment status for casual workers is dealt with again in **CHAPTER 7** at **7.2**, whilst the engagement of seasonal workers is discussed in **CHAPTER 7** at **7.14**. The essential question is whether, in between periods during which the person is working, it can be argued that there is an 'umbrella' or 'global' contract under which the parties have agreed together (expressly or impliedly) that the work will resume at some future date. The determination of this issue usually requires an examination of the working periods themselves, their length and regularity (or absence of such), the length of the gaps between them and whether there is any understanding between the parties (express or implied) that the casual worker will resume working after a period during which no work was done.

The Control Test [1.14]

The degree of control exercised by an employer over a worker will be a key factor in the determination of their employment status, taken in conjunction with other factors. The more control the employer exercises over the person's work, both in an overall sense and on a day-to-day basis, the more likely it is that the person will be their employee. An individual is likely to be viewed as an employee if they:

- Take instructions from a boss.

- Are under a duty to obey orders.

- Are supervised as to the mode of working to the extent that they do not have the opportunity to exercise their own initiative except to a limited degree.

- Cannot delegate their responsibilities other than in a very limited way.

- Must consult management about such things as timing of holidays.

- Have all their tools and equipment supplied by the employer and work wholly or mainly on the employer's premises (see **1.21** below).

In the case of *Clifford v Union of Democratic Mineworkers [1991] IRLR 518*, the Court of Appeal commented that control would be a particularly important factor in cases that otherwise lacked clarity since it might demonstrate the reality of the working relationship.

One of the early cases that looked at employment status was *Ready Mixed Concrete (South East) Ltd v Minister of Pensions and National Insurance, High Court (Queen's Bench Division), [1968] QB 497*. In this case, three elements were identified that were essential for the existence of a contract of employment. These were:

1. That the worker has agreed that, in exchange for a wage or other remuneration, he will provide his own work and skill in the performance of a service for the 'master', i.e. the employer (this is known today as mutuality of obligation and is discussed in **1.10**).

2. That the worker has agreed, either expressly or impliedly, that he will be subject to the employer's control in the performance of his duties to a sufficient degree to make the employer the 'master' (the 'control test').

3. That the other provisions of the contract are consistent with its being a contract of service.

The approach that the Court took in the *Ready Mixed Concrete* case is sometimes referred to as the 'multiple test'.

With regard to the 'control test' (the second point from the *Ready Mixed Concrete* case above), the High Court commented that control over how the work should be done on a day-to-day basis was not an essential pre-requisite for a contract of employment to exist (although such control, where it existed would clearly be relevant). Provided there was some sufficient framework of control, a contractual relationship of employer/ employee could exist (see also the *Durcan* case below in **1.18**). This approach is logical in that there are many occasions where the employer has no direct involvement in how an employee carries out their day-to-day duties but nevertheless exercises a considerable degree of control over the employment relationship as a whole. Examples would include many professional staff such as doctors working in hospitals. The key point to note therefore is that, unless there is an overall framework of control within which the person works, the terms of the person's engagement cannot be characterised as a contract of employment.

The Integration (or Organisation) Test [1.15]

A variation on the control test is the integration test (sometimes known as the organisation test). Under this test, the extent to which the person's work is a fully integrated part of the employer's business can be relevant to determining employment status. Key factors will include whether the worker is subject to all the employer's policies, procedures and rules, for example disciplinary and grievance procedures.

Practical Example [1.16]

The case study below demonstrates the potential for distinction under the control test and integration test:

Fred and Freda are both freelance management training specialists working for various organisations on ad hoc contracts. Company X engages Fred on a temporary contract for six months having decided to provide additional management training to a large number of their staff during the coming year. Fred undergoes a period of induction with the Company and is issued with their training manual, training notes and visual-aid material. He is instructed by the Company's training manager to use these materials and to adhere to the Company's existing training programmes and style of delivery in order to ensure consistency across the whole of the management training programme (which has been planned and scheduled by line management). Thereafter Fred's work involves running a series of training courses in the company mould. The Company employs several permanent trainers, and Fred's work sometimes involves his working alongside another trainer, whilst at other times he runs courses alone. In both cases his instructions are to adhere strictly to the pre-arranged course content and delivery style.

At around the same time, Company Y engages Freda for a temporary period of six months to conduct a training needs analysis across all sections of the organisation. After a brief introduction to the Company and its background, Freda develops a plan and makes arrangements to interview a cross-section of Company employees over the next few weeks. She is responsible for making and carrying out these arrangements, the only stipulation being that she should report back at the end of each week with a list of the various interviews that she has conducted. The agreement is that, by the end of the six-month contract, Freda will have produced a comprehensive and detailed report containing recommendations as to the type of training the Company should be planning for the following year, the priorities, the expected outcomes of this training, the reasons for the recommendations, projected costs and a list of potential training providers. Although Freda attends the Company's offices every day, she often spends part of the day at home, preparing the material for her report on her own home-based computer.

Irrespective of any contractual documentation, what is the employment status likely to be of Fred and Freda respectively?

The distinction in the above example is fairly obvious. Fred's work is fully integrated into the Company's enterprise, i.e. he is working alongside company employees performing the same job as them from day to day. The Company's training manager is exercising full control over his daily activities and providing him with clear and specific instructions as to what to do and how to do it. There is no facility for him to decide of his own volition what materials to use, how to deliver the training or to change the way things are done. Equally, it is not open to him to decide which days to work or which courses to run, as these matters are determined by his line manager.

Freda's work on the other hand, falls outside the scope of the Company's normal day-to-day business activities. She is working on a job that is clearly a one-off project which, although undertaken for the business, is an accessory to it rather than being integrated into it.

Freda is responsible for her own day-to-day work, its methodology, timing and the manner of carrying it out. She is in a position where she is able to use, and indeed expected to use, her own initiative in order to achieve an agreed outcome at the end of the six-month period. The report will contain what she believes to be the priority issues and appropriate recommendations, without any external control or input from the Company's line management.

In the above scenario, Fred is very likely to be regarded in law as an employee of Company X during his six-month engagement, whilst Freda is unlikely to be regarded as an employee of Company Y given the absence of any day-to-day control over her work by the Company.

The Manner of Performance   [1.17]

In the case of *Narich Pty Ltd v Commissioner of Payroll Tax [1984] ICR 286*, lecturers who conducted weight-watching classes were held to be employees because of the high level of control and direction exercised over their work – a factor which led the Privy Council to describe them as being 'tied hand and foot' as to the manner of their performance. The lecturers' contracts contained provisions that laid down the precise manner in which they should teach the classes and a provision that any failure to adhere to these teaching methods would lead to immediate termination of their contracts. Even though the lecturers were authorised in the contract to provide a substitute, and despite the contract itself stating they were independent contractors, the Privy Council concluded that they were employees.

Key Case   [1.18]

The integration test has often been applied to determine the status of professional workers where the employer is unable in practice to direct how the worker should perform the work. Examples include doctors, dentists and the like. One example is the case of *City & East London FHS Authority v Durcan [1996] EAT 721/96.*

Facts

Mr Durcan was a dentist who ran his own dental practice. Quite separately, he provided emergency dental cover for the Family Health Services Authority (FHSA) on Tuesday evenings between 7 pm and midnight for which he was paid a flat fee. This took place at the Royal London Hospital. Subsequently the FHSA sought to reduce Mr Durcan's hours at the hospital and he complained to a tribunal that this was a breach of contract entitling him to resign and claim constructive dismissal. In order to pursue such a claim, however, Mr Durcan had first to show that he was an employee of the FHSA, rather than someone providing services to the FHSA on a self-employed basis.

Findings

The EAT upheld Mr Durcan's claim that he was employed by the FHSA on Tuesday evenings, despite the fact that his contract allowed him to provide a substitute if he could not work on a particular Tuesday. The key factors leading to this conclusion were that:

- Although Mr Durcan was required to exercise his professional discretion in carrying out his work, he was, in an overall sense, subject to the control of the FHSA.

- Mr Durcan was not working on his own account whilst providing emergency cover at the hospital, but was instead part of the FHSA's organisation.

- Mr Durcan used the hospital's premises, equipment and medicines.

- There was sufficient mutuality of obligation between the parties to indicate the existence of an employment contract.

Inconsistent approaches   [1.19]

To demonstrate how court and tribunal decisions can be inconsistent in the area of employment status, the EAT in the case of *Sreekanta v Medical Relief Agency (Stoke-on-Trent) Ltd EAT 536/91* upheld a tribunal's decision that a doctor who worked part-time on Thursday nights for many years for the Medical Relief Agency was not an employee of the Agency. The tribunal had found that the Agency had only a very small element of control over the doctor's work. He was not obliged to perform the work personally as he was authorised to arrange for a substitute if he did not wish to work on a particular Thursday night. This contrasts with the decision in the *Durcan* case above in which Mr Durcan also had the freedom to provide a substitute for his Tuesday evening sessions.

The economic reality test [1.20]

Another issue that courts and tribunals will consider in reviewing the issue of control is the extent to which an individual is financially independent of the organisation for whom they work, and/or the degree of financial risk the individual is exposed to when working for the employer. The underlying issue is whether the worker who is performing the work is in business on their own account. If the answer is in the affirmative, the contract will not be capable of being a contract of employment. Sub-sets of this argument (based on the decision in *Market Investigations Ltd v Minister of Social Security [1969] 2 QB 173 QBD*, would include the following questions:

- Has the individual taken on a degree of financial risk in agreeing to perform work for the organisation?

- Does the individual hold responsibility for investment and management?

- Does the individual have the opportunity to make a profit from effective management of the work?

- Does the individual provide his own tools and equipment? (see **1.21** below).

- Does the individual hire his own helpers? (see **1.22** below).

In the case of *Lee v Chung and Shun Shing Construction and Engineering Co Ltd [1990] IRLR 236*, these factors were taken into account in establishing that a skilled worker who earning his living by working for several businesses was in fact an employee of one of them (for the purposes of health and safety law), notwithstanding the fact he worked for more than one employer at the same time. This was based on evidence that Mr Lee was not an independent contractor venturing into business on his own account – there was no degree of financial risk, no opportunity for him to profit and no responsibility for investment and management. Furthermore, his tools were provided by the employer and he did not hire his own helpers.

In some cases, however, even where there is a substantial degree of control exercised by one party to a contract over the other, the contract will not be held to be a contract of employment. Examples could include sub-postmasters who run their own business on their own premises (over whom the Post Office would exercise considerable control) (*Hitchcock v Post Office [1980] ICR 100*) and managers of grocery or newsagents' shops who are under the control of a principal who may dictate the lay out of the shop, the supply and display of the stock and the training of the staff (*Brand v Paper Chain (East Anglia) Ltd EAT 653/92*). In such cases it is likely that the individual will be deemed to be self-employed on the grounds that they have a financial interest in the business which they run and the ability to enhance their income by the exercise of sound business practices.

The provision of tools and equipment and whether the employer provides the premises [1.21]

Another factor that can impact on an individual's employment status in certain circumstances is whether it is the employer or the worker who provides any tools, equipment or other resources required for the performance of the job. For example if an individual is engaged to work from home, it may be either the employer or the individual who supplies the computer and software required for the job. A skilled trades-person may supply their own tools, or alternatively may be supplied with tools or protective clothing by the employer. In *Airfix Footwear Ltd v Cope [1978] IRLR 396*, Ms Cope worked from home making heels for shoes. The employer provided the patterns, tools and equipment. Following a dispute over her tax status, the EAT held that she was an employee for the purpose of statutory employment protection.

Whether helpers are hired by the employer or by the worker [1.22]

If an individual is contracted to perform a job and that person requires 'helpers' to assist them in the completion of the work, the identity of the party who hires the helpers will be yet another factor relevant to the determination of the person's employment status. Normally, in a relationship governed by an employment contract, the employer would determine whom to recruit to support the person in their work, even though the individual might have some input into the selection process If, however, an individual is invited to supply their own helpers, then that would point towards worker status.

Jim Jamieson was a project manager with ABC Petroleum Ltd, responsible for managing the construction of an oil facility for the Condor Field in the North Sea, a project which commenced in 2001 and was expected to last for two years. In order to satisfy head office requirements to keep staff levels to a minimum, he engaged a number of individuals as contractors, rather than hiring them as direct employees of the organisation. One of these individuals, Jack Jackson who was a self-employed freelance design engineer, was engaged on a fixed-term contract for eighteen months with the following terms:

'You will be engaged as a self-employed contractor on the Condor project for a period commencing on 1 September 2001 and continuing until 28. February 2003. The Company may wish to extend your engagement thereafter, but this is not guaranteed.'

The contract also stated:

'You will be paid a rate of £500 per day, payable on receipt of correct monthly invoices, and you will be responsible for all your own taxation and other statutory payments.'

Jack's work as a senior design engineer was an integral part of the project. He supervised a group of four employees, who were hired prior to his commencement with the company. He worked five, sometimes six, days a week, and was allocated a company car due to his senior status.

Just over a year later, however, due to an overspend on the project budget and pressure from head office, Jim decided that he had no choice but to shed some staff. Consequently, he gave Jack one month's notice to terminate his contract effective from 30 November 2002. In order to pacify Jack, Jim agreed also to pay him a bonus of ten further days' pay to compensate him for the loss of the use of his company car. The reason he gave Jack was 'redundancy'.

In these circumstances, what, if any, claim would Jack have against ABC Petroleum?

In these circumstances, Jack would (for a start) have a claim for breach of contract. The contract under which he was engaged was clearly for a fixed eighteen month period and there were no notice clauses permitting early termination. When the company terminated the contract early, this was a breach of contract. The reason for the early termination is irrelevant – the fact is that the terms of the contract were broken. Jack would be able to claim damages for the outstanding three months, based on the number of days he would actually have worked less an amount equivalent to the extra ten days pay which he received. He would also be entitled to compensation for loss of the use of the company car for the outstanding period.

Jack may also be able to claim unfair dismissal by arguing in the first instance that he was, in reality, an employee of the company. His engagement meets several of the key criteria required for employment status:

- There was 'mutuality of obligation' between the parties, i.e. the employer committed to provide regular work for Jack for the 18-month period, and Jack accepted the obligation to perform the work.

- Jack was engaged to carry out work which was an integral part of the employer's business.

- Jack worked full-time, and was not working for any other organisation.

- Jack bore no personal financial risk in his position with the company.

- Jack's engagement was subject to control and direction from the company.

- The company provided all Jack's resources.

- Jack enjoyed the benefit of a company car.

- The responsibility for hiring Jack's team of assistants lay with the company, and not with Jack.

How the Individual is Paid [1.24]

Where someone is engaged on the basis of a fixed weekly wage or monthly salary, that will be an indicator of employment (taken into account along with all the other relevant factors governing the working relationship). In contrast, factors that might point towards self-employment would include:

- A right to participate in the profits or responsibility for any losses.

21

- A right to set the rate payable for the job.

- Payment of a lump sum for a specific job.

- Payment of commission only, depending entirely on the individual's productivity or success (for example in selling).

- Payment of submission of invoices instead of payment of a wage or salary.

The financial arrangements are of course only one aspect of a working relationship and it is important to bear in mind that this matter alone will not be determinative of an individual's employment status.

Income Tax and National Insurance Contributions [1.25]

If an individual has income tax and national insurance contributions deducted at source under the PAYE scheme, this will point towards employment. Similarly paying someone gross will suggest that they are self-employed. However, this matter will not be conclusive on its own and a more accurate way of viewing an individual's tax status in relation to employment status is to view the matter in reverse, i.e. if an individual is an employee, then tax should be deducted under PAYE whilst someone working under a contract for services may be paid gross. In any event, the Inland Revenue's assessment of whether an individual is employed or self-employed for tax purposes is not binding on employment tribunals who may be considering the same individual's status for the purpose of employment protection rights, although no doubt it would be persuasive.

VAT Registration [1.26]

In contrast to the above, if an individual is registered for VAT purposes, that will be a strong indication of self-employment. Once again, however, there is no guarantee that this would be the outcome in the event of a challenge by the individual.

Professional Indemnity Insurance [1.27]

Self-employed workers are often required by organisations that hire their services to produce evidence that they are covered by their own professional indemnity insurance policy. This would not be required from employees, as employers are obliged themselves to take out employer liability insurance to cover any loss or damage to others caused by their employees in the course of their employment. Thus a requirement for an individual to hold professional indemnity insurance would be an indicator of self-employment.

Company Perks and Benefits [1.28]

Most employees receive certain contractual perks and benefits by dint of their employment. These can include diverse benefits such as occupational sick pay (i.e. continuation of wage or salary in the event of sickness absence), long-term permanent health insurance, private medical insurance cover, maternity, paternity and parental leave beyond the statutory minimum provided for in legislation, holidays over and above the minimum four weeks laid down in the *Working Time Regulations 1998 (SI 1998 No 1833)*, occupational pension benefits, use of a company car, free or subsidised lunches, free parking, sports and social facilities, and so on.

Individuals engaged on a contract for services, however, are often not privy to such benefits. Essentially the presence or absence of such company perks and benefits will be broadly relevant to the determination of employment status, but of course these factors will not be decisive on their own.

Application of Disciplinary and Grievance Procedures [1.29]

If an employer maintains, and uses, a contractual power to apply any in-house disciplinary or grievance procedures to a particular worker, that will be a contributory factor pointing towards employee status.

It follows that it may be in the interests of managers to avoid applying such procedures to an individual whose status is that of worker (rather than employee). In the case of an agency worker, for example, the worker could be directed to take a workplace grievance to their agency, and for a representative of the agency to then raise the matter with the employer on their behalf. This three-party arrangement would avoid creating the impression that the person was a direct employee of the company to whom the agency worker was assigned.

The intention of the parties [1.30]

The intention of the employer and the person engaged when entering into the contract will, of course, be relevant to the question of employment status, but will not necessarily be determinative. The actual substance of the working relationship will always be more important in the eyes of a court or tribunal tasked with deciding an individual's actual status. In any event, the status of what is essentially a contract of employment cannot be altered just because one or both of the parties has attached a particular label to it. Even if an employee has specifically asked his employer to have their employment status changed to that of self-employed, that will not act to prevent the person from arguing at a later date that they were in reality still an employee.

Nevertheless, if employment status is unclear or ambiguous following an analysis of the other factors, the intention of the parties may be sufficient to swing the decision one way or the other, provided there is no evidence to suggest that the employer had intended or sought to contract out of employment legislation.

Key case   **[1.31]**

This was the outcome in the case of *Stevedoring & Haulage Services Ltd v Fuller & ors Court of Appeal 09.05.01*, discussed below:

Stevedoring and Haulage Services Ltd v Fuller & ors unreported 09.05.01

Facts

A number of casual dockers who had been engaged under employment contracts had taken voluntary redundancy and subsequently accepted offers of casual work on an ad hoc basis. An express term in the documents relating to the offer of casual work stated that the dockers would not be employees, and there would be no obligation on the employer to offer work and no obligation on the workers to accept any work offered.

In practice, the casual dockers worked the majority of days and were offered work in preference to other casual workers. The employer operated a rota system under which the dockers were rewarded if they were available for work but were not offered it, and penalised if they were unavailable for work that was offered. The employer provided training and protective clothing and the dockers worked under the employer's control and direction. Furthermore, they did not work for any other employer.

When the dockers applied to an employment tribunal for written statements of the particulars of their employment, the employer contested their employment status, arguing that since they were not

---

employees, they had no entitlement to the provision of a written statement.

Findings

Overturning the employment tribunal's decision, the Court of Appeal held that the workers were not employed under contracts of employment. The documents that had been signed meant that there could be no mutuality of obligation between the parties, and without mutuality of obligation there could be no employment contract. Instead, the documents provided no more than a framework for a series of successive ad hoc contracts. In the light of the express term that there was no obligation on the employer to offer work and no obligation on the workers to accept any work offered, the tribunal had been incorrect to imply that there was an overriding contract of employment containing mutual contractual obligations.

The above case shows that the outcome of any challenge to employment status can often be unpredictable and surprising.

Summary of points impacting upon employment status [1.32]

In summary, the question of an individual's employment status will depend on all the circumstances of the particular case. It is unlikely that any single factor on its own will be decisive, although in recent years the questions of mutuality of obligation and degree of control over the individual's work have usually been held to be paramount. Certainly an employer-employee relationship will exist only if there is a reasonable level of obligation on the worker to provide their services personally (with no more than a very limited power to delegate) and a reasonable obligation on the employer to provide work on an ongoing basis.

Sometimes it will be fairly obvious that someone is an employee whilst in other cases the worker will be unable to argue that they work under a contract of employment in which case they will have only limited employment protection rights. Individuals who are genuinely in business on their own account may be unable to argue the status of worker, let alone that of employee. To quote one eminent judge (Mummery J in the High Court):

'This is not a mechanical exercise of running through items on a checklist to see whether they are present in, or absent from, a given situation. The object of the exercise is to paint a picture from the accumulation of detail. The overall effect can only be appreciated by standing back from the detailed picture which has been painted, by viewing it from a distance and by making an informed, considered, qualitative appreciation of the whole. It is a matter of evaluation of the overall effect of the detail ... Not all details are of equal weight or importance in any given situation ...'.

Checklist   **[1.33]**

The following is a check-list for employers who wish to draft contracts with individuals that are not contracts of employment, i.e. they wish to stipulate that the individual is a 'worker' and not an 'employee:

- State in the contract that it is not a contract of employment and it is not the intention of the parties to create such a contract.

- Make sure that the contract makes it clear that there is no obligation on the employer to offer any minimum amount of work, and no obligation on the worker to accept work when it is offered – and ensure this is the reality of the working relationship.

- Allow the right in the contract for the individual to provide a substitute to perform the work if they are unable or unwilling to work on a particular day, and ensure this is permitted in practice.

- Minimise the right for management to direct how, when and where the person's work is to be performed.

- Avoid integrating the individual into the organisational structure or giving them management responsibility over others who are employees of the organisation.

- Permit the individual to perform some or all of the work from home, or to use their own facilities, equipment and tools.

Rights for Employees/Workers/the Self Employed [1.34]

Employees (i.e. those engaged on a contract of employment) enjoy the full range of employment rights. Certain rights are dependent on a minimum period of continuous service, for example the right to claim unfair dismissal depends on the employee having a minimum of one year's service and the right to a statutory redundancy payment following dismissal by reason of redundancy is subject to a minimum of two years' service. A full list is provided in **CHAPTER 6**, at **6.3**.

Legislation that applies to workers [1.35]

Workers who are not employees of the organisation for whom they provide their services are entitled to more limited employment protection rights than those who are employed on a contract of employment.

There has, however, been a trend in recent years for new legislation, particularly legislation emanating from Europe, to be drafted to cover workers as well as employees. Additionally all anti-discrimination legislation and some other laws protect workers as well as employees. The following is a list of employment legislation that applies to workers as well as employees:

Sex Discrimination Act 1975

All workers, including self-employed individuals who provide their services personally are protected against discrimination on grounds of sex and marital status.

Equal Pay Act 1970

All workers, including self-employed individuals who provide their services personally are protected against gender discrimination in relation to their pay and contractual terms.

Race Relations Act 1976

All workers, including self-employed individuals who provide their services personally are protected against discrimination on grounds of colour, race, nationality, ethnic origins and national origins.

Disability Discrimination Act 1995

All workers, including self-employed individuals who provide their services personally are protected against discrimination on grounds related to any disability they have.

Working Time Regulations 1998

All workers are entitled to limit their working hours to no more than an average of 48 hours per week averaged over a reference period of 17 weeks (26 weeks or 52 weeks in certain circumstances). They also have the right to certain minimum rest breaks, to limit night working and to be granted four weeks paid holiday leave each year.

National Minimum Wage Act 1998

All workers, except those genuinely in business on their own account, are entitled to be paid a rate that is no less than the national minimum wage in force at the time, currently £4.10 per hour for adult workers.

Part-Time Workers (Prevention of Less Favourable Treatment) Regulations 2000 (SI 2001 No 1551)

Employees and workers who work part-time have the right not to be treated less favourably on the grounds of part-time status than equivalent full-time employees or workers performing similar work (see **CHAPTER 3**, at **3.10**).

Certain parts of the Trade Union and Labour Relations (Consolidation) Act 1992 relating to less favourable treatment on grounds of union membership

Part II of the Employment Rights Act 1996

All workers, other than those performing work for a client or customer, have the right not to suffer an unlawful deduction from their pay – i.e. a deduction to which they have not signified their agreement in advance.

Employment Relations Act 1999, ss 10–15

Workers have the right to be accompanied by a fellow worker or trade union official of their choice at a formal grievance or disciplinary hearing.

Public Interest Disclosure Act 1998

All workers (including the self-employed) have the right not to be dismissed or subjected to a detriment on grounds that they have made a protected disclosure alleging certain types of wrongdoing on the part of the employer.

Rights for self-employed individuals [1.36]

Self-employed individuals have few employment rights, although where a self-employed person provides their services personally, they do enjoy protection under anti-discrimination legislation.

Conclusion [1.37]

The distinction between employee status and worker status is an important one since the rights and entitlements of employees are greater than those of workers engaged on a contract for services. Often however, the distinction is unclear, and individuals may challenge their employment status as a preliminary matter to a claim for unfair dismissal, redundancy pay or some other statutory right available only to employees. Employment tribunals have, over time, developed a range of tests that are used to assess the employment status of an individual. Usually the outcome of a challenge to employment status will depend on a detailed examination of all the relevant elements of the working relationship. In particular the presence or absence of mutuality of obligation between the parties, and the extent to which the employer exercises control and direction over the person's work will be important factors. The decisions of courts and tribunals have not always been consistent and the law in this area is continuously developing.

Employers who are unsure whether the employment status of a particular individual whom they have engaged could be successfully challenged at an employment tribunal would be advised to err on the cautious side and assume that the person might be classed as their employee, and would thus have the full range of statutory employment rights.

Questions and Answers [1.38]

Question

What is the distinction between an 'employee' and a 'worker' for the purpose of employment protection legislation?

Answer

An 'employee' is someone who has entered into or is working under a contract of employment, whereas a 'worker' is engaged on a contract

---

for services which implies the appointment of an independent contractor or a person working on a freelance basis.

Question

What is the importance of the distinction between an employee and a worker?

Answer

Employees enjoy the full range of statutory employment protection rights, whereas workers engaged on a contract for services have more limited rights.

Question

Do self-employed people have any employment protection rights?

Answer

Self-employed entrepreneurs who provide their services directly to their clients or customers have, with one exception, no employment protection rights. The exception is that individuals who provide their services personally for a client or customer are protected against sex, race and disability discrimination, even though they are not eligible for other employment protection rights. It is, however, possible in some instances for a self-employed person to be classed as a 'worker' for the purposes of certain employment protection legislation, provided they are providing their services personally to someone other than their own client or customer. In this case a self-employed worker would be able to enjoy a limited range of employment protection rights.

Question

Can an employer dictate when they engage someone what that person's employment status will be?

Answer

The label the employer puts on the contract is not regarded as conclusive proof of the worker's employment status. If an individual's employment status is challenged at an employment tribunal (usually by a worker who wishes to establish that their contract is or was a contract of employment), the tribunal will examine the actual working arrangements and working relationship between the employer and the worker. The aim of this will be to judge whether, in reality, the working relationship was typical of an employment contract. Essentially, the interpretation of who is an employee and who is a worker will depend on all the circumstances of the particular case.

Question

What are the advantages to the employer of engaging individuals on a contract for services as opposed to a contract of employment?

Answer

An employer may wish to engage individuals on a contractor or self-employed basis where the work is of an uncertain or limited duration, where the amount of work fluctuates, where the employer needs extra resources to cover periods of leave or where the employer wants to be able to call on additional resources in order to cut down on overtime payments to employees. The obvious advantage to the employer is that workers who are not employees have no unfair dismissal or redundancy pay rights.

Question

How is employment status determined in the event of a challenge to an employment tribunal?

Answer

Determining whether an individual is employed under a contract of employment or engaged on a contract for services is a complex issue. An employment tribunal must consider all aspects of the working relationship as no single feature will be decisive. Where the wording of the contract and the reality of the working arrangements appear to the tribunal to be at variance with each other, the reality of the working arrangements will usually prevail. The presence or absence of mutuality of obligation and the degree of control exercised over the person's work will be key factors.

Question

What does 'mutuality of obligation' mean in relation to a dispute over employment status?

Answer

In order for a contract of employment to exist there must be an obligation on the employer to provide work and a corresponding obligation on the individual to perform the work. Unless there is a minimum of obligations on both sides, the working relationship cannot be characterised as an employment contract.

Question

How will a tribunal assess whether the working relationship between an employer and a worker contained sufficient mutuality of obligation to create a contract of employment?

Answer

The tribunal would look at the reality of the working arrangements as well as the wording of the contract. Evidence that there was no obligation on the employer to offer work, and no obligation on the worker to accept work when offered it, would be crucial. The length of time the individual had worked for the employer, whether they worked for other organisations during that time and whether the working hours and patterns were set and regular would also be relevant. Another key feature would be whether the individual was free to provide a substitute. Where this was a feature of the working relationship, it would suggest that the worker was not obliged to provide their services personally, and it would therefore be unlikely that the contract under which they work would be assessed as a contract of employment.

Question

If an employer makes it clear in a worker's contract that the person may provide a substitute if they are unable to perform the work personally, would this be conclusive proof that the contract was not an employment contract?

Answer

Although the ability for a worker to provide a substitute in the event of inability to do the work personally will often mean that the contract under which they are working cannot be characterised as an employment contract, this principle is not an absolute one. Although there has to be some obligation to perform the work personally for a contract of employment to exist, a limited or occasional power of delegation will not necessarily change the fact that the working relationship is one of employer/employee.

Question

What is the employment status of casual workers likely to be in law where the casuals work on a purely ad hoc basis?

Answer

The absence of mutuality of obligation often means that casual workers cannot be viewed as employees of the organisation for whom they perform services. Unless it can be argued that an umbrella contract exists in between periods of actual work, it is unlikely that a casual worker could claim employee status. However, the determination of this issue usually requires an examination of the working periods themselves, their length and regularity (or absence of such), the length of the gaps between them and whether there is any understanding (express or implied) that the casual will resume working after a period during which no work was done.

Question

If a contractor or self-employed person is working under the control and direction of management, what impact might this have on their employment status?

Answer

The degree of control exercised by an employer over a worker will be a key factor in the determination of the worker's employment status, taken in conjunction with other features of the working relationship. The more control the employer exercises over the person's work, the more likely it is that they will be an employee of the organisation. An individual is particularly likely to be viewed as an employee if they take instructions from a boss, are under a duty to obey orders and are supervised as to the mode of working to the extent that they do not have the opportunity to exercise their own initiative except to a limited degree.

Question

What is the 'integration test' as regards the determination of an individual's employment status?

Answer

The integration test (sometimes known as the 'organisation test') involves an analysis of the extent to which an individual's work is a fully integrated part of the employer's business. Key factors will include whether the worker is subject to all the employer's policies, procedures and rules, for example disciplinary and grievance procedures. The more 'integrated' a worker is, the more likely it is that they will be classed as an employee for the purposes of employment protection legislation (when viewed together with other aspects of the working relationship).

Question

Does it matter whether the employer or the worker provides any tools, equipment or other resources required for the performance of the job?

Answer

The question of who provides any tools, equipment or other resources required for the performance of the job is yet another factor that can impact on the determination of an individual's employment status. This would, however, be viewed alongside many other aspects of the working relationship before any decision on employment status could be made.

Question

If an individual is paid gross, without deductions for income tax or national insurance, is this conclusive proof that they are not an employee of the organisation for whom they provide their services?

Answer

No, not necessarily, as an employment tribunal would take many other factors into account when determining the matter. A more accurate way of viewing an individual's tax status in relation to employment status is to view the matter in reverse, i.e. if an individual is an employee, then the employer must deduct tax and national insurance under PAYE whilst someone working under a contract for services may possibly be paid gross.

Question

What would be the effect, if any, of granting company benefits to a self-employed worker, or of applying in-house procedures such as a disciplinary procedure?

Answer

The presence or absence of company perks and benefits will be broadly relevant to the determination of an individual's employment status. Equally, the application of company procedures such as a disciplinary procedure to an individual would tend to point towards employment status. These factors would not, however, be decisive on their own and would be assessed alongside many other factors.

Question

How can an employer make a realistic and accurate assessment of an individual's true employment status in the event of a dispute?

Answer

The question of an individual's employment status will depend on all the circumstances of the particular case and no single factor will be decisive. In recent times, however, the questions of mutuality of obligation and degree of control over the individual's work have usually been held to be paramount. An employer-employee relationship will exist only if there is a reasonable level of obligation on the worker to provide their services personally (with no more than a very limited power to delegate) and a reasonable obligation on the employer to provide work on an ongoing basis. If mutuality of obligation and a reasonable degree of control are present, then all the other elements of the working relationship would have to be assessed to establish whether, on the balance of probabilities, the individual's contract was one of employment, or a contract for services.

2. Contracts of Employment

Introduction [2.1]

A contract of employment may be open-ended (the so-called 'permanent contract'), or temporary. Permanent contracts are of unlimited duration and are designed to continue until one of the parties gives the other notice to terminate the contract, or until the employee reaches retirement age. This is the traditional, and still the most common, form of employment contract, and can be either full-time or part-time.

A temporary contract is one which, from the outset, is agreed between the employer and the employee as a contract that will run for a limited duration. A temporary contract can also be either full-time or part-time. There is no universally accepted or legally binding definition of a temporary contract and temporary contracts may be of various types, for example a fixed-term contract. Equally, seasonal workers (see **CHAPTER 7**, at **7.14**) and some self-employed people (see **CHAPTER 8**) would typically be engaged on temporary, rather than permanent, contracts.

An employee's length of continuous service begins from the first day of their employment and continues until the contract is brought to an end. Continuity of service is important because a number of statutory employment protection rights depend on the employee having gained a minimum period of service.

As regards the distinction between a full-time and a part-time contract, there is no definition in statute as to what constitutes full-time employment. A full-time contract is therefore one under which the employee works the number of hours that their employer has defined as the full-time standard for the organisation. Correspondingly, a part-time employee is one who works fewer hours per week or per month than someone working the company's standard full-time hours.

It is important to consider, before examining the management of fixed-term and part-time contracts in more detail, what constitutes a contract of employment, different forms of contract, what a contract consists of (express and implied terms) and what terms the employer is obliged to put into writing.

What is a Contract of Employment? [2.2]

The existence of a contract of employment establishes the relationship of employer/employee between the parties. All the terms and conditions, rules, obligations and entitlements related to the employee's employment (other than statutory rights) will be established by reference to the contract. Workers who are not employees are not engaged on a contract of employment, but rather a contract for services (see **CHAPTER 1** at **1.1**).

Conditions for a Contract to Exist [2.3]

In order for a contract to exist, four conditions must be met. These are:

Agreement between the parties [2.4]

For a contract to exist, there must be agreement between the parties. This usually means that there must have been an offer of employment by the employer and an acceptance of that offer by the employee. The contract will come into force as soon as an unconditional job offer has been unconditionally accepted, provided that the person making the offer had the authority to enter into a binding contract on behalf of the employer.

If the offer is conditional (for example conditional upon satisfactory references, the satisfactory outcome of a pre-employment medical examination or the achievement of a defined qualification), then the contract will not normally take effect until the condition is satisfied. In the event that both parties agree that performance of the contract is to commence before one of the pre-conditions has been fulfilled, and if subsequently the condition is not satisfied, this would give the employer proper grounds to terminate the contract. Where, however, an offer of employment is absolute, i.e. there are no pre-conditions, any withdrawal of the offer after it has been accepted but before the person has started work would constitute a breach of contract. The individual would then be able to recover damages equivalent to the period of notice to which they were entitled under the contract.

Legal Relations [2.5]

The parties must have entered into the agreement with the intention of creating legal relations. This means that both parties must have intended that both the agreement itself and the terms that it contains were to be legally binding. If this is not the case, the contract will not be effective.

Consideration **[2.6]**

The contract must be supported by 'consideration' which means that something of benefit must pass from each of the parties to the other when the contract is performed. The practical interpretation of 'consideration' in the context of an employment contract is that the employer must agree to pay the employee and/or provide certain benefits, whilst the employee must agree to perform work for the employer. Thus, where someone performs a service on a purely voluntary basis, and is not paid for that service, there can be no contract of employment.

Certainty **[2.7]**

The individual terms of a contract must be sufficiently clear and certain for a court to be able to give them meaning.

The Inter-Relationship Between Contracts of Employment and Statutory Obligations **[2.8]**

Employee rights that have been created by the passing of legislation are automatically incorporated into every contract of employment, whether permanent or fixed-term, full or part-time. It is not open to employers to attempt to exclude an employee's statutory rights. Any contractual clause purporting to deny an employee such rights will be unenforceable.

This means in effect that employees automatically have a range of employment rights conferred upon them by statute including, for example, rights under the *Employment Rights Act 1996*, the *Sex Discrimination Act 1975*, and the *Part-Time Workers (Prevention of Less Favourable Treatment) Regulations 2000 (SI 2000 No 1551)*. Apart from any terms incorporated into a contract as a result of statute, a contract of employment is likely to consist of a range of terms, both express and implied.

Different Forms of Contract **[2.9]**
Part-time Contracts of Employment **[2.10]**

The key difference between a part-time contract and a full-time contract is the number of hours the employee works per week or month. Part-time contracts include job-sharing contracts, where two or more employees, each working part-time, share the responsibilities, duties and benefits of one full-time job.

Part-time employees, irrespective of the number of hours they work per week or month, are entitled to the same statutory employment rights as full-time employees. They are also protected against unfavourable treatment on grounds of part-time status as regards the terms of their contract of employment.

Engaging staff on part-time contracts can have many advantages for the employer, including:

- Hours of operating can readily be extended by using part-time workers to cover early mornings, late evenings, lunch-time cover, weekend shifts, etc.

- There will be more flexibility for the employer in dealing with peaks and troughs in the workload.

- Because a larger number of people will be employed, it will be easier for the employer to arrange cover for holidays and sickness absence.

- The pool for recruitment will be wider as there may be many experienced people who, although unable or unwilling to work full-time, would be available to come to work on a part-time or job-sharing basis.

- Experienced female staff can be attracted back to work following maternity leave or a career break for family reasons, as the opportunity to work part-time may provide them with the flexibility to combine family and work commitments.

- People who work a shorter day are likely to have more energy than those working very long hours. This in turn can lead to lower stress levels within the workforce.

- Salary costs are likely to be reduced, due to a decreased need for premium overtime payments payable to full-time staff working additional hours.

Part-time working is explored fully in **CHAPTER 3**.

Temporary Contracts of Employment [2.11]

Where temporary workers are employed directly (as opposed to workers engaged through another employer, e.g. an employment agency), their statutory entitlements are the same as those of permanent employees. There is no fixed definition of a 'temporary employee' in law. The significance of a temporary contract as opposed to a permanent contract is that:

- Both the employer and the employee agree from the outset that the contract will be of a limited duration.

- The employee may not work long enough to gain certain statutory employment protection rights, for example the right not to be unfairly dismissed which requires the employee to have a minimum of one year's continuous service, and the right to a statutory redundancy payment which is dependent on the employee having a minimum of two years' service.

One point to bear in mind is that if an employee works on a succession of temporary contracts with no gaps between them, they will gain statutory employment protection rights in the same way as an employee engaged on a permanent contract. There is also a range of circumstances in which employees can preserve their continuity of service even if there have been gaps between contracts – an issue that is explored fully in **CHAPTER 6** at **6.9**.

Uses of Temporary Contracts [2.12]

There are many potential uses of temporary contracts:

- They allow employers to alter their staffing levels to match their business needs, which can be particularly useful during periods of organisational change or uncertainty.

- Where the work is thought to be of limited duration, it is often more appropriate to engage someone on a temporary contract. This is also fairer on the employee in that it does not create false expectations of long-term employment.

- Where there is a one-off project, the engagement of a temporary employee is usually more appropriate.

- Temporary contracts are useful to cover periods of leave, such as holidays and maternity leave, and peaks in the workload.

- Engaging a temporary employee can eliminate or reduce the requirement for permanent employees to work overtime, thus removing the need for existing staff to work excessive hours and cutting down on premium overtime payments.

- A temporary contract can be offered as a pre-condition for permanent employment, thus allowing a period of time during which the employer can assess the person's suitability for permanent employment.

Temporary and fixed-term contracts are explored fully in **CHAPTER 4**.

Probationary Periods [2.13]

It is common practice for employers to stipulate in permanent employment contracts that employment is subject to a probationary period – usually between three and six months. This in effect means that permanent employment status is confirmed only after the employee has completed the probationary period to the employer's satisfaction.

The contract of employment should state clearly:

- Whether a probationary period is applicable.

- How long the probationary period is for.

- Whether any special conditions will apply during the probationary period.

The employer may elect to stipulate in the contract that certain employee perks, for example paid sickness absence leave, will not commence until after satisfactory completion of the probationary period. It would be advantageous also for the employer to stipulate that the company's normal disciplinary procedure will not apply until the probationary period has been completed and the employee's position confirmed. This will allow the employer to dismiss an unsatisfactory employee at the end of a three or six-month probationary period without having to go through every aspect of the disciplinary procedure, which might otherwise necessitate a protracted and complex series of actions.

The probationary period has no meaning in law, as the employee's length of service for statutory purposes commences on the first day of their employment. It is, however, a useful management tool that can be beneficial for the purpose of assessing the new employee's suitability for the post into which they have been recruited (or promoted), and for reviewing and implementing any training necessary for the person to perform the job to an acceptable standard.

The Express Terms of a Contract of Employment [2.14]

The express terms of a contract of employment are those that have been specifically agreed between the employer and the employee, whether verbally or in writing. This notion of agreement is fundamental to the formation of the contract. Essentially anything that has been *agreed* between the employer and the employee will form part of the contract, whether or not the term is in writing. It follows that terms and conditions that are imposed unilaterally on an employee will not be contractually binding, unless and until the employee has agreed to them. Where a term of the contract has been agreed, this creates an obligation on the part of the employer to honour the term, and a corresponding right on the part of the employee to enforce it. In the same way, the contract creates obligations on the part of the employee that must be honoured.

Express terms take precedence over implied terms in a contract of employment unless there are exceptional circumstances. Clearly this makes sense since the express terms represent what the parties have specifically agreed, whereas implied terms represent what the parties are taken to have agreed (see **2.26** below).

Incorporated Terms [2.15]

Apart from statutory terms, certain other terms may be incorporated into employment contracts by means of reference to a separate document. Typically, disciplinary procedures and policies and sickness absence procedures that are to have contractual effect may be incorporated in this way.

Varying the Terms of a Contract of Employment [2.16]

Once the terms of a contract of employment are agreed between the employer and the employee, they are legally binding on both parties. This means that none of the terms of the contract can be changed without the agreement of the other party. Employers who wish to change any of the terms of an employee's contract must therefore obtain the employee's agreement to the change, either at the time the change is proposed, or in advance by means of a flexibility clause in the contract of employment itself.

The Terms of Employment That Must be In Writing
[2.17]

The law does not require a contract of employment to be in writing, although employers are under a statutory obligation to issue written particulars of the key terms and conditions of employment to every employee.

Written Statement of Particulars of Employment [2.18]

Under *section 1* of the *Employment Rights Act 1996*, an employer is obliged to provide all employees whose contract is to continue for one month or more a written statement setting out the main terms and conditions of their employment. This is known as a written statement of particulars of employment, or a written statement of the key terms and conditions of employment, or sometimes just as the 'written statement'.

The obligation to provide a written statement applies to part-time employees as well as full-time employees. Temporary employees are also entitled to receive a written statement, so long as their contract is to last for a minimum period of one month.

Only employees and not other workers (see **CHAPTER 1**) are entitled to be given a written statement. Employees are entitled to receive a written statement within two months of the commencement of their employment.

The Difference Between a Contract of Employment and a Written Statement [2.19]

The difference between a contract of employment and a written statement is that the contract will consist of *all* the terms that have been agreed between the employer and the employee (including any terms agreed verbally), plus any implied terms, whereas the written statement is a document issued by the employer to the employee covering some of the terms of the contract. If the written statement contains terms to which the employee has not agreed, then these terms will not be legally binding even though they are included in the statement. Normally the terms contained in a written statement are consistent with what has been agreed as part of the contract, but in the event of a dispute, the written statement will not always be taken as proof of what was agreed (although it does provide evidence). The fact remains, however, that unless the employee has agreed to the terms contained in the written statement, they will not be binding as part of the contract.

Key Case [2.20]

An example of the type of problem that can arise as a result of employers not obtaining their employees' agreement to all the terms of the contract is demonstrated in the case of *Lovett v Wigan Metropolitan Borough Council Court of Appeal 12.01.01*.

Lovett v Wigan Metropolitan Borough Council Court of Appeal 12.01.01

Facts

The applicant was interviewed and offered the job of mechanical engineer, which he accepted. The terms of his engagement were subsequently confirmed to him in an offer letter. One of the terms of his employment, which was later to form the basis of a dispute, was in relation to career progression. The applicant had been told simply that progression beyond pay scale 6 would be dependent upon his 'gaining the appropriate qualifications and experience'.

Three months after the applicant had begun working, the Council issued him with a written statement of particulars of employment. Attached to the written statement was a document that detailed the Council's policy on career progression which was stated to form part of the contract. In this document, it was stated that progression beyond scale 6 would be subject to the attainment of specified qualifications and experience (which the applicant had previously agreed to), and to 'the needs of the department' (which he had not known and not agreed to). Despite the appearance of the additional clause, the applicant signed a copy of the written particulars to indicate his receipt of the documentation.

During the years that followed, the applicant did not progress up the pay scales beyond scale 6, despite his raising complaints about this on several occasions. In 1997, he was dismissed, and brought various complaints to tribunal including a claim for breach of contract.

Findings

The Court of Appeal upheld the applicant's contention that the terms of the contract were those discussed and agreed at the job interview and subsequently confirmed in the offer letter. The applicant had not been informed before accepting the job that progress beyond scale 6 would depend on the needs of the department, as well as his gaining the appropriate qualifications and experience. Because he had not agreed to this term, it did not form part of his contract.

The employer put forward the alternative argument that the applicant had, when he signed a copy of the written particulars and continued to work, agreed to a variation of the original contractual terms. The Court,

> however, refused to uphold this argument and confirmed that the
> written statement of particulars was not of itself a contractual document,
> but was issued to comply with a statutory requirement.
>
> The case was remitted to a fresh employment tribunal to decide
> whether the applicant had in fact gained the necessary qualifications and
> experience for progression up the pay scales. Subject to this condition,
> his claim for breach of contract would succeed.

The *Lovett* case did not create any new principle of law, but served as a
timely reminder that a written statement of particulars issued by an
employer to an employee cannot of itself effect a variation to the terms of
a contract of employment until and unless the employee has expressly
agreed to any change contained within it.

Full Written Contract [2.21]

Although there is no statutory obligation on employers to put *all* the terms
of a contract into writing, it is strongly advisable to issue a full written
contract and ensure it is signed by both parties. This minimises the risk of
misunderstandings and disputes at a later stage.

It is possible of course and indeed common for employers to formulate a
written contract of employment that also contains all the information
required for the written statement. This avoids the need to create a separate
document containing written particulars of employment.

The Terms That Must be in Writing [2.22]

The following information must, by law, be included within the written
statement:

1. The names of the employer and the employee.

2. The date employment began, and whether any previous employment
   counts towards the employee's continuous service.
   Previous employment may count towards continuous service where
   there has been a transfer of the business in which the employee
   works to another employer (under the *Transfer of Undertakings
   Regulations (Protection of Employment) Regulations 1981 (SI 1981 No
   1794)*, or where the employee has moved from one company to an
   associated company without a break in service.

46

3. The scale or rate of pay and the pay intervals (e.g. weekly, monthly)
    The rate of pay must not be below any minimum specified from time to time in the *National Minimum Wage Act 1998*.

4. Any terms and conditions relating to hours of work
    This should include terms relating to normal working hours and any overtime requirements. There is, however, no need to specify exact hours of work so long as the written statement makes it clear what the employee's obligations are. The clause governing hours may stipulate that the employee must be available to work any reasonable hours required for the performance of the job (subject to the working time restrictions laid down in the *Working Time Regulations 1998 (SI 1998 No 1833)*).

    Such a clause would, however, be unusual, and in most instances inappropriate, in the case of a part-time employee. It would be more appropriate and helpful to both parties to state the precise days and times during which a part-time employee has agreed to work.

5. Entitlement to holidays, including public holidays, and holiday pay
    This should include clarification of employees' entitlement to be paid for holidays accrued but not taken on termination of employment.

6. Any terms and conditions relating to sickness absence, including any provision for sick pay
    This provision relates to the provision of occupational sick pay, i.e. continuation of the employee's wage or salary during periods of sickness absence. The provision of statutory sick pay is a separate matter governed by statute.

7. Any terms and conditions relating to pensions and pension schemes
    The written statement should say whether or not an occupational pension scheme is in operation, and if so whether a contracting-out certificate is in force.

8. The length of notice which the employee is entitled to receive and obliged to give to terminate the contract of employment (see **2.24** below).
    Minimum notice periods are prescribed in law, but the written statement may impose longer periods on one or both parties.

9. The job title
    Either the job title or a brief description of the work must be provided. There is no legal obligation on employers to provide a job

description (although to do so represents good management practice). If a job description is provided, it is advisable to incorporate an 'any other duties' clause to ensure flexibility.

10. The likely duration of a period of temporary employment
     If the temporary contract is for a fixed-term, the precise finish date must be stated (see **CHAPTER 4** at **4.6**), Alternatively, if the contract is to come to an end on the occurrence of a particular event, for example the return to work of another employee who is absent from work on maternity leave, this should be clearly notified in writing to the temporary employee (see **CHAPTER 4** at **4.26**).

11. The place of work
     The employee's normal place of work, including the employer's address, should be stated. If there is a requirement for the employee to work at different places, this must also be specified.

12. Details of any relevant collective agreements which directly affect the employee's terms and conditions of employment
     This must specify who the parties are to the collective agreement.

13. Details of overseas assignments
     Where an employee is to be assigned to work overseas for a period of more than one month, they must be provided with written information on the duration of the assignment, the currency in which their salary will be paid, details of any special terms, conditions and perks relevant to the assignment and terms governing the employee's return to the UK.

14. The name or designation of the person to whom the employee should apply if they have a work-related grievance
     This can either be the name or job designation of the appropriate person. Technically, this requirement comes into play only if the employer employs 20 or more employees.

15. Disciplinary rules
     The requirement to provide a note of any disciplinary rules that exist applies at present only to employers who have 20 or more employees. The Government has proposed, however, to abolish the threshold of 20 in 2003.

There is no defined format or style for these terms and conditions of employment although the law states that certain terms should be contained within one document known as a 'principal statement'. Specifically, a single statement must include details of: the names of the parties, the date employment began, pay, hours, holiday entitlements, job title and place of work.

Model Written Statement [2.23]

Written Statement of Particulars

between

[Company name], having a place of business at [address] (hereafter referred to as 'the Company').

and

[Name of employee]

Start Date

Your start date with the Company was [date]. No previous employment with the Company, and no employment with any previous employer, will count as part of your period of continuous employment with the Company.

Job Title and Duties

Your job title is [job title]. Your duties are as detailed in the attached job description, although it is a condition of your contract that you agree to undertake duties other than those specified in the job description which it is reasonable for the Company to ask you to perform.

[Flexibility clause] Furthermore, your duties may from time to time be reasonably modified as necessary to meet the needs of the Company's business.

Hours of Work

Your normal hours of work are from/to [normal hours including lunch break] [from Monday to Friday/other days of the week]. This constitutes a normal working week of [number of hours] hours.

[Flexibility clause] You may, however, be asked to work longer days, different hours and/or to be available to work at weekends according to the Company's requirements. It is a condition of your contract of employment that you agree to work reasonable overtime or vary your hours of work when asked to do so.

[Alternative clause] Irrespective of the basic working week, you are expected to work whatever hours are reasonably required of you to meet the demands of your job, subject to the provisions contained in the *Working Time Regulations 1998 (SI 1998 No 1833)*.

Rate of pay

You will be paid a salary of [£— per month/week/hour]. This will be paid in arrears on a [weekly/monthly] basis on the last working day of each [week/month] [by cheque/bank credit transfer into your nominated bank or building society account].

[Alternative clause] Since your part-time hours are variable, you will be paid [£ per hour] for all hours actually worked. This will be paid in arrears on a [weekly/monthly] basis on the last working day of each [week/month] [by cheque/bank credit transfer into your nominated bank or building society account].

[Alternative clause] For any hours worked over and above your normal working hours, you will normally be granted equivalent time off in lieu at a time to be agreed with your line manager.

[Alternative clause] You will normally be paid overtime for any hours worked over and above your normal working hours. This will be at a rate of pay equivalent to [your normal rate of pay/one and a half times your normal rate of pay/double your normal rate of pay].

[Alternative clause] You will not be entitled to receive any additional remuneration in the event that you work additional hours beyond your normal hours of work.

The Company reserves the right to make deductions from your salary, and/or to require you to make a payment to the Company in any of the following circumstances:

- where a loan has been made to you by the Company;
- where you owe the Company money (for any reason);
- where your salary or expenses have been over-paid (for any reason);

- where you leave the Company (for any reason) having taken holiday entitlement in excess of the amount of holidays accrued during the final year or part-year of your employment.

Expenses

The Company will reimburse you for all reasonable expenses wholly and exclusively incurred by you in the performance of your duties, provided that you furnish the Company with a properly completed expense claim form, together with receipts or other evidence of expenses.

Place of employment

Your normal place of work is at [Address of normal workplace].

[Flexibility clause] The Company may, however, require you to work at other locations anywhere in the [region/UK] and it is a condition of your employment that you agree to do so when asked.

[Flexibility clause] You may from time to time be asked to work elsewhere on a temporary basis, for example to cover periods of holiday or sickness absence.

[Alternative clause] Due to the nature of your employment, you may be required to travel and work anywhere within the UK or further afield as requested by the Company. This may be on a temporary or permanent basis. It is a condition of this contract that you agree to do this when asked.

[Alternative clause] Your job is totally mobile and therefore requires that you agree to travel and work in different locations and premises within the [region/UK]. Your base for administrative and pay purposes is [address of place of work/head office].

Holiday Entitlement

The Company's holiday year runs from [January to December]. You are entitled to [four] weeks paid holiday per calendar year. This is calculated on a pro rata basis of [1.67] days leave per calendar month.

The timing of your holidays must be agreed in advance with your line manager who will retain final discretion over whether and when to grant holiday dates. You should give your line manager a minimum period of notice of any dates on which you wish to take holidays. The notice period must not be less than twice the length of holiday you wish to take, for example if you wish to take two weeks holiday, you must give at least four weeks notice.

Holidays must be taken in the year in which they are earned (i.e. not carried over to another holiday year).

[Alternative clause] The Company shuts down for business for a two week period [around Christmas and New Year/during the summer], and you will be required to take two of your four week holiday entitlement at that time. The exact dates of these holidays will be notified to you in advance each year.

[Alternative clause] The Company reserves the right to nominate specific dates on which you are to take your annual leave. In these circumstances the Company will give you notice which will be not less than twice the number of weeks holiday that the Company wishes you to take.

Proportionate holiday entitlements will be granted to those joining the Company during the year, and to employees who leave part way through a holiday year. Precise details of the method of calculating holiday entitlement in such cases are available from your line manager.

In addition to your annual holiday entitlement, you will also receive [eight/ nine/ten] paid public holidays. These days will vary each year. You may be required to take your public holidays on a day other than the calendar day on which they fall at the Company's discretion.

[Alternative clause] Since you work part-time, your annual and public holiday entitlements will be pro-rated in accordance with the number of hours/days you are contracted to work.

[Alternative clause] Since your temporary employment is to last less than a year, your entitlement to paid holidays under the *Working Time Regulations 1998* will accrue on a monthly basis and be paid to you on the termination of your employment.

Pay in lieu of holidays not taken will not be made except (where appropriate) on termination of employment. Payment in lieu of holidays accrued but not taken as at the date of termination of employment will be calculated on a pro-rata basis and paid along with your final salary.

The Company reserves the right, upon the termination of your employment for any reason, to deduct from your final salary payment an amount equivalent to normal pay for any periods of statutory or contractual holiday entitlement which you have taken before your termination date, but not earned.

Illness

If you are unable to come to work on account of sickness or injury (or for any other reason), you must inform your line manager of the reason for your absence as soon as possible, and in any event no later than the end of the first working day on which your absence occurs.

If your sickness absence lasts for seven or fewer calendar days, you must complete a self-certification form immediately upon your return to work.

If your sickness absence lasts longer than seven calendar days, you must produce a medical certificate stating the reason for your absence and subsequent medical certificates for the total duration of the period of absence.

The Company reserves the right to require you to produce a medical certificate and/or undergo a medical examination with an occupational doctor at any time during your employment.

If you are absent from work due to sickness, you will be paid statutory sick pay (SSP) in accordance with the rates defined in statute. You are required to cooperate with the Company in the maintenance of necessary SSP records. For the purposes of calculating your entitlement to SSP, the 'qualifying days' are those days on which you are normally required to work.

[Alternative clause] You will not normally be entitled to receive any salary whilst you are absent from work due to sickness or injury.

[Alternative clause] During periods of sickness absence, provided you comply with the Company's rules on notification and certification, the Company will pay you a sum equivalent to your normal salary for a period of [one month/three months/six months, etc]. In this case, any SSP payable will be offset against normal salary payment.

[Optional clause]

Long Term Absence

The Company operates a long term sickness benefit scheme which may provide financial assistance in respect of sickness beyond six months duration for eligible employees. Full details of the scheme are available [from named person/in the company handbook].

Pension

[Alternative clause] The Company does not operate an occupational pension scheme.

[Alternative clause] The Company operates a [contributory/non-contributory] pension scheme which you are entitled to join after (number of months' service). Details of the scheme can be found in the Company's pension scheme booklet.

Termination of Employment

Your appointment is made subject to a probationary period of [three months/six months], during which time notice of termination will be one week on either side.

Thereafter you may terminate this agreement at any time by giving the Company [one week's one month's/three months] notice in writing.

[Alternative clause] Since this contract is for a fixed-term of [number of weeks or months], it is a condition of this contract that you agree to work for the full term specified in the contract.

The Company may terminate your employment at any time by giving written notice as follows:

- During the first two years of your employment, one week's notice;
- After two years' continuous employment, one week's notice for each full year of service up to the twelfth year of continuous employment;
- Twelve weeks' notice after twelve years of continuous employment.

[Alternative clause] The Company reserves the right to terminate this contact before the expiry of the fixed-term in the event that the needs of the business change, or due to other operational reasons. In this case you will be given not less than [two weeks/one month's] notice.

The Company may terminate your employment at any time without notice or payment in lieu of notice in the case of gross misconduct or other serious breach of contract on your part.

The Company reserves the right to give you payment in lieu of notice upon termination of your employment (rather than your working out your notice period). This provision, which is at the Company's discretion, applies whether notice to terminate the contract is given by you or by the Company.

The Company also reserves the right, at its sole discretion, to require employees who have resigned with notice, or who have been given notice to terminate their contract by the Company, not to attend work for the duration of the notice period. In this eventuality, the contract of employment will continue until the end of the notice period and the employee will continue to receive full pay and contractual benefits. Under these circumstances, the employee will not be permitted to take up employment elsewhere during the notice period.

Fixed-term Contract

This contract is for a fixed term of [number of weeks/months]. The contract will expire on [date].

Grievances

If you have any problem, complaint or grievance relating to your employment, you should raise it in the first instance, either orally or in writing, with your line manager with a view to resolving the matter. Failing satisfaction at that level, you may, if you wish, take the matter further by writing to the next level of management within three days. If at this next level the matter still remains unresolved, you may seek an interview with, or write to the managing director. The decision of the managing director will be final.

You may be accompanied by a fellow employee or trade union official of your choice at any formal grievance hearing.

Conduct

It is a condition of your contract that you will not engage in any conduct which is or might be detrimental to the interests of the Company.

Discipline

The Company's disciplinary procedure will apply to you, however during the first year of your employment, the application of the procedure is at the Company's discretion. A copy of the procedure is attached.

Data protection

In relation to the *Data Protection Act 1998*, you agree to the processing of personal data by the Company for the purposes of calculating your remuneration and maintaining records on attendance, health, discipline, grievances and adherence to all company policies, procedures and rules such as are necessary for the performance of your contract.

Acceptance

I have read and understood this written statement and the disciplinary rules and agree to accept the appointment under these terms.

Signed [employee's signature]   Date:

Signed by or on behalf of the Company   Date:

Notice Periods for Temporary Workers   **[2.24]**

Where a temporary employee is engaged for a period of one month or more, the employer must state in writing what the notice periods will be (as part of the written statement of particulars explained in **2.22** above). If the temporary contract is to last less than two years, the notice period for the employer to terminate the contract can be as little as one week. Thereafter, statutory minimum notice periods for the employer to terminate the contract rise at the rate of one week per completed year of service up to a maximum of twelve weeks. Whatever the notice periods are, they must be put in writing whether the employment is temporary or permanent (except in the case of a temporary contract lasting for less than one month).

In the case of a fixed–term contract lasting one month or more, the employer may either state in writing that the contract may be terminated before the expiry of the fixed–term with a defined period of notice, or alternatively that the contract will expire automatically on a specified date and that no notice clauses for early termination apply. In the latter case, it is as if notice to terminate has been given when the contract has been entered into.

Paradoxically, there is no reason why an employer cannot put notice clauses into a fixed–term contract, even though it seems somewhat inconsistent to set out a contract for a defined period of time and then say that notice to terminate it can be given before that period of time has elapsed. The inclusion of a notice clause would give the employer the option, in the event that the requirements of the business change, to terminate a fixed-term contract early without being in breach of contract. In *Dixon v BBC [1979] ICR 281*, the Court of Appeal held that the inclusion of a notice provision allowing the employer to terminate a fixed-term contract before the agreed termination date did not affect its status as a fixed-term contract.

The notice period required from the employee must also be stated in writing whenever the contract is for one month or more. However, the employer may wish to give careful consideration as to whether or not to introduce a clause into a fixed-term contract permitting the employee to terminate the contract early. Clearly, it will give the employer more certainty and security if a fixed-term contract does not contain an option for the employee to terminate early. The contract can state that it is a condition of the contract that the employee agrees to work through to the termination date defined in the contract, i.e. for the full term specified in the contract.

The Importance of Ensuring Employees Understand their Contractual Obligations [2.25]

Over and above the requirement for the employer to provide the key terms of an employee's contract in writing, the employer may of course wish to specify additional written terms of employment. These may be provided in the written statement itself, in a separate document such as a disciplinary procedure, a company handbook, a policy manual or in a collective agreement. Such terms could cover, for example, medical examinations, personal and property searches, confidentiality clauses, restrictive covenants, safety, general security measures, equal opportunities, mobility, dress codes and rules on the use of e-mail and the internet. It is sound practice to provide as much information to employees in writing as possible in order to confirm entitlements and avoid disputes at a later date.

Where policies and procedures are provided in a document other than the written statement of particulars, it is important that the employer should make it clear whether or not the policy or procedure has contractual force. A policy that is not incorporated into contracts of employment will be regarded more as a management guideline, and will not give rise to contractually enforceable terms and conditions.

The Implied Terms of a Contract of Employment [2.26]

The implied terms of a contract of employment are those that are not spelt out in writing but are presumed to have been the intention of the parties when the contract was entered into. Even though nothing is in writing, implied terms are binding on both the employer and the employee.

It is well established in law that the express terms of an employment contract take precedence over implied terms. The House of Lords ruled in *Johnson v Unisys Ltd [2001] IRLR 279*, that implied terms can supplement the express terms of a contract, but cannot overrule them. Earlier case law has held that an implied term in a contract can qualify or govern the manner in which an express term is put into effect. For example, in *Johnstone v Bloomsbury Health Authority [1991] ICR 269*, the Court of Appeal ruled that an express term in the contract that allowed the employer to require the employee (a doctor) to work up to 48 hours overtime in any one week (over and above his standard 40 hour week) was qualified by the duty to take care of the employee's health and safety. The employer had exercised the right to require the employee to work overtime in a way that had caused him to become ill, which represented a breach of their duty of care.

Similarly, in *United Bank Ltd v Akhtar [1989] IRLR 507*, the EAT ruled that a mobility clause in the employee's contract had to be exercised in a way that did not destroy or seriously damage the implied duty of mutual trust and confidence between the parties. Although the employer was entitled contractually to require the employee to move to a different location, their right to invoke the discretionary express term was qualified by the implied duty of trust and confidence.

How Terms Come to be Implied into Contracts　　　　[2.27]

Terms may be implied into a contract in any of the following ways:

1. As a result of the conduct of the parties, i.e. both the employer and the employee act as if the term was agreed
   If both the employer and the employee conduct themselves in a manner that is consistent with a particular term having been agreed, then the term may, by implication, come to form part of the contract. For example, if an employer imposed a pay cut on an employee and if the employee continued to work normally and accepted their normal pay at the end of the week or month, then the conduct of the employee would suggest that they had accepted the reduction to their pay.

2. Because they are necessary to give the contract 'business efficacy'
   This means that the term is necessary in order to make the contract workable, or that it is common sense that the term should be

implied. An example of a term implied in this way would be the requirement for an employee supplied with a company car to have a current driving licence.

3. Because they are so obvious that the parties took them for granted
    An example of a term implied under this heading could be the requirement for an employee to be honest in their dealings with their colleagues.

4. As a result of custom and practice in the organisation or within the industry as a whole

Custom and Practice [2.28]

For a term to be implied into employees' contracts as a result of custom and practice, it must be:

- Reasonable, i.e. fair and not arbitrary or capricious.

- Certain, i.e. precisely defined.

- Notorious, i.e. well known and established over a long period of time.

There is no legal timeframe after which a company perk or procedure can be said to be a contractual right. A term will only be implied into a contract on the basis of custom and practice if the practice has been regularly adopted in a particular company or industry over a number of years. Certainly a single incident will not give rise to an implied term. The notion is that, because the term has regularly been applied and employees have come to expect it, it has evolved into a contractual right.

Employers' Implied Duties [2.29]

Over a period of time, courts and tribunals have implied terms into employment contracts that impact on both employers' and employees' obligations. The most important of these duties on employers are:

- The duty to maintain trust and confidence in the employment relationship (see **2.30** below).

- The duty of support (see **2.31** below).

- The duty of care (see **2.33** below).

- The duty to provide and monitor a reasonably suitable working environment in which employees can perform their work (see **2.35** below).

- The duty to enable employees to obtain redress for any grievance they may have (see **2.36** below).

There are also implied duties applicable to employees, such as:

- The duty to obey lawful and reasonable instructions (see **2.38** below).

- The duty to exercise reasonable care and skill in carrying out their duties (see **2.39** below).

- The duty to maintain trust and confidence (see **2.40** below).

- The duty of fidelity (see **2.41** below).

The Duty to Maintain Trust and Confidence in the Employment Relationship **[2.30]**

This wide ranging duty obliges employers not to treat employees arbitrarily or capriciously. The duty of trust and confidence encompasses the concept of treating employees with respect and maintaining a working relationship that is based on trust. The duty also incorporates refraining from any type of conduct that would have the effect of making an employee's working life intolerable.

The earliest case to deal with the duty of trust and confidence was *Courtaulds Northern Textiles Ltd v Andrew [1979] IRLR 84* in which the EAT ruled that it was a fundamental breach of contract for an employer to act in a manner 'calculated or likely to destroy or seriously damage the relationship of trust and confidence between the parties'.

In a subsequent case (*Woods v WM Car Services (Peterborough) Ltd [1981] ICR 666*), the EAT held that a breach of the duty of trust and confidence would be judged according to whether 'the employer's conduct as a whole [towards an employee] ... is such that its effect, judged reasonably and sensibly, is such that the employee cannot be expected to put up with it ...'

Examples of a breach of the duty of trust and confidence could include:

- Severe bullying.

- An unjustified failure or refusal on the part of management to deal promptly and adequately with a genuine complaint about bullying or violence in the workplace.

- Unreasonable withholding of discretionary benefits.

- False, malicious or negligent accusations of improper conduct.

- The unreasonable exercise of an express contractual term or flexibility clause in the contract.

- Suspension from work without proper cause where the matter leading to the suspension could be dealt with adequately in another way (*Gogay v Hertfordshire County Council [2000] IRLR 703*).

- The sudden, unilateral introduction of a new policy or rules without consultation or agreement.

The scope of the implied duty of trust and confidence is limitless, but a breach will only occur if the conduct of the employer is unreasonable to the extent that it makes continuing in the working relationship impossible or intolerable for the employee.

The duty of support   **[2.31]**

Employers are obliged to provide reasonable support to their employees, to enable them to perform their duties to the required standard. For example, this duty would include the duty to provide adequate training, to give support to help employees deal with genuine problems with their work or working relationships, and the duty to take appropriate steps to protect an employee who is the victim of bullying or harassment.

Key Case   **[2.32]**

An example of a breach of contract arising out of an employer's failure to provide support is that of *Whitbread plc t/a Thresher v Gullyes [1994] EAT 478/92*.

Whitbread plc t/a Thresher v Gullyes [1994] EAT 478/92

Facts

Ms Gullyes had been employed as a branch manager of an off-licence for almost four years, and was successful and happy in that post. She was offered a vacancy at a larger branch that no other manager had been prepared to take on, and which had suffered from staff and operational problems. She accepted the transfer with misgivings and on the basis that she would be transferred to another branch if she so requested. The employer was fully aware that Ms Gullyes did not have the experience to manage the branch without considerable support.

Ms Gullyes found the new job very demanding and had to work an average of 76 hours a week, with little staff support. When she was away on holiday, the area manager transferred two of her most experienced staff to other branches without consulting her. On her return, she found she could not cope, and so requested a transfer. She was refused, and consequently resigned and complained of unfair constructive dismissal.

Findings

The tribunal held that the employer had failed to provide the support and back-up that Ms Gullyes needed in the new job, and that her position had been made untenable by the removal of the two experienced staff members. Thus Ms Gullyes had been placed in a position where she was prevented from performing her contract to any acceptable extent. The EAT upheld the findings of the tribunal, ruling that the employer had acted in fundamental breach of the implied term that obliged employers not to frustrate the ability of an employee to carry out their duties to an acceptable standard. They also ruled that there had been a breach of the implied duty of trust and confidence.

The Duty of Care [2.33]

The common law duty of care obliges employers to take care of their employees' health, safety and welfare, and to provide a safe workplace and safe system of work. This duty runs parallel to a range of statutory duties, in particular those imposed by the *Health and Safety at Work etc Act 1974*.

It is important to note that the common law duty to take care incorporates the duty to take care of employees' mental health. This means that employers are responsible for ensuring employees are not put at risk as a result of excessive work pressures which could lead to stress-related illnesses which in turn would be likely to lead to mental injury. This issue is becoming more prevalent in modern times as a result of workplace stress.

Key Case   **[2.34]**

The following case was the first to bring this issue to the fore.

Walker v Northumberland County Council 1995 IRLR 35

Facts

Mr Walker was employed as a social worker dealing with cases of child abuse. His workload had been steadily increasing over a number of years such that in 1986 he had a nervous breakdown. When, the following year, he had recovered sufficiently to return to work, he was promised additional resources to help him with his workload. Despite this, the support he had been promised failed to materialise and he had a second breakdown six months later. Mr Walker sued the Council arguing that they were in breach of their implied duty of care to provide a safe working environment and to provide effective support to alleviate his workload.

Findings

Mr Walker was able to succeed in his claim for damages because he was able to establish four factors:

- That the employer had breached their duty of care towards him by being negligent.

- That he had suffered an injury. Stress alone does not constitute an injury in this context, but the nervous breakdowns the employee suffered were deemed to constitute damage to his mental health.

- That the injury to his health was caused by stress at work, and not by external factors (the causation test). The onus on an employee is to show that, on the balance of probabilities, the employer's breach of the duty of care materially increased the risk of harm. Absolute proof is not required, although medical evidence will play an important part.

- That the injury to his health was reasonably foreseeable (the foreseeability test). Reasonable foreseeability can occur as a result of either the work itself or the individual's personal vulnerability to the work or working conditions.

The Court found that the Council could not be held liable for Mr Walker's first breakdown as, in their view, the employer could not have reasonably foreseen that he was exposed to a significant risk of mental illness through performing his job.

In relation to the second nervous breakdown, however, the Court held that the Council could have reasonably foreseen that injury to Mr Walker's health was a real risk, given that the kind of workload and work pressures that led to the first breakdown had persisted and no effective support to alleviate his workload had been provided. Damages of some £175,000 were awarded to Mr Walker.

In a case such as the *Walker* case above, it can be difficult for the employee to provide sufficient evidence to satisfy the tests of causation and foreseeability. Nevertheless a number of other cases for damages for psychiatric injury have subsequently succeeded in the courts.

The implied duty to take care also means that employers are obliged to act reasonably in dealing with any complaint or grievance about health or safety matters raised by employees.

The Duty to Provide and Monitor a Working Environment which is Reasonably Suitable for the Performance of Employees' Contractual Duties [2.35]

Key Case

This duty emerged from the case of *Waltons & Morse v Dorrington [1997] IRLR 488* reported below.

Waltons & Morse v Dorrington [1997] IRLR 488

Facts

Ms Dorrington had worked as a secretary for a firm of solicitors for eight years. She was a non-smoker. After an office reorganisation, she was moved to an open-plan area and began to suffer discomfort on account of cigarette smoking by colleagues. When she raised the matter with management, a policy was introduced banning smoking in the open-plan area where she worked. That did not resolve the problem, however, because smoke from nearby areas continued to affect the air quality and cause her discomfort. Having complained again and received an unsympathetic response, she resigned and brought a claim for constructive dismissal to an employment tribunal based on the allegation that her employer was in breach of her contract.

Findings

On assessing the evidence put forward, the tribunal concluded that the air quality had been intolerable for a non–smoker. On appeal, the EAT implied a term into the employee's contract that the employer must provide a reasonably tolerable working environment for employees to perform their work, and that the employer in this case was in breach of that duty. They also found that the employer was in breach of the implied term to provide employees a reasonable opportunity to obtain redress for a grievance. Thus there had been a breach of contract entitling Ms Dorrington to resign, and she succeeded in her case.

Although the duty to provide a reasonably suitable working environment was established in a case involving smoking, it could be applied to a much wider range of circumstances. One interpretation could be that it would also incorporate a duty to provide a working environment in which employees can perform their duties free from any form of bullying or harassment. In the case of *Moores v Bude-Stratton Town Council [2000] IRLR 676*, the EAT held that there was a duty on employers to provide and maintain a reasonably tolerable working environment, and that this duty applied to protect an employee from unacceptable treatment and behaviour and unauthorised interference with their work.

The duty to enable employees to obtain redress for any grievance they may have [2.36]

Key Case

The EAT, in the case of *W A Goold (Pearmak) Ltd v McConnell & anor [1995] IRLR 516*, implied a term into employment contracts that employers should 'reasonably and promptly afford a reasonable opportunity to their employees to obtain redress of any grievance they may have'.

Goold (Pearmak) v McConnell [1995] IRLR 516

Facts

Mr McConnell and Mr Richmond were employed as jewellery salesmen. They were paid on a salary plus commission basis. In 1992, when the sales methods changed, their commission dropped considerably. Both employees brought this to the attention of their manager in the form of a grievance, but nothing was done.

Later, a new managing director was appointed, and the two employees took their grievance to him. After some discussions, he said that nothing could be done immediately. The employees then tried to speak to the company chairman, but were told by his secretary that a meeting would have to be arranged through the managing director. With all routes effectively blocked, the two employees resigned and brought a complaint of constructive dismissal to an employment tribunal, alleging that the employer's failure to deal with their grievance constituted a fundamental breach of contract.

Findings

The tribunal found that the employees' grievance had been left to 'fester in an atmosphere of prevarication and indecision', and that the way in which the employees had been treated amounted to a breach of contract. The EAT upheld this decision and found that there was an implied term in contracts of employment that employers would 'reasonably and promptly afford a reasonable opportunity to their employees to obtain redress of any grievance they may have'.

Following the *Goold* case, irrespective of whether the contract of employment contains express terms governing grievance procedures, employees are contractually entitled to have any genuine grievances dealt with by their management. Managers should always take any complaint from employees about problems with their work, terms and conditions and working relationships seriously and make sure the complaint is promptly and fully investigated and properly dealt with. This will avoid the possibility of a claim that the implied duty to provide redress for grievances has been breached.

Employees' Implied Duties [2.37]

The Duty to Obey Lawful and Reasonable Instructions [2.38]

It is inherent in every contract of employment that employees should obey any lawful and reasonable instructions issued by their employer. This implied term must of course be read in the context of any express terms contained in the contract that define the nature and scope of the employee's job duties. If, however, an instruction is unreasonable (or unlawful), then the employee is under no duty to comply with it.

The Duty to Exercise Reasonable Care and Skill [2.39]

There is an implied term in every contract that the employee must exercise reasonable care and skill in the carrying out of their duties. If there is a serious breach of this duty, this may justify dismissal, as in the case of *Taylor v. Alidair Ltd [1978] IRLR 82*. In this case, an airline pilot had landed his plane so badly that it was seriously damaged. The pilot was deemed to be in breach of the implied duty to take reasonable care and skill, and his dismissal (for one single incident) was ruled fair by a tribunal.

The Duty to Maintain Trust and Confidence [2.40]

The duty of trust and confidence applies both to the employer and the employee. This means that the employee is contractually bound not to act in a way that fundamentally breaches the bond of trust that must exist in any employment relationship. Any act of very serious misconduct or blatant breach of company rules is likely to breach the duty of trust and confidence giving the employer the right to dismiss the employee summarily.

The Duty of Fidelity [2.41]

Employees are under an implied duty of fidelity, i.e. a duty to render faithful service. This includes the duty not to misuse or disclose confidential information belonging to their employer. This implied duty will apply whether or not there is an express clause in the contract governing confidential information.

The duty not to disclose confidential information applies throughout employment. Even after an employee has left their employment, the duty not to disclose information that amounts to a trade secret continues in force.

It is advisable for employers, despite the existence of this implied term, to introduce specific express rules governing the use of confidential information. This will be particularly important for employees who have access to sensitive information as part of their jobs. Express contractual terms governing confidentiality will have four key advantages:

- They will help employees to understand their obligations under the duty of confidentiality.

- They can clarify what information is to be treated as confidential.

- They can specify how employees should keep key information confidential.

- They will help the employer to enforce the rules on confidential information in the event of a breach by an employee.

Conclusion [2.42]

Whether a contract of employment is permanent or temporary, full-time or part-time, employees will have certain entitlements and duties under both the express terms of the contract that they have entered into and as a result of terms implied into the contract through common law and (possibly) custom and practice. Each contractual term creates an obligation of the part of the employer or a duty on the part of the employee. Correspondingly, both parties have the right to enforce the terms of the contract which will continue until either both parties agree to vary the contractual terms, or until one or other of the parties serves notice on the other to terminate it.

Questions and Answers [2.43]

Question

What is the definition of a temporary contract?

Answer

There is no universally accepted or legally binding definition of a temporary contract. A temporary contract is one which, from the outset, is agreed between the employer and the employee as a contract that will run for a limited duration. A temporary contract can involve either full-time or part-time working.

Question

What is the definition of a part-time contract?

Answer

An employee engaged on a part-time contract is one who works fewer hours per week or per month than someone working the company's

---

standard full-time hours. There is no definition in statute as to what constitutes full-time employment and it is therefore up to each employer to determine the number of hours that will represent the full-time standard for the organisation.

Question

What is the key function of a contract of employment and what are the necessary criteria for one to exist?

Answer

The existence of a contract of employment establishes the relationship of employer/employee between the parties. All the terms and conditions, rules, obligations and entitlements related to the employee's employment will be established by reference to the contract. In order for a contract to exist, there must be agreement between the parties, an intention to create legal relations, and consideration.

Question

At what point in time does a contract of employment come into force?

Answer

A contract of employment will come into force as soon as an unconditional job offer made by an employer has been unconditionally accepted. Withdrawal of an unconditional offer that has been accepted will therefore constitute a breach of contract, entitling the 'employee' to claim damages equivalent to the contractual notice period.

Question

What is 'consideration' in the context of an employment contract?

Answer

The practical interpretation of 'consideration' in the context of an employment contract is that the employer must agree to pay the employee and/or provide certain benefits, whilst the employee must agree to perform work for the employer. Without consideration, no contract of employment can exist.

Question

How does statutory legislation impact upon the terms of an employment contract?

Answer

Employee rights that have been created by the passing of legislation are automatically incorporated into every contract of employment, whether permanent or temporary, full or part-time. It is not open to employers to attempt to exclude an employee's statutory rights through the terms of the contract. Any contractual clause purporting to deny an employee such rights will be unenforceable.

Question

What is the difference between a full-time and a part-time contract of employment?

Answer

The key difference between a part-time contract and a full-time contract is the number of hours worked per week or month. Part-time employees are protected against unfavourable treatment on grounds of part-time status as regards the contractual terms of their employment. Part-time employees, irrespective of the number of hours they work, are also entitled to the same statutory employment rights as full-time employees.

Question

What are the key implications of a temporary contract?

Answer

The significance of a temporary contract as opposed to a permanent contract is that both the employer and the employee agree from the outset that the contract will be of a limited duration, and, depending on the actual duration of the contract, the employee may not gain sufficient length of service to become eligible for certain statutory employment protection rights. For example the right not to be unfairly dismissed requires the employee to have a minimum of one year's continuous service, so employees engaged for less than a year would not gain unfair dismissal protection unless their temporary contract was extended or renewed without a gap.

Question

What is the effect of a probationary period on an employee's statutory and contractual rights?

Answer

Although it is common practice for employers to stipulate in permanent employment contracts that employment is subject to a probationary period, this has no meaning in law as the employee's length of service for statutory purposes commences on the first day of their employment. However, it is open to the employer to stipulate that certain aspects of the employment contract will not come into play until after the satisfactory completion of the probationary period, for example payment of occupational sick pay during periods of sickness absence, or the application of the disciplinary procedure.

Question

What are express terms in a contract of employment?

Answer

The express terms of a contract of employment are those that have been specifically agreed between the employer and the employee, whether verbally or in writing. The notion of agreement is fundamental to the formation of the contract. Where a term of the contract has been agreed, this creates an obligation on the part of the employer to honour the term, and a corresponding right on the part of the employee to enforce it.

Question

Must all the terms of a contract of employment be in writing?

Answer

There is no obligation to put every single term of the contract of employment in writing. However, under *section 1* of the *Employment Rights Act 1996*, an employer is obliged to provide all employees whose contract is to continue for one month or more a written statement setting out the main terms and conditions of their employment. Temporary employees will therefore be entitled to receive a written statement, so long as their contract is to last for a minimum period of one month. The obligation to provide a written statement applies to part-time employees as well as full-time employees.

Question

What is the difference between a contract of employment and a written statement of particulars?

Answer

The difference between a contract of employment and a written statement of particulars is that the contract will consist of *all* the terms that have been agreed between the employer and the employee (including any terms agreed verbally), plus any implied terms, whereas the written statement is a document issued by the employer to the employee covering some of the terms of the contract. Usually what is in the written statement forms part of the contract, but unless the employee has agreed to the terms contained in the written statement, they will not be binding as part of the contract.

Question

What are the terms of employment that must be stated in writing?

Answer

The terms that must be in writing are: the names of the employer and employee; the date employment began and whether any previous employment counts towards continuous service; the rate of pay and pay intervals; terms relating to hours of work, holiday entitlement and holiday pay, sickness absence and sick pay, and pensions; periods of notice; the job title; the likely duration of a temporary contract; the place of work; details of any relevant collective agreements; details of overseas assignments; and (where the employer employs 20 or more employees) the person to whom the employee should apply if they have a work-related grievance and details of any disciplinary rules that apply in the organisation.

Question

Is it necessary or appropriate to give an employee engaged on a temporary contract written details of notice periods?

Answer

Where a temporary employee is engaged for a period of one month or more, the employer must state in writing what the notice periods will be (as part of the written statement of particulars). In the case of a fixed-term contract, the employer may either state that the contract may be terminated before the expiry of the fixed-term with a defined period of notice, or that the contract will expire automatically on a specified date and that no notice clauses for early termination apply. In the latter case, it is as if notice to terminate has been given when the contract has been entered into.

Question

What are the implied terms of a contract of employment?

Answer

The implied terms of a contract of employment are those that are not spelt out in writing but are presumed to have been the intention of the parties when the contract was entered into. Terms can come to be implied into an employment contract as a result of the conduct of the parties, because they are necessary in order to make the contract workable, because they are so obvious that the parties took them for granted, or as a result of custom and practice.

Question

How long does it take before a company benefit or procedure can be regarded by employees as forming part of their contractual entitlements as a result of custom and practice?

Answer

There is no legal timeframe after which a company perk or procedure can be said to be a contractual right. A term will only be implied into a contract on the basis of custom and practice if the practice has been regularly adopted in a particular company or industry over a number of years. The notion is that, because the term has regularly been applied and employees have come to expect it, it has evolved into a contractual right.

Question

What does the implied duty of trust and confidence mean for employers?

Answer

The implied duty of trust and confidence obliges employers not to treat employees arbitrarily or capriciously. It encompasses the concept of treating employees with respect and maintaining a working relationship that is based on trust. The duty also incorporates refraining from any type of conduct that would have the effect of making an employee's working life intolerable. Examples of a breach of trust and confidence would include bullying, unreasonable withholding of discretionary benefits and false accusations of improper conduct.

Question

Are there implied duties that apply to employees, as well as those that impact on employers?

Answer

Yes, there is a number of implied duties applicable to employees, including the duty to obey lawful and reasonable instructions, the duty to exercise reasonable care and skill in carrying out duties, the duty to maintain trust and confidence and the duty of fidelity.

3. Part-Time Workers

Introduction [3.1]

Part-time working is becoming more popular and widespread in the UK. At the end of 2000 there were approximately seven million people working part-time in Britain compared with five and half million some ten years earlier. This represents approximately a quarter of the total workforce. The majority of part-time workers are women – approximately 80 per cent – but there is evidence to suggest that more and more men would like to work part-time if the opportunity arose.

Part-timers may be employees, i.e. individuals engaged on a contract of employment by the organisation for whom they work, or workers such as self-employed contractors, agency temps, casuals and homeworkers. The distinction is explored fully in **CHAPTER 1**.

The Advantages of Part-Time Working [3.2]

Unfortunately, many line managers' perceptions about part-time working tend to be negative. Some take the view that part-time working and job-sharing will lead to insurmountable operational difficulties and problems in supervision. Whilst it is true that part-time working and job-sharing need to be carefully thought out and well managed, most of the practical difficulties that such flexible working practices can create are capable of being effectively resolved through the application of common sense, effective communication and forward planning.

It is a fact of modern working life that many people would like to reduce their working hours for a variety of reasons. Work-life balance has become an important issue both for the Government and for employers of all sorts, public and private, large and small. The days when part-time working was the prerogative of women engaged in unskilled jobs are long gone. Enlightened managers will recognise that flexible working practices, including the promotion of part-time working and job sharing, are an important element of business that demand recognition.

Managers who adopt a positive, rather than a negative, attitude towards part-time working will find that their operational needs can be better met. Just because work is arranged differently with employees working variable patterns and numbers of hours does not mean that the work will be done any less effectively or efficiently. Indeed, there is much evidence to suggest that the reverse is true. There are many advantages to both employers and individuals if opportunities for part-time working are promoted:

- There will be more flexibility for the employer in dealing with peaks and troughs in the workload, for example seasonal highs, short-term contracts etc.

- Cover can be made available at set times of the week when it is known there will be an increased customer demand, for example over lunch-times.

- Use of part-timers can help ensure machinery and equipment is fully utilised.

- Because a larger number of people will be employed, it will be easier for the employer to arrange cover for holidays, sickness absence, and maternity and parental leave.

- Part-time employees are less likely to need time off work for medical appointments etc.

- The employer's hours of operating can readily be extended by using part-time workers to cover early mornings, late evenings, weekend shifts, etc.

- The pool for recruitment will be wider as there may be many experienced people who, although unable or unwilling to work full-time, would be available to come to work on a part-time basis.

- Experienced female staff can be attracted back to work following maternity leave or a career break, as the opportunity to work part-time may provide them with the flexibility to combine family and work commitments. Many talented individuals are unable to commit to a full-time job because of childcare or other family responsibilities, but may be available for work on a part-time basis.

- Valued staff members who are either unable or unwilling to continue to work full-time can be retained.

- Part-time working may be suitable for people with certain disabilities, for example if an employee becomes disabled or is recovering from an accident or illness, they may be capable of working part-time and keen to return to work on that basis even though they are not able to work full-time.

- People who work a shorter day are likely to have more energy than those working very long hours. This in turn can lead to lower stress levels within the workforce.

- Wage costs are likely to be reduced, due to a decreased need for premium overtime payments payable to full-time staff working additional hours.

- Because part-time working suits many people, employee morale, motivation and levels of job satisfaction are likely to be enhanced.

Employers can therefore gain substantially by adopting a positive approach towards part-time working generally, and by promoting flexibility to switch from full-time to part-time working and vice versa for all employees, both male and female.

Possible disadvantages of part-time working for employers include higher recruitment, training and administrative costs, and possibly an increase in staff turnover (in proportion to the numbers employed). Given the many benefits of part-time working listed above, it may well be that these disadvantages are strongly outweighed.

The Scope of Part-Time Working [3.3]

Research indicates that part-time working is no longer restricted to unskilled or mundane jobs as was the case in the past. Instead, part-time working is becoming accepted as a normal business activity across virtually all types of employment and industry. The old-fashioned attitude that an employee could not be committed to their job unless they worked full-time is gradually disappearing and enlightened managers are fast realising that it is not the number of hours an employee works that are the key to the success of the business, but rather the quality of the employee's work. Clearly there is no logical reason why a part-time employee should not be fully committed to their job, or why they should not produce a very high standard of work during the hours they are present in the workplace. It could even be argued that part-time employees are likely to have more commitment and more energy than their full-time counterparts due to the lower likelihood that they will become over-worked, over-tired and stressed as a result of the long-hours culture still prevalent in many British organisations.

Part-Time Employees' Statutory Rights [3.4]

Part-time employees, irrespective of the number of hours they work per week or month, are entitled to the same statutory employment rights as full-time employees.

Prior to February 1995, there were three 'categories' of employee as regards entitlement to claim statutory rights such as unfair dismissal and statutory redundancy pay. Employees who worked sixteen or more hours per week enjoyed the full range of statutory employment rights after two years continuous service with the same employer, whilst those working between eight and sixteen hours per week had to work for five years to qualify for these same rights. Employees who worked for less than eight hours per week could never qualify.

This state of affairs was successfully challenged by the Equal Opportunities Commission (EOC) who brought a claim to the European Court of Justice (ECJ) arguing that the hours thresholds that applied to employees' rights to claim unfair dismissal and redundancy pay were contrary to European equality law.

The ECJ took the view that the hours thresholds as they stood were indirectly discriminatory against women who at that time constituted 87 per cent of part-time workers in Britain. The logic of this ruling was that, in order to qualify for the right to claim unfair dismissal and statutory redundancy pay within two years of starting work, an employee had to meet the condition of working full-time, and this condition was one with which a considerably smaller number of women than men could comply in practice. Since women were obviously placed at a disadvantage as a result of the application of this condition, it was indirectly discriminatory on grounds of sex, and the ECJ held that the condition could not be objectively justified.

Following the decision in this case, the Government implemented a change to the law via the *Employment Protection (Part-Time Employees) Regulations 1995 (SI 1995 No 31)*. As a result of the change, part-time employees now accrue continuity of service in the same way as full-time employees, and enjoy the same statutory rights in respect of unfair dismissal, statutory redundancy pay, maternity leave, the right to receive a written statement of particulars of employment and a range of other statutory employment rights. In particular, the right to claim unfair dismissal is now available to full-time and part-time employees equally after one year's continuous service, and the right to a statutory redundancy payment following dismissal by reason of redundancy is available to all employees over the age of 18 provided they have a minimum of two years continuous service.

It is worth noting also that part-time employees enjoy the same rights under health and safety legislation as full-timers.

The issue of indirect sex discrimination against part-time workers is addressed fully in **CHAPTER 9**.

The Part-Time Workers (Prevention of Less Favourable Treatment) Regulations [3.5]

It is unlawful, following the implementation of the *Part-time Workers (Prevention of Less Favourable Treatment) Regulations 2000 (SI 2000 No 1551)* on 1 July 2000, for an employer to offer part-time workers less favourable terms and benefits than equivalent full-timers just because they work part-time. In addition, such an approach may be in breach of sex discrimination legislation if the majority of part-time staff in the company's employment are women. This is based on the argument that, where there are more women than men working part-time within an organisation, the application of less favourable terms and conditions of employment to part-timers causes an indirect detriment to women, thus discriminating indirectly against them on the grounds of sex. The subject of indirect sex discrimination against part-timers is explored fully in **CHAPTER 9**, at **9.24**.

The Key Provisions of the Part-Time Workers (Prevention of Less Favourable Treatment) Regulations and Accompanying Guidance [3.6]

The *Part-Time Workers (Prevention of Less Favourable Treatment) Regulations 2000 (SI 20000 No 1551)*, implemented in July 2000, emanate from the EC Part-Time Workers' Directive whose key aims are:

● To prohibit discrimination against part-time workers.

● To improve the quality of part-time work.

● To encourage employers to take a positive attitude towards part-time working.

● To contribute to the flexible organisation of working time taking into account the needs of both employers and workers.

The prohibition of discrimination against part-time workers was enacted through the *Part-Time Workers Regulations 2000,* made under the *Employment Relations Act 1999.* The other measures, aimed at encouraging employers to increase the status of part-time work and facilitate access to part-time working have been enshrined in a DTI document titled '*The Law and Best Practice*' . This document contains Guidance Notes which give advice on how to comply with the law and a section titled '*Best Practice Guidance*' which suggests ways in which employers can widen access to part-time work. The DTI document does not have legal status, but a failure to follow its recommendations may lead an employment tribunal to make a finding that an employer acted unfairly. Further information is available on the DTI's web-site at www.dti.gov.uk/er/ptime.htm.

The Scope of the Regulations [3.7]

The Regulations confer rights on 'workers', i.e. not only employees but also other workers who provide their services personally to the employer. This means that (for example) part-time workers engaged on a fixed-term contract, people working from home on a part-time basis, part-time contractors, agency workers and part-time apprentices are all entitled not to suffer discrimination in their contractual terms when compared to an equivalent full-time worker. However, comparisons must in general, be made with a worker engaged on the same type of contract (see **3.13** below).

There is no minimum period of qualifying service for a worker to be entitled to the protection afforded by the *Part-Time Workers Regulations*, and no age limits. However, the Regulations do not apply during recruitment and therefore do not confer rights on job applicants to request or demand part-time working. However, a refusal to consider a job applicant for recruitment on a part-time basis may fall foul of the indirect sex discrimination provisions in the *Sex Discrimination Act 1975, s 1(2)*. This subject is discussed fully in **CHAPTER 9**.

Definition of Full-Time and Part-Time Working [3.8]

The definitions of full-time and part-time working provided in the Regulations are not altogether helpful. *Regulation 2 of the Part-Time Workers (Prevention of Less Favourable Treatment) Regulations 2000 (SI 20000 No 1551)* states that a full-time worker is one who:

'is paid wholly or in part by reference to the time he works and, having regard to the custom and practice of the employer in relation to workers employed by the worker's employer under the same type of contract, is identifiable as a full-time worker'.

A part-time worker is then defined as someone who:

'is paid wholly or in part by reference to the time he works and, having regard to the custom and practice of the employer in relation to workers employed by the worker's employer under the same type of contract, is not identifiable as a full-time worker'.

In practice what this means is that there is no statutory definition of full-time working by reference to any set number of hours and it is therefore up to each employer to determine what constitutes full-time working for their organisation. Any worker whose working hours are fewer than the standard full-time working hours in the particular organisation will then be a part-time worker. Thus, someone working 35 hours a week may be regarded as a part-time worker in organisation A if the full-time norm in that company is 40 hours a week, but, on moving to organisation B, may become a full-time worker if the custom and practice in organisation B is that 35 hours a week is the full-time norm.

How Workers can Enforce their Rights under the Regulations [3.9]

There is a provision (*Reg 6* of the *Part-Time Workers Regulations*) that allows part-time workers to request and receive a written statement from their employer giving the reasons for any less favourable treatment of them as part-time workers (see **3.24** below).

Workers who believe their rights under the Regulations have been infringed or who have been subjected to a detriment for raising a complaint about inequitable treatment under the Regulations, can take a complaint to an employment tribunal. There is no minimum qualifying period of service. Equally, any employee dismissed for attempting to assert their rights under the *Part-Time Workers Regulations* has the right to claim unfair dismissal irrespective of their length of service. Such a dismissal will be automatically unfair.

Where an employment tribunal makes a finding that a worker's rights under the *Part-Time Workers Regulations* have been infringed, they may award compensation in an amount that they consider 'just and equitable' taking into account the infringement itself and any loss attributable to the infringement. An example of a loss attributable to an infringement could be loss of earnings in circumstances where a part-time employee was denied a promotion on account of their part-time status and where the decision not to promote the employee could not be justified on objective grounds.

The Concept of Less Favourable Treatment [3.10]

The *Part-Time Workers (Prevention of Less Favourable Treatment) Regulations 2000 (SI 20000 No 1551)* make it unlawful to treat part-time workers less favourably than equivalent full-time staff unless the less favourable treatment can be justified on objective grounds. The question of justification is discussed fully in **3.23** below. Less favourable treatment is described in two ways:

- As regards the terms of the individual's contract of employment.

- Any other detriment by any act, or deliberate failure to act, of the part of the employer.

Thus the Regulations apply to workers' contractual terms and also make it unlawful for an employer to subject a part-time worker to any other type of unfavourable treatment on grounds of their part-time status. This non-discrimination principle in effect means that a wide range of treatment that may not form part of the worker's contractual terms is covered, for example criteria for promotion, access to training, etc.

The Pro-rata Principle [3.11]

The *Part-Time Workers (Prevention of Less Favourable Treatment) Regulations 2000 (SI 20000 No 1551)* stipulate that employers should apply the pro-rata principle unless it is inappropriate to do so. *Reg 1(2)* states that the pro-rata principle means:

> 'that where a comparable full-time worker receives or is entitled to receive pay or any other benefit, a part-time worker is to receive or be entitled to receive not less than the proportion of that pay or other benefit that the number of his weekly hours bears to the number of weekly hours of the comparable full-time worker'.

Certain contractual benefits would, arguably, be difficult, if not impossible, to apply pro-rata. One obvious example would be the provision of company car where an attempt at literal application of the pro-rata principle would have rather outlandish results! The employer may be able, however, to identify an alternative way of dealing with this dilemma, for example by providing the part-time worker with a less expensive model of car than the type allocated to equivalent full-time employees, or by providing a financial allowance equivalent to the pro-rata benefit of the car.

If no such solution presents itself, the employer may consider whether there is objective justification for not allocating the benefit to the part-time worker. Unless there is objective justification for not providing the benefit, the employer should grant the part-time employee the equivalent benefit to that enjoyed by comparable full-time employees in order to avoid unlawful discrimination against the part-time employee. Paradoxically, although it is unlawful to treat a part-time worker less favourably than a comparable full-time worker, the reverse is not the case, i.e. it is not unlawful to treat part-timers *more* favourably than equivalent full-time staff. Employers should therefore take care not to discriminate against part-timers when assessing how to deal with any benefits to be conferred on part-time workers that cannot be easily pro-rated.

Comparing Part-Time Workers to Full-Time Workers   **[3.12]**

The underlying principle contained in the *Part-Time Workers Regulations* is that part-time workers should not be treated less favourably than equivalent full-time workers on the grounds of their part-time status unless such treatment can be justified on objective grounds.

To bring a claim under the Regulations, the part-timer has to make a comparison with another worker who is a full-timer. This is the same principle as that enshrined in the *Sex Discrimination Act 1975* (under which a woman must compare her treatment to that of a man in similar circumstances) and the *Race Relations Act 1976* (under which an individual must compare their treatment with that of someone of a different racial group in similar circumstances).

Under the *Part-Time Workers (Prevention of Less Favourable Treatment) Regulations 2000 (SI 20000 No 1551), Reg 2(4)*, the comparator must be someone who:

- Is employed by the same employer (there is no provision for a comparison with someone who works for an associated employer).

- Is employed full-time.

- Is employed under the same type of contract (see **3.13** below).

- Is engaged to do the same or broadly similar work, having regard where appropriate to the worker's qualifications, skills and experience.

- Works at the same workplace, or, where there are no equivalent full-timers at the same workplace, works for the same organisation at a different workplace.

There is no provision for a comparison to be made with a hypothetical comparator as is the case in the *Sex Discrimination Act 1975* and the *Race Relations Act 1976*.

The Same Type of Contract   **[3.13]**

The provisions that the part-time worker and the full-time worker must be engaged by the same employer and employed under the same type of contract limit the scope for comparison for many part-timers. Under *Reg 2(3)* of the Regulations, certain types of contract are identified as being of different types, namely:

- Contracts of employment.
- Contracts for services.
- Contracts of apprenticeship.

Examples [3.14]

- A worker assigned by an employment agency to work for one of their clients on a part-time basis would have to compare their treatment with a full-time worker engaged by the same agency and assigned to the same client.
- A self-employed part-time worker engaged on a contract for services would be unable to compare their treatment with a full-time employee of the same organisation who is doing the same job.

When the *Part-Time Workers Regulations* were first introduced, a distinction was made between permanent (or open-ended) contracts and fixed-term contracts. This meant that an employee engaged on a fixed-term contract to work part-time could only compare their treatment with a full-time employee who was also engaged on a fixed-term contract, and not with someone employed on a permanent contract. This distinction was removed when the *Fixed-Term Employees (Prevention of Less Favourable Treatment) Regulations 2002* were implemented in October 2002. Thus, a part-time worker making a claim under the Part-Time Workers Regulations can compare their treatment to that of a full-time worker irrespective of whether the contracts of either worker are permanent or fixed-term.

No Full-Time Workers Employed [3.15]

One aspect of the *Part-Time Workers (Prevention of Less Favourable Treatment) Regulations 2000 (SI 2000 No 1551)* that came under fire from many interested bodies at the time the Regulations were being drafted was the inability of part-time workers to make a claim if they worked for an organisation that did not employ any full-time workers doing the same type of work. A common example is employment in the cleaning industry. It is common for the entire workforce of cleaners engaged in companies providing cleaning services to industry to be employed part-time. Irrespective of any individual cleaner's views on whether the treatment afforded to them by their employer is favourable or unfavourable, there can be no claim under the *Part-Time Workers Regulations*, simply because there is no full-time worker with whom their treatment can be compared.

The Terms and Conditions of a Part-Time Contract   [3.16]

The Regulations apply to all benefits conferred by a worker's contract, including some or all of the following:

- Hourly rates of pay (see **3.26** below).

- Overtime rates (see **3.27** below).

- Benefits under any contractual sick pay and maternity pay schemes. Where such schemes are operated for full-time employees, part-time employees would be entitled to receive the same rate of sick pay or maternity pay (on a pro-rata basis), to qualify for payment after the same length of service, and to be paid for the same length of time.

- Annual leave entitlement beyond the statutory minimum of four weeks per annum.

- Public holidays (see **3.32** below).

- Contractual maternity or parental leave beyond the minimum provided for in statute.

- Access to any career break scheme operated by the employer.

- Access to and benefits from any occupational pension scheme.

- Access to and benefits from any profit sharing scheme or share-option scheme operated by the employer.

- Any other contractual benefits, such as private medical insurance, staff discounts, subsidised loans, company cars, etc.

Non-Contractual Benefits   **[3.17]**

The provision in the Regulations that stipulates that employers must not subject part-time workers to any detriment because of their part-time status means that there must not be any less favourable treatment of part-timers as regards any non-contractual benefits.

Promotion   **[3.18]**

This 'non-discrimination principle' would for example come into play if a part-time employee was refused a promotion on account of part-time status, and the employer was unable to justify the refusal. Managers should not assume that part-timers do not want promotion or that they are not suitable for promotion, whether the promoted post is part-time or full-time.

Access to Training [3.19]

As regards access to opportunities for training, employers should not exclude part-timers just because they work part-time. The DTI's Guidance Notes that accompany the Regulations suggest that training should be structured wherever possible to be at the most convenient times for the majority of staff, including part-timers.

Practical Example [3.20]

XYZ Company employs a number of part-time employees who work various patterns of days and hours. Their terms and conditions of employment contain a general provision that part-time employees will receive a proportionate share of the pay and other company benefits applicable to full-time employees doing similar work. However, the precise entitlement of each employee is not spelled out in any detail.

In order to improve efficiency, the company has arranged a series of training programmes for its staff to be provided by an external training provider. The training sessions are scheduled to take place on Fridays and are open to all staff whether they work full-time or part-time. The general manager has put out a note to all employees encouraging them to attend the Friday sessions as part of their personal career development, and there is a strong hint that future promotions within the company will be linked in part to the achievement of certain core elements of the training programme. The actual arrangements for attendance, and release of staff to attend, are left to each departmental manager to organise.

A number of part-time employees who work Mondays, Tuesdays and/ or Wednesdays have complained that they are missing out on the training because they are unable to attend on Fridays. The general manager has stated that it would not be cost effective, given the relatively small number of part-time staff involved, to run each module of the training programme twice on different days of the week.

Another issue that arises a few weeks after the training sessions have been launched is the question of pay for the Friday training sessions, which normally last from 10.00 am to 4.00 pm. It has been agreed that managers need not insist that full-time staff work their full hours on these days (normal hours of work for a full-timer are 9.00 am to 5.00 pm) although they continue to be paid normally. James is a part-timer who usually works from 9.00 am to 1.00 pm on Fridays. He has attended two of the training sessions so far and, on discovering that his pay has remained unchanged despite the longer working day, he claims that he is entitled to be paid for the extra time involved in attending the course.

These matters have come to the attention of the general manager who has elected to discuss two questions with his senior management team. These are:

Is the company under an obligation to re-organise the training for the part-time staff who are unable to attend on Fridays?

What is the pay entitlement for James and other part-timers who attend one of the training sessions on a Friday?

Following the implementation of the *Part-Time Workers' Regulations*, workers must not be excluded from training just because they work part-time, unless there is objective justification for their exclusion. The question in this case is whether the company can justify not offering the training to the part-timers who are unable to attend on Fridays on cost or other objective grounds. This in turn will depend on the company's size, resources and the actual proportionate cost of arranging some of the training sessions on other days of the week. It seems unlikely that the cost of rescheduling would in fact be substantial, and so the exclusion of part-timers in these circumstances may well be unlawful.

Options that the company could consider would include re-scheduling the training to make it more flexible, offering at least some of the sessions on different days of the week, organising an additional equivalent series of modules at a convenient time for the part-timers, or offering other training methods, such as distance learning courses, as an alternative.

As regards pay for attendance on the Friday sessions, James would be entitled to be paid from 9.00 am to 5.00 pm on the days when he attends one of the training sessions. To do otherwise would constitute less favourable treatment of him as a part-time worker.

Redundancy Programmes [3.21]

The Guidance Notes that accompany the Regulations provide that in the event of a redundancy programme, part-timers should not be treated less favourably than their full-time equivalents, unless different treatment can be justified on objective grounds. Clearly this means that redundancy selection criteria must not discriminate against part-time employees, and any policy that has the effect of favouring the retention of full-time employees as compared to part-time employees is likely to be unlawful. The criteria used to select employees for redundancy should in any event be objective and fair and should be applied objectively and consistently without regard to whether the person works full-time or part-time.

Another important point to bear in mind in relation to redundancies is that where an employer elects to offer enhanced redundancy payments beyond the minimum redundancy payments required by law, part-time employees should be granted the same entitlement as full-timers calculated on a pro-rata basis.

Checklist [3.22]

The DTI's '*Law and Best Practice*' document provides further guidance:

- Part-time workers should not be denied promotion opportunities or treated less favourably than equivalent full-time staff in relation to promotion. Thus past or present part-time status should not on its own constitute a barrier to promotion, whether the promoted post is full or part-time.

- Where workloads are to be reorganised, part-time workers should not be treated less favourably than full-time workers unless there is objective justification for different treatment.

- Part-time workers should be afforded access to any profit-sharing or share option schemes and benefits such as subsidised loans or mortgages, staff discounts etc, if these benefits are available to full-time staff. Benefits under such schemes should be pro-rated where appropriate.
  Where a benefit, such as health insurance, cannot be applied pro-rata, this should not on its own be viewed as an objective justification for withholding it from part-time employees.

Justification For Treating Part-Timers Less Favourably than Full-Timers [3.23]

The *Part-Time Workers Regulations* contain a provision that allows employers to treat part-timers less favourably than their full-time counterparts if there is objective justification for such less favourable treatment.

No definition is given in the Regulations as to what 'objective justification' should consist of, but some help is at hand from the DTI Guidance Notes which state that:

'Less favourable treatment will only be justified on objective grounds if it can be shown that the less favourable treatment:

(1) is to achieve a legitimate objective, for example, a genuine business objective;

(2) is necessary to achieve that objective; and

(3) is an appropriate way to achieve the objective.'

This approach is similar to that used by tribunals when assessing whether a provision, criterion or practice adopted by an employer that is indirectly discriminatory on grounds of sex is objectively justified by factors unrelated to gender.

It can be seen that employers need to exercise caution in attempting to justify any less favourable treatment of part-time workers on the grounds of their part-time status. One possible justification could be where the cost of providing a contractual benefit to a part-time worker would be disproportionately high, for example where an employer provided full-time employees with private medical insurance, and the cost of providing similar cover to an employee who worked one day a week was the same as insurance cover for a full-time employee.

In relation to pay, the Guidance Notes suggest that paying a part-time worker a lower hourly rate of pay than a full-timer doing the same work might be objectively justified if the reason for the lower pay rate was poorer performance, as measured by a fair and consistent appraisal scheme.

It is important to note that showing a particular benefit could not be applied pro rata will not be enough to constitute objective justification for less favourable treatment of part-time workers.

Part-Timers' Right to a Written Statement of Reasons for Less Favourable Treatment [3.24]

Any part-time worker who believes that they have been less favourably treated on grounds of their part-time status is entitled under *Reg 6* of the Regulations to request a written statement of the reasons for the less favourable treatment from their employer. This request must be in writing.

On receipt of such a written request, the employer is obliged to comply within 21 days. Any written statement provided can be used as evidence in any proceedings taken under the Regulations and it is therefore in the interests of the employer to ensure that the content of such a written statement is clear and honest. A failure or refusal to provide a written statement, or the provision of a statement that is vague or ambiguous, may lead an employment tribunal to draw an inference that the employer has infringed the worker's rights under the Regulations.

The aim of including this provision in the Regulations was to reduce the likelihood of a claim being taken to an employment tribunal.

Model Written Statement Giving Reasons for less Favourable Treatment of a Part-Time Worker [3.25]

The following is a model reply letter to a query from a part-time employee asking why their rate of pay is less than a full-time worker performing the same job.

'Dear [name]

I acknowledge receipt of your letter dated [date] requesting written reasons for certain treatment of you as a part-time worker, namely that you are paid less than some full-time workers performing the same job as you.

The reasons why your rate of pay is lower than some equivalent full-time workers are as follows:

1. The company operates a system of pay increments that depend on length of service. You have completed three years of service and are therefore on the third point on the scale. Other employees, both full and part-time, will be on a higher point on the scale if they have longer service than you. This means that their higher rate of pay may be due to longer service.

2. As you know the company operates a merit pay scheme based on individual performance ratings recorded at the time of the annual appraisal interview. I have checked your record and noted that at the time of your last annual appraisal you were rated at level X, which means a performance standard marginally below the expected standard. You may recall that your line manager discussed various aspects of your performance with you at the time, and set targets for improvement. As a result of your performance, you were not awarded a merit pay increase last year, whilst other employees (both full and part-time) whose performance was rated more highly would have received a merit pay increase.

In conclusion, the reasons for your pay rate being lower than certain other workers in the department has nothing to do with your part-time status, but is, as you can see, based on your length of service and performance.

I hope this answers your query to your satisfaction, however if you have any further questions, please contact the undersigned.

Yours sincerely'

Pay for Part-Timers [3.26]

The *Part-Time Workers (Prevention of Less Favourable Treatment) Regulations 2000 (SI 2000 No 1551)* stipulate that part-time workers must not receive a lower basic rate of pay than comparable full-time workers (see **3.12** above on who is a comparable full-time worker) if the reason for the lower rate of pay is the worker's part-time status.

This of course does not prevent employers from paying different workers different rates of pay for other reasons, for example where one employee has longer service, better qualifications or has demonstrated a higher level of performance than another employee (provided this has been objectively and fairly measured via a well-designed appraisal scheme).

Overtime Payments [3.27]

As regards overtime payments, the ECJ ruled in *Stadt Lengerich v Helmig [1995] IRLR 216* that a part-time worker was not entitled to premium overtime payments until they had worked the equivalent number of hours of a full-time worker within the same organisation. The ECJ took the view that there is no discrimination where part-timers are paid for overtime hours at single time whilst full-timers earn a premium rate for overtime hours, simply because part-time employees in these circumstances receive the same overall pay as full-time employees for the same number of hours worked.

This principle has been incorporated into *Reg 5* of the *Part-Time Workers Regulations* which stipulates that any premium rate of overtime payable to full-time employees need not be applied to a part-time employee until the part-time employee has exceeded the organisation's normal full-time hours in any given period.

The equality of treatment to which part-time employees are entitled under the *Part-Time Workers Regulations* would also apply to any bonuses paid by the employer, for example a Christmas bonus, a performance bonus, etc. Once again, the pro-rata principle would apply.

Overtime example [3.28]

Company X pays full-time employees double-time for any overtime worked beyond 40 hours in any one week. Employee A works 42 hours during a particular week and is paid his normal pay plus two hours at double time. Employee B, who is contracted by the same company to work 28 hours a week, works 30 hours in a particular week. Employee B's entitlement would be to his normal weekly wage for the 28 hours, plus two additional hours at single time (and not double time). To qualify for double time, employee B would have to work more than 40 hours in a particular week. Thus if employee B, like employee A, worked 42 hours in a particular week, he would be entitled to be paid for 40 hours at single time plus two hours at double time.

Model Clause [3.29]

It is useful to insert a clause in the contracts of part-time employees to ensure this point is understood. For example, a contract of employment could state:

> 'In the event that you work additional hours beyond your contracted hours, you will not qualify for premium overtime rates unless you work more than [number of hours of full-time staff] hours in any one week, i.e. the equivalent of full-time hours'.

Working Out Holiday Entitlements [3.30]

Under the *Working Time Regulations 1998 (SI 1998 No 1833)*, all workers have the right to a minimum of four weeks paid holiday leave per annum. This can, if the employer so wishes, include any public holidays that are granted and paid for. Thus if an employer who operates on the basis of a five-day working week grants ten paid public holidays per year to all workers, the minimum amount of additional paid leave entitlement that would have to be granted would be a further ten days. This is because the combination of 10 days paid annual leave and 10 days paid public holiday would satisfy the statutory obligation to grant four weeks – i.e. 20 days – paid leave per annum.

Clearly, the pro-rata principle applies to the calculation of holiday entitlement in respect of part-time staff. Thus for example if a part-timer works three days a week (in an organisation where full-time working is five days per week), their entitlement to statutory annual leave would be three fifths of four weeks which, measured in days, would be twelve days.

If the number of days resulting from such a calculation includes a fraction of a day, this should be rounded up to the next whole day.

Pay Entitlement During Statutory Annual Leave [3.31]

Workers who take statutory annual leave and who are paid a regular weekly wage or monthly salary are entitled to be paid their normal rate of pay during their leave. However, where a worker's income is variable due to their hours of work being variable, special provisions are in place (*Employment Rights Act 1996, ss 221–223*). These provide that where an employee's remuneration varies according to the amount of work done, the amount of a 'week's pay' for statutory purposes is to be averaged out based on the employee's actual remuneration over the previous twelve weeks. Remuneration in this context must include any commission paid or similar payment that varies in amount.

This provision would be relevant to part-timers who worked variable hours according to the needs of the employer's business. In effect the employer would have to calculate the person's entitlement to holiday pay by:

1. Counting the total number of hours the part-timer has worked over the previous twelve weeks. If during any of the twelve weeks in question, the part-timer has not worked at all, the employer must take earlier weeks into account so as to ensure the calculation is

done over a twelve week period. This computation produces the 'relevant twelve week period'.

2. Calculate the average hourly rate of pay in respect of all the hours worked during the relevant twelve-week period.

3. Pay the worker the resultant hourly rate in respect of the period of statutory annual leave that follows the relevant twelve-week period.

Public Holiday Entitlement for Part-Time Workers [3.32]

Contrary to popular belief, there is no statutory obligation on employers to grant paid public holidays to employees, although many employers do so in practice. If it is an employer's practice to grant full-time employees a set number of days paid leave on public holidays (over and above annual holiday entitlement), this benefit must also be offered on a pro-rata basis to part-time employees.

Care should be taken as to the application of paid time off on public or bank holidays for part-time workers. Many UK public holidays fall on Mondays, which means that part-time workers who, for example, work only on Wednesdays and Thursdays could lose out unless an adjustment is made to their overall leave entitlement to allow them to receive the same pro-rata number of paid days leave as an equivalent full-time worker. If a part-time worker receives less benefit in terms of paid public holidays than an equivalent full-time worker, this will be unlawful under the *Part-Time Workers (Prevention of Less Favourable Treatment) Regulations 2000 (SI 2000 No 1551)*.

Practical Example [3.33]

Company XYZ operates on the basis of a five-day working week for all employees. However, a number of part-timers are employed, many of whom work on only two days per week, usually Tuesdays and Wednesdays or Wednesdays and Thursdays which happen to be the company's busiest days. It is the company's practice to grant full time staff ten paid public holidays per year, the dates of which are variable and determined by management at the beginning of each calendar year. This entitlement to ten paid public holidays is classed by the company as a contractual benefit over and above entitlement to paid annual holiday leave.

The company's part-timers who work two days per week will be entitled by dint of the *Part-Time Workers Regulations* to two fifths of the contractual benefits afforded to equivalent full-time workers. Thus the part-timers' right to paid public holidays will be two fifths of ten days, i.e. four days paid holiday per year.

The employer may have to make adjustments to the part-timers' actual paid leave entitlement to ensure that the four-day public holiday entitlement is granted, especially if fewer than four public holidays happen to fall on Tuesdays, Wednesdays and Thursdays in a particular year. The result may be that the employer has to grant the part-time worker additional days paid leave in lieu of the public holidays.

Workers Becoming Part-Time or Wishing to Become Part-Time   [3.34]

The *Part-Time Workers (Prevention of Less Favourable Treatment) Regulations 2000 (SI 2000 No 1551), s 3* contain provisions that allow workers who move from full-time working to part-time working within the same organisation to compare the terms and conditions of their new part-time contract with their previous full-time terms and conditions. This of course applies only where the new part-time contract is for the same type of work as the previous contract. The worker's right is not to be afforded less favourable terms and conditions on a pro-rata basis than those that were applicable under their previous contract. The right applies irrespective of whether part-time working comes about as a result of a consensual variation to the terms of the contract or following a termination of the contract coupled with an offer to re-engage on revised terms.

This same right also applies to workers who, by agreement with their employer, return to work on a part-time basis after a period of absence from work, provided the absence has been no longer than twelve months. Thus, workers who have agreed with their employer that they will return on a part-time basis to the same job, or a job at the same level, after a period of maternity leave, parental leave, sickness absence, extended holiday or after a career break will have the right to enjoy terms and conditions not less favourable than those they would have enjoyed if they had returned full-time. Any standard changes, for example a pay increase, that have occurred during the period of their absence, must also be applied to the worker on their return on a pro-rata basis.

Workers Wishing to Move to Part-Time Working [3.35]

The *Part-Time Workers Regulations* did not introduce any statutory right for employees to demand a move from full-time to part-time working. The provisions detailed in **3.34** above kick in only when the employer has *agreed* that a worker may switch to part-time working. As a separate measure, however, the Government has published proposals to introduce a right for the parents of young children under six years of age (both men and women) to request flexible working, and a corresponding obligation on the part of their employer to give serious consideration to the request. The right to request flexible working will include requests for a change to the number of hours worked, i.e. a switch from full-time to part-time working.

Furthermore, a refusal to agree to permit a woman to move from full-time to part-time working may be indirectly discriminatory on the grounds of sex since fewer women than men can work full-time due to childcare and other family commitments. This topic is explored fully in **CHAPTER 10**.

One important point to consider when an employee is granted a move from full-time to part-time working is that the amount of work output expected must be reduced accordingly. This can involve either a reduction in the overall quantity of work or the removal from the job description of certain discrete elements of the job. Clearly this needs to be reviewed and agreed clearly with the employee in advance of the part-time arrangement commencing. Any scheme promoting part-time working will be very quickly discredited if an employee who has moved to part-time working is expected to produce the same amount of work in fewer hours, or if colleagues are simply left to pick up the pieces of the work that the employee can no longer do. These are issues that management needs to address when reviewing the feasibility of part-time working for a particular job. One answer may be job-sharing, which is explored fully in **3.40** below.

Despite the absence of legislative provisions conferring rights on workers to elect to work part-time, the DTI's *Law and Best Practice* document contains a number of recommendations on this matter. It is advisable for employers to take these recommendations into account and indeed it may be advantageous for them to do so given the additional flexibility that part-time working can bring to the organisation.

Checklist [3.36]

The following points are based on the DTI's main recommendations. Employers should:

- Consider seriously any request for part-time working or job-sharing and explore the possibilities for accommodating an employee's request thoroughly. This could include agreeing to part-time working for a trial period and then reviewing whether it is working in practice.

- Before refusing a worker's request to move to part-time working, consider seriously whether there is an objective business reason for such a refusal (in order to avoid indirect sex discrimination).

- Maintain a database of workers who are interested in moving to a job-shared post (for larger organisations).

- Maximise the range of posts designated as suitable for part-time working or job-sharing.

- Adopt measures to ensure that information about full and part-time vacancies is effectively circulated throughout the organisation.

- Look for ways in which transfers from full-time to part-time work (and vice versa) can be facilitated.

- Take steps to arrange training in a way that is convenient for part-time workers.

- Monitor the organisation's use of part-time workers if possible.

Different Forms of Part-Time Working   [3.37]

Part-time working may involve any of the following arrangements:

- Working a defined number of hours on a set number of days which make up less than the organisation's normal full-time hours, for example from 09.00 am to 2.00 pm Monday to Friday.

- Working mornings or afternoons only on agreed days of the week.

- Working full-time on some but not all days of the week.

- Working a pattern to fit in with school hours, for example 09.00 am to 3.00 pm.

- Working twilight shifts, for example from 5.00 pm until 10.00 pm.

- Providing lunch-time cover, for example from 12.00 pm to 2.00 pm on some or all days of the week.

- Working on Saturdays and/or Sundays only where the business is open seven days a week.

- Working full or part-time every second week.

Contractual Terms for Part-Time Workers [3.38]

The contract of employment (or contract for services) should make it quite clear how many hours the part-time employee or worker is expected to work. There are a number of issues to consider, each of which should be clearly stated in the contract:

- The number of hours the employee is contracted to work within a defined period of time, e.g. within a week, a month or a year.

- When the hours are to be worked, i.e. on which days of the week and between what hours.

- Whether there is to be any authority for the employer to vary the terms of the part-time employee's contract, e.g. make changes to the hours or days worked, or to the number of hours worked.

- Whether or not there are paid breaks if the working day is six hours or less. The *Working Time Regulations 1998 (SI 1998 No 1833)* impose the requirement for all workers to be given a break of at least 20 minutes where the working day exceeds six hours.

- The position with regard to time off and pay for public holidays.

- (If the part-timer works on a job-share) the extent of any obligation on the part-timer to cover for their partner's absences.

Model Clauses [3.39]

Examples of contractual clauses are as follows:

'You are required to work a total of ten hours per week. Your precise hours are: Tuesday from 09.00 am to 1.00 pm, Wednesday from 09.00 am to 12.00 pm and Friday from 10.00 am to 1.00 pm. You are not entitled to any paid rest breaks during these work periods'.

'You are required to work a total of 23 hours per week. Your precise hours are: Monday from 09.00 am to 4.00 pm, Wednesday from 09.00 am to 1.00 pm, Friday from 09.00 am to 2.00 pm and Saturday from 09.00 am to 4.00 pm. Where your working day exceeds six hours (on Mondays and Saturdays), you will be entitled to a 30-minute paid break during your shift, the exact time of which should be agreed with your line manager. Where your working day is less than six hours, you will not be entitled to any paid breaks during working hours'.

'Your normal hours of work are Monday to Friday from 09.00 am to 1.00 pm. This represents a total of twenty hours. However, it is a condition of your contract that you agree to work up to an additional five hours per week if asked to do so by your line manager. Any additional hours over and above your normal working hours will be paid to you at single time'.

'Your normal weekly hours are sixteen hours per week. Your actual hours will be determined by your line manager who will notify you at least ten working days in advance of the beginning of each week what your working hours will be for that week.'

'Your normal working hours are Monday to Friday from 2.00 pm to 6.00 pm, representing a twenty hour week. The company reserves the right, however, to alter your start and finish times, or the number of weekly hours you work, according to the needs of the business'.

'Your normal working hours will be 25 hours per week, from 12.00–17.00 hours Monday to Friday inclusive. It may be possible to vary the number or timing of these hours from time to time on reasonable request. This is subject to your line manager's agreement in writing'.

Job Sharing [3.40]

Job sharing is an arrangement in which two employees share the responsibilities, duties, hours, pay and benefits of one full-time job in proportion to the hours that each of them works. Job-sharing contracts are part-time contracts in law and a job-sharer will therefore be entitled to benefit from the provisions of the *Part-Time Workers (Prevention of Less Favourable Treatment) Regulations 2000 (SI 2000 No 1551)* (see **3.6** above). Despite the fact that job-sharers are engaged to perform parts of the same job, each of them must be treated as an individual in respect of their contractual rights, obligations and conduct.

It follows that each job-sharer's contract should clearly define that person's individual terms (as for any contract) and the working relationship with the other job share partner. It is important that the contract should also cover the extent of any obligation on the person to cover for their job-share partner's absences, and the procedures that will be adopted if one partner leaves or is transferred elsewhere within the organisation.

Job sharing can come about in a variety of ways:

- An individual employee may reach agreement with their line manager that an additional part-time employee will be appointed to share an existing job.

- The employer may elect to advertise a full-time post as being suitable for job sharing.

- Two people may apply jointly for one full-time job.

- An employee returning to work after maternity leave may request a move to part-time working (see chapter 10 for a full discussion on this topic).

Advantages and Disadvantages of Job Sharing [3.41]

Job sharing as a flexible working practice can bring many benefits to employers and employees alike. Many organisations introduce job-sharing arrangements to further equal opportunities or as a means of retaining staff who are no longer able or willing to work full-time. Clearly it is better for an employer to retain an experienced member of staff on a part-time basis than to lose them altogether.

Job sharing provides the employer with considerable flexibility in terms of meeting operational needs. Furthermore, it often leads to increased work output – the employer will gain the benefit of the skills, experience, creativity and work effort of two people rather than one especially where the job-sharers have complementary or contrasting skills. The familiar 'two heads are better than one' cliché springs to mind! Additionally, evidence suggests that job sharers bring increased energy, commitment and productivity to the job.

There are, however, certain disadvantages, namely:

- Some possible loss of continuity if the job-sharers need to deal with a narrow range of customers.

- Differences of approach between two job-sharers – which, viewed from a different perspective, could also bring benefits to the organisation.

- Two people instead of one have to be recruited, trained and administered.

- There may be difficulties finding compatible job-share partners.

- There is obvious inconvenience if one of the job-share partners leaves.

Nevertheless, the benefits of promoting job sharing can be substantial as all the advantages of part-time working listed in **3.2** above will accrue to the employer provided there is a genuine management commitment to making job-sharing work. The practical problems can, to a great extent, be minimised by effective communication and forward planning.

Job Sharing Arrangements [3.42]

The most common job-share arrangements are where:

- Job-sharer A works all day Monday and Tuesday plus Wednesday morning, whilst job-sharer B works on Wednesday afternoon and all day Thursday and Friday.

- Job sharer A works mornings whilst job sharer B works afternoons.

- Each of two job sharers works alternate weeks. In this eventuality, a clause should be included in each job sharer's contract recognising that the employee will have continuity of employment through the weeks when they are not working.

There is, however, no rule that prevents two job-share partners working different numbers of hours, for example one may work five hours a day and the other three hours a day, or one may work two days a week and the other three days.

It is a sensible idea to construct job sharing so that there is some overlap between the two job sharers, i.e. time when both job-sharers are at work together. This will:

- Enhance communication between the job sharers.

- Help them to build a good working relationship.

- Allow work to be handed over smoothly from one job-sharer to the other.

- Maximise continuity and consistency.

- Minimise any problem areas.

The split may be made simply by dividing up the total amount of work to be done, or alternatively by identifying discrete elements of the job and allocating different job duties to each job sharer. The decision on how to divide up the responsibilities and duties and hours of a particular job is best made in consultation with the job sharers themselves. People have different preferences and it may be that one of two job sharers enjoys a particular aspect of the job more than the other. Where it is possible to take personal preferences into account when designing the job share, that will clearly benefit the job sharers and enhance their motivation. Furthermore, if some flexibility is built into the working arrangement, both the employer and the employees will gain in terms of reliability of cover and the employees' willingness to vary their hours.

Suitability for Job Sharing [3.43]

The suitability of jobs for sharing should be reviewed by management on a periodic basis and a positive attitude adopted towards making job sharing work throughout the organisation. In some organisations, all posts may be potentially suitable for job sharing whilst in others job sharing may need to be restricted to certain jobs. Managers should not, however, assume that a particular job is or is not suitable for job-sharing without first conducting an objective review of the job's component responsibilities and duties. If job sharing has not previously been tried, a pilot scheme could be established across defined jobs. In particular, whenever a full-time job becomes vacant, it should be assessed for job-sharing potential and the various options for splitting the job up considered.

Arrangements When One Job Share Partner Leaves [3.44]

One of the thorniest issues relating to job-sharing is the procedure to follow when one of the job-share partners either leaves the organisation, or is offered a promotion or transfer elsewhere within the organisation.

It is important for employers to determine the procedure that will be followed in this eventuality. Part of the commitment to making job-sharing work will lie in management's willingness to take on board the responsibility for finding a new job-share partner whenever one leaves.

It is recommended that in this situation, management should commit to the following actions:

- The remaining job share partner should first be asked whether they would like to take on the post on a full-time basis.

- No pressure should be put on the remaining job-share partner to work longer hours, whether temporarily or permanently.

- If the remaining job-share partner does not wish to perform the job on a full-time basis, the employer should commit to do its best to find a replacement partner within a reasonable period of time.

- The employer should involve the remaining job-share partner in the selection process for a new partner (in order to increase the chances of a compatible working relationship).

- In the event that a suitable job-share partner cannot be found within a reasonable period of time and after reasonable efforts have been made, the employer should reserve the right to move the remaining job-sharer to alternative part-time work elsewhere in the organisation so that the post can be filled on a full-time basis. This right should be incorporated into job-sharers' contracts of employment.

Checklist of Items to Consider when Setting up Job-Sharing [3.45]

Management should review the following issues when setting up job-sharing, preferably in consultation with the job sharers:

- The total number and pattern of hours to be worked to meet the needs of the business.

- The specific contractual hours to be worked by each job-sharer.

- How much the job sharers' hours should overlap.

- Whether there is to be a trial period, and if so for how long.

- Whether there should be flexibility of hours written into the contracts of the job-sharers to cover any absences from work on the part of the other partner, for example for holidays, sickness, parental leave etc, and if so how many additional hours each partner would be expected to work in such circumstances, and for how long.

- How to work out a fair pro-rata allocation of contractual terms and perks to the job-share partners (in particular if one partner works longer hours than the other).

- Whether the work to be carried out by the job sharers will be individually allocated, or whether the overall objectives and targets of the job can be collectively defined with the detail of who does what being left to the job sharers to decide.

- Whether there are any specific responsibilities or duties to be allocated exclusively or predominantly to one or other of the job sharers.

- Whether any performance related pay, bonuses or merit payments will be applied to the job as a whole or to each individual job sharer separately.

103

- How the job sharers will be appraised and how performance targets (if there are any) should be applied to the job share.

- How training needs will be assessed and met, i.e. whether training will apply to the post as a whole or whether training needs will be determined on an individual basis (or a combination of both).

- What steps can be taken to ensure compatibility between job-share partners' methods of working.

Clearly it is important whenever job duties are shared between two people that both of them are willing to share both the responsibilities and the day-to-day tasks of the job. Each must be prepared to accept that their job-share partner's way of working may not mirror theirs precisely. Cooperation and tolerance will obviously be required, coupled with a willingness to engage in open two-way communication with each other and with management. These are issues which need to be addressed by management during recruitment and induction training.

Term-Time Working [3.46]

Some employees with school-age children may be unable or unwilling to take a full-time job, but may be available for employment during the term-times of the school year. Making term-time employment available will allow the employer to gain access to an increased pool of potential employees from whom to recruit talented staff. In effect, engaging someone on a term-time contract will mean that the employee will work a reduced number of weeks during the year. Term-time contracts may involve either full or part-time working during the school terms only, with leave being taken during the periods of the school holidays.

Although there are benefits for the employer in introducing term-time working, there may also be disadvantages. The main inconvenience is during periods of school holidays when the employer may need to recruit temporary workers to cover term-time employees' absence.

Administration of term-time working [3.47]

There are two ways to administer term-time employees' pay:

1. Pay the employee a weekly wage during the weeks they work, with no remuneration being payable during the school holidays;

Schemes that pay on the straightforward basis of pay for weeks worked mean that a term-time employee will receive no pay during the school holidays. However, there is no reason why the employer cannot offer term-time employees the option to come into work during part of the school holiday period and be paid accordingly. Many term-time workers will not want or need to take every week off during the school holidays.

Weekly pay should be calculated simply by dividing the annual salary for the job by 52 and then paying the term-time employee that weekly wage for each week actually worked (or a pro-rata amount for a part-week worked). In these circumstances, however, the employer will have to ensure that four weeks out of the employee's annual leave are paid at the normal weekly wage, in order to comply with the statutory annual leave provisions in the *Working Time Regulations 1998.*

2. Pay the employee a salary made up of twelve equal monthly payments.

This approach has the advantage of avoiding a sharp fall in the employee's income during periods of leave. If this arrangement is adopted, there should be provision written into the contract of employment to allow the employer to claw back any money overpaid in the event that the employee should resign at the end of the school summer holiday.

Where the salary of the term-time employee is to be paid in twelve equal monthly instalments, the appropriate amount can be calculated as follows:

- First establish the normal full-time annual salary for the job.

- Divide this annual salary by 52 to establish the weekly wage.

- Multiply the resulting figure by the number of weeks during the year that the employee will be working.

- Add four weeks to take into account the four week statutory holiday entitlement under the *Working Time Regulations.*

- This produces the appropriate annual salary which should then be divided by twelve to produce twelve equal monthly salary payments.

For the employer's convenience, it is advisable to include a clause in term-time employees' contracts that stipulates that the employee's annual holiday entitlement must fall within the school holidays, and may not be taken during term-times.

Other terms and conditions of employment should be the same as for full-time staff.

Policies on Part-Time Working and Job-Sharing [3.48]

It is advisable and beneficial for employers to devise and implement a policy and procedure on part-time working and job-sharing. The policy should set out the aims of part-time working and job-sharing and the general approach of the company, whilst the procedure should detail practical and administrative matters. Taken together, the policy and procedure can clarify thinking and practice on part-time working for everyone within the organisation.

Obviously any policy or procedure must be compatible with the organisation's other policies, practices and contractual documentation. Care should therefore be taken to adapt the following model policy/procedure to the organisation's particular needs.

The Equal Opportunities Commission's Recommendations [3.49]

The Equal Opportunities Commission (EOC) has produced a useful good practice guide titled '*How to manage flexibility in the workplace*'. This document contains a number of recommendations on part-time working and job-sharing. In relation to what a policy should include, the following is a summary of the key points:

- Employers should make flexible working open to both sexes equally.

- No arbitrary restrictions should be imposed on the types of jobs open to job sharing. A cut-off point limiting flexible working or job sharing to junior posts could, as the EOC points out, lead to a glass ceiling preventing women from reaching senior positions.

- There should be no fixed limit on the number of jobs that can be worked flexibly.

- Job sharing should not be dependent on the employee having a minimum length of service.

- The employer should be willing to take steps to find a job-share partner whenever a request for job-sharing is received. Such a request should not be refused unless real attempts have first been made to advertise the job share opportunity and these attempts have proved unsuccessful.

- Employers should make sure training opportunities are made available to employees who work part-time.

Model Policy [3.50]

Policy statement

The company recognises the benefits that can be gained from part-time working and it is the aim of the company to facilitate and promote part-time working and job-sharing at all levels for all employees whenever it is practicable to do so.

Part-time working is appropriate where:

- There is insufficient work for a particular job to be done on a full-time basis.
- The workload and duties of a job can potentially be undertaken in less than full-time hours.
- The workload and duties of a job allow it to be split into separate components, thus permitting job sharing.
- Special initiatives are needed to attract and retain skilled staff.

Where a full-time employee wishes to move to part-time working, irrespective of their reasons for so wishing, the company will give serious consideration to the request irrespective of the status of the job, its level of seniority, or the individual's personal circumstances or length of service. It is the company's policy to facilitate access to part-time working at all levels within the organisation wherever possible and to take all reasonable steps to accommodate a request for part-time working.

The company cannot, however, guarantee that a particular request for a move from full-time to part-time working will be granted. Each case will be reviewed according to its own circumstances and an objective decision will be made based on the company's business needs and requirements and the nature of the employee's job.

The company will also publicise information on the availability of part-time and full-time positions in the organisation in order to facilitate transfers from full-time to part-time work and vice versa.

Definition of a part-time workers and job sharers

A full-time worker is someone who works 40 hours per week (the company's standard working hours).

A part-time worker is anyone who works fewer hours per week than the company's standard working hours.

A job-sharer is a worker who works part-time and who, together with another worker, shares the hours, tasks, responsibilities, pay and benefits of a full-time job.

Procedure

1. All line managers should adopt a positive attitude towards part-time working and should give serious consideration to any request for part-time working or job sharing.

2. When reviewing a job vacancy or assessing the workload of the department or of an individual job, line managers should routinely consider how certain duties in the department could be covered on a part-time basis, or divided up in different ways.

3. Any employee who wishes to apply for a move to part-time working or job-sharing in the same job should submit a written request to their line manager, detailing how they believe part-time working or a job-share arrangement could work.

4. In deciding whether a particular job can be done on a part-time or job-share basis, the line manager should focus on the job and not on the job holder.

5. When considering whether a particular job could be performed satisfactorily on a part-time or job-share basis, the line manager should take into account a range of factors such as the different elements of the job, the size of the workload, the need for continuity, any specialist skills required, etc.

6. On receipt of a request to move to part-time working, the line manager should discuss the request with the employee concerned to establish what options may be feasible. The line manager should ensure that the employee is fully aware of all the implications of moving to part-time work, in particular the effect on their level of pay and other benefits.

7. Line managers should not expect a part-time worker to cover all the duties of a full-time post. Agreement should be reached on either a reduced quantity of work, or the removal from the job description of certain discrete elements of the job in order to ensure it can be effectively performed part-time.

8. Employees moving to part-time work will be given written details of the changes to their terms and conditions of employment within four weeks of the revised hours taking place.

9. In the event that an employee's request to move to part-time working is refused, the employee's line manager will communicate this decision to the employee in writing and will state the reasons why part-time working cannot be supported in the particular circumstances.

10. The final authority to decide whether part-time working or job sharing can be granted in respect of a particular job lies with the line manager. However, in the event of a refusal that the employee considers unreasonable, the employee will have the right to use the company's grievance procedure in the usual way.

11. In the event that it is unclear whether part-time working in a particular post would be a workable option, the line manager may agree to a trial period during which the job will be done on a part-time or job-share basis. Where this is agreed, the employee's hours will be varied for a stated temporary period only and this will not be interpreted as a contractual agreement giving the employee the right to work part-time on a permanent basis. If, at the end of the trial period, the line manager considers that the trial has not been successful, the job will revert to its previous full-time status and the employee will be encouraged to resume full-time working.

12. In the event that a job is shared, and if one job-share partner leaves or is transferred or promoted to another post, the manager should deal with the remaining job-share vacancy as follows:

    • The remaining job-sharer should first be offered the opportunity to move to full-time employment, but no pressure should be put on them to agree to this.

    • If the remaining job-sharer does not wish to work full-time, then the manager should embark on the company's normal recruitment procedure in order to find a replacement for the employee who has left.

    • All job-share vacancies should in the first instance be advertised internally.

    • In the event of a failure to recruit a suitable replacement job-sharer within three months, the line manager has the right to transfer the remaining job-sharer into alternative part-time work in order to allow recruitment of a full-time employee into the post.

Rights and benefits for part-time workers

- Part-time employees, irrespective of hours worked, accrue continuous service and gain statutory employment protection rights on the same basis as full-time employees.

- Annual holiday entitlement for part-time workers will be calculated on a pro rata basis. Additionally, part-time workers will be entitled to be granted the pro-rata equivalent of eight paid public holidays each year, rounded up to the nearest half-day.

- Part-time employees will be entitled to receive occupational sick pay on the same basis as full-time employees. The amount of sick pay will be based on the part-time employee's normal basic rate of pay.

- All employees, regardless of the number of hours they work, are eligible to join the company's pension scheme.

- Part-time employees will be eligible for appraisal, training and promotion in the same way as full-time employees.

Conclusion [3.51]

Employers can gain substantially by adopting a positive approach towards part-time working, and by promoting flexibility to switch from full-time to part-time working and vice versa for employees at all levels, both male and female. Managers who adopt this positive attitude towards part-time working will find that their operational needs can be better met because part-time working can bring many benefits to both employers and individuals.

Part-time employees have the same statutory employment protection rights as full-time employees. Additionally, all part-time workers (including workers engaged on a self-employed or contract basis) have the right to the same contractual benefits on a pro-rata basis as full-time workers engaged on the same type of contract and performing the same or similar work.

It is advisable therefore for employers to conduct a review of the terms and conditions applicable to their part-time workers, including both those who are employed directly and workers engaged indirectly or on a self-employed basis. It is important to be sure that there are no material differences between full-time and part-time workers as regards both contractual rights and non-contractual benefits.

Questions and Answers [3.52]

Question

In relation to employees' statutory rights such as the right to claim unfair dismissal and the right to statutory redundancy payments, what distinction is there between full-time and part-time employees?

Answer

Part-time employees, irrespective of the number of hours they work per week or month, are entitled to the same statutory employment rights as full-time employees. The hours distinctions that once applied were abolished in 1995 following a case taken to the European Court of Justice (ECJ) in which the ECJ took the view that the hours thresholds as they stood at that time were indirectly discriminatory against women.

Question

Is it lawful to confer different terms of employment on part-time workers from those granted to full-timers performing the same work?

Answer

Following the implementation of the *Part-Time Workers (Prevention of Less Favourable Treatment) Regulations 2000 (SI 2000 No 1551)*, it is unlawful for an employer to offer part-time workers less favourable terms and benefits than equivalent full-timers on the grounds that they work part-time, unless there is objective justification for such treatment. Different terms and benefits can be offered to individuals working full-time or part-time provided the reason for any less favourable treatment of a part-time worker is not part-time status.

Question

What is the legal definition of a part-time worker?

Answer

There is no statutory definition of full-time working or part-time working and it is therefore up to each employer to determine what constitutes full-time working for their organisation. Any worker whose working hours are fewer than the standard full-time working hours in the particular organisation will be a part-time worker.

Question

What course of action is open to a part-time worker who believes that they have been treated unfavourably on the grounds of their part-time status?

Answer

Part-time workers have the right to request and receive a written statement from their employer giving the reasons for any less favourable treatment of them as part-time workers. In addition, a worker who believes their rights under the Regulations have been infringed or who has been subjected to a detriment for raising a complaint about inequitable treatment under the *Part-Time Workers Regulations*, can take a complaint to an employment tribunal. There is no minimum qualifying period of service to bring such a complaint.

Question

What type of 'less favourable treatment' is unlawful under the *Part-Time Workers Regulations?*

Answer

Less favourable treatment is described in two ways, firstly as regards the terms of the individual's contract of employment and secondly as 'any other detriment by any act, or deliberate failure to act, of the part of the employer'. Thus the Regulations apply to workers' contractual terms and also make it unlawful for an employer to subject a part-time worker to any other type of unfavourable treatment on grounds of their part-time status.

Question

What should an employer do if a particular contractual benefit cannot be pro-rated, for example the provision of medical insurance or allocation of a company car?

Answer

The employer may be able to identify an alternative way of dealing with this dilemma, for example by providing the part-time employee with a less expensive model of car than the type allocated to equivalent full-time employees, or by providing a financial allowance equivalent on a pro-rata basis to the full-timers' benefit. If no such solution presents itself, the employer may consider whether there is objective justification for not allocating the benefit to the part-time worker. If there is no such objective justification, the employer should grant the part-time employee the equivalent benefit to that enjoyed by comparable full-time employees in order to avoid unlawful discrimination against the part-time employee. It is not, paradoxically, unlawful to treat a part-time worker *more* favourably than a comparable full-time worker.

Question

What type of comparison must a part-time worker make in order to show less favourable treatment under the *Part-Time Workers Regulations?*

Answer

To bring a claim under the *Part-Time Workers Regulations*, a part-timer has to make a comparison between their treatment and the treatment of another worker who works full-time for the same employer. The comparator must be engaged under the same type of contract, be engaged to do the same or broadly similar work and must (normally) work at the same workplace.

Question

Is it obligatory in law to offer part-time employees training?

Answer

The *Part-Time Workers Regulations* impose an obligation on employers not to exclude part-timers from training just because they work part-time. This does not go so far as placing a statutory obligation on employers to offer training to part-time employees, but instead deems that part-timers must be treated no less favourably in this respect than equivalent full-time employees.

Question

In the event that an organisation needs to make a number of employees redundant, can part-time employees be selected first before the selection of any full-timers is contemplated?

Answer

No, such an approach would be unlawful under the *Part-Time Workers Regulations*. Redundancy selection criteria must not discriminate against part-time employees, and any policy that has the effect of favouring the retention of full-time employees as compared to part-time employees is likely to be in breach of the Regulations.

Question

Is it permissible to pay a part-time worker a lower rate of pay than a full-timer performing the same job, or must the level of pay be the same on a pro-rata basis?

Answer

Pay and other conditions of employment can be different for a part-timer provided the reason for the difference can be objectively justified by factors that are unrelated to the fact the person works part-time. Objective factors could include length of service, qualifications and level of performance. For example, the Guidance Notes that accompany the *Part-Time Workers Regulations* suggest that paying a part-time worker a lower hourly rate of pay than a full-timer doing the same work might be objectively justified if the reason for the lower pay rate was poorer performance, as measured by a fair and consistent appraisal scheme.

Question

Are part-time staff entitled to overtime payments in the same way as full-timers?

Answer

Where an employer pays a premium rate of overtime to full-time employees who work additional hours, the same premium rate need not be applied to a part-time employee until the part-time employee has exceeded the organisation's normal full-time hours in any given period. Overtime hours worked by a part-time employee up to the equivalent of full-time hours can therefore be paid at single time.

Question

How many days holiday is a part-time worker entitled to in law?

Answer

Under the *Working Time Regulations*, all workers are entitled to a minimum of four weeks paid annual holiday. The pro-rata principle applies to the calculation of holiday entitlement in respect of part-time staff. Thus for example if a part-timer works three days a week (in an organisation where full-time working is five days per week), their entitlement to statutory annual leave would be three fifths of four weeks which, measured in days, would be twelve days. Fractions of a day should be rounded up to the next whole day.

Question

If a part-time worker's hours vary from week to week, how should holiday pay be calculated when annual leave is taken?

Answer

Where an employee's remuneration varies according to the amount of work done, the amount of a 'week's pay' for statutory purposes is to be averaged out based on the employee's actual remuneration over the previous twelve weeks. The worker's average hourly rate of pay in respect of all the hours worked during the relevant twelve week period should be calculated and the worker paid the resultant hourly rate in respect of the period of statutory annual leave that follows the relevant twelve week period.

Question

Is an employer obliged in law to grant part-time employees paid time off on public holidays?

Answer

Contrary to popular belief, there is no statutory obligation on employers to grant paid public holidays to employees, although many employers do so in practice. If it is an employer's practice to grant full-time employees a set number of days paid leave on public holidays (over and above annual holiday entitlement), this benefit must also be offered on a pro-rata basis to part-time employees.

Question

What do the *Part-Time Workers Regulations* say about transfers from full-time to part-time work?

Answer

The Regulations do not go so far as placing a statutory obligation on employers to agree to allow workers to move from full-time to part-time working. However, in the event that agreement is reached for a worker to move to part-time working either immediately or after a period of absence not exceeding twelve months, the worker has the right not to be afforded less favourable terms and conditions on a pro-rata basis than those that were applicable under their previous contract.

Question

What are the issues that should receive attention when drafting a part-time employee's contractual terms related to hours of work?

Answer

There are a number of issues to consider including: the total number of hours per week or month the employee is contracted to work; when the hours are to be worked, i.e. on which days of the week and between what hours; whether there is to be any authority for the employer to vary the employee's hours; whether or not there are paid breaks if the working day is six hours or less; the position with regard to time off and pay for public holidays; and (if the part-timer works on a job-share) the extent of any obligation on the part-timer to cover for their partner's absences.

Question

What is a job–sharing contract?

Answer

Job sharing is an arrangement in which two employees share the responsibilities, duties, hours, pay and benefits of one full-time job in proportion to the hours that each of them works. Job-sharing contracts are part-time contracts in law and a job–sharer will therefore be entitled to benefit from the provisions of the *Part-Time Workers Regulations*. Despite the fact that job-sharers are engaged to perform parts of the same job, each of them must be treated as an individual in respect of their contractual rights and obligations.

Question

How should management go about splitting a job up for the purpose of organising a job–sharing arrangement?

Answer

The split may be made simply by dividing up the total amount of work to be done, or alternatively by identifying discrete elements of the job and allocating different job duties to each job sharer. The decision on how to divide up the responsibilities and duties of a particular job is best made in consultation with the job sharers themselves. People have different preferences and it may be that one of two job sharers enjoys a particular aspect of the job more than the other. Where it is possible to take personal preferences into account when designing the job share, that will clearly benefit the job sharers and enhance their motivation.

Question

What actions can realistically be taken when one of two job-share partners leaves their job?

Answer

It is important for employers to determine the procedure that will be followed when one of two job-share partners leaves the company or is transferred to a different job. This procedure should incorporate offering the remaining job share partner the opportunity, if they wish, to take on the post on a full-time basis (but no pressure should be put on them to agree to this). Otherwise the employer should seek to recruit a replacement job-share partner and involve the remaining job-share partner in the selection process. In the event that a suitable job-share partner cannot be found, the employer should reserve the right to move the remaining job-sharer to alternative part-time work elsewhere in the organisation, so that the post can be filled on a full-time basis. This right should be incorporated into job-sharers' contracts of employment.

Question

What is a term-time contract and how is an employee's pay administered when they work only during the school terms?

Answer

Engaging someone on a term-time contract means that the employee will work a reduced number of weeks during the year. Term-time contracts may involve either full or part-time working during the school terms only with leave being taken during the periods of the school holidays. Term-time employees' pay can either be administered by paying the employee the weekly wage for the job during the weeks they work, with no remuneration being payable during the school holidays, or by paying a salary pro-rated to the number of weeks actually worked divided into twelve equal monthly payments. In both cases, the employer must account for the four weeks statutory annual holiday entitlement provided for in the *Working Time Regulations*.

Question

Should employers operate a policy and procedure on part-time working?

Answer

It is advisable and beneficial for employers to devise and implement a policy and procedure on part-time working and job-sharing. The policy should set out the aims of part-time working and job-sharing and the general approach of the company, whilst the procedure should detail practical and administrative matters. Taken together, the policy and procedure can clarify thinking and practice on part-time working for everyone within the organisation.

4. Fixed-Term Workers

Introduction [4.1]

According to a survey conducted in 1998, around half of all temporary workers work on fixed-term contracts. There is a higher incidence of fixed-term working in the public sector than in the private sector with fixed-term contracts being particularly common in nursing and teaching.

Traditionally, temporary working was viewed as a type of employment typified by low-skilled and low-paid groups of workers. This view is no longer valid, however, as the highest growth in temporary working in recent years has been amongst professional, technically qualified and managerial staff. It is still the case that the majority of temporary workers are women (between 50 and 60 per cent).

There is no universally accepted or legally binding definition of a temporary contract. Furthermore, temporary contracts, which may be performed on either a full-time or a part-time basis, may be of different 'types', for example:

- A fixed-term contract, i.e. a contract whose termination date is defined and agreed in advance (see **4.6** below).

- A contract for performance, i.e. a contract that will expire automatically on the completion of an agreed job or project (see **4.24** below).

- A contract that will come to an end on the happening of a defined future event (see para below).

- A seasonal contract, i.e. a contract activated for the duration of a specified season of the year, or during a particularly busy period of the year for the organisation in question (see **CHAPTER 7**, at **7.14**).

- A casual contract, where the individual is engaged on an ad-hoc, as required basis (see **CHAPTER 7**, at **7.2**).

- Any other type of contract that is stated to be temporary, but where the termination date is not specifically defined.

This chapter aims to explore the features and implications of temporary contracts, in particular fixed-term contracts, the rights of employees who are engaged on temporary contracts, and the legal implications involved when such contracts terminate without renewal. The focus here is on temporary workers employed directly by the organisation. The subject of temporary staff hired through a third party, for example an employment agency, is dealt with in **CHAPTER 5**.

Statutory Rights of Fixed-Term Employees and Continuity of Employment [4.2]

In general, individuals employed on a temporary or fixed-term basis enjoy the same statutory employment protection rights as employees engaged on permanent contracts, provided they are directly employed by the organisation for whom they work (see chapter 1 for a detailed discussion on the employment status of various types of workers). However, since many statutory employment rights are dependent on the individual obtaining a defined minimum period of continuous service, temporary employees engaged on a single contract may not work long enough to become eligible for certain statutory employment benefits.

It should be borne in mind, however, that an employee who works on a series of consecutive temporary or fixed-term contracts will acquire continuity of service in the same way as an individual engaged on a single contract. This will be the case irrespective of whether the successive contracts are on the same, or different, terms and conditions.

Additionally, in certain circumstances, gaps between contracts can count towards the employee's continuous employment with the employer, a topic that is dealt with fully in **CHAPTER 6**.

Employer's Duty to Specify the Duration of the Contract in Writing [4.3]

There is a statutory duty on all employers to provide temporary employees (both full and part-time) whose contract is to continue for more than one month, with a written statement designating (amongst other things) the period for which their employment is expected to continue. These provisions are contained in the *Employment Rights Act 1996, s 1(4)(g)*. If the length of the person's employment is uncertain, then this fact should be stated together with an approximate indication of the expected duration of the contract. If the contract is to be for a fixed-term, the written statement must specify the date when it is to end.

Employees are entitled to receive a written statement within two months of the commencement of their employment. Full details of written statements of particulars of employment are available in **CHAPTER 2**, at **2.18**.

Model Offer of Temporary Employment [4.4]

The following model may be used to draft an offer of temporary employment:

'Dear (*name*).

XYZ Company is pleased to offer you temporary employment as (*job title*) in (*department*), commencing on (*proposed start date*). The main terms of your employment are as follows:

- Your employment will be for a temporary period of (*number of weeks or months*). The Company cannot guarantee any further employment at the end of this temporary period of employment, but may, at its discretion and depending on the availability of a suitable vacancy, elect to offer you a further term of employment.

- (*Alternative clause*) Your employment is for the duration of a fixed task/project, namely (*type of task or name of project*). Thus your employment will terminate automatically at such time as this task/project is completed. We expect this to be in the region of (*number of weeks or months*).

- (*Alternative clause*) Your employment with the Company is a temporary appointment for the purpose of covering the absence of (*name of employee*) who is (*or will be*) on (*maternity leave/sickness absence, etc*). Your temporary employment will therefore terminate when (*name of absent employee*) returns to work. Although it is uncertain at this stage how long the employee's absence will last, we anticipate that it will be approximately (*number of weeks or months*). We will endeavour to keep you informed as to the likely date of the termination of your contract.

- During the period of this temporary contract, your employment may be terminated at any time for any reason by either party, by giving (*one week's notice/two week's notice*) in writing.

- Your rate of pay will be £ (*amount*) per week/month.

- Your normal hours of work will be (*days and hours to be worked*).

The other terms of your temporary employment will be notified to you separately. If, in the meantime, you have any queries on the above, please contact the undersigned.

Yours sincerely

(Name of manager)'.

The Advantages and Disadvantages of Employing Temporary Workers [4.5]

There are various reasons why the employment of temporary workers, including fixed-term employees, may be of advantage to the employer, for example:

- Where it is known that the need for a particular type of work will be for a limited duration.

- Where extra staff are needed to cover seasonal or other peaks in the workload.

- Where there is a specific need to perform a one-off task or project.

- Where the employer is going through a period of change or uncertainty, for example if a merger is underway, and final arrangements for future levels of staffing have not been finalised.

- Where the employer wishes to cut down on premium overtime payments to permanent staff.

- Where there is a need for evening or weekend hours to be worked and the employer wishes to avoid asking permanent staff to work those hours.

- Where the employer requires cover for other employees who are on leave for example on maternity leave, parental leave or sickness absence.

- Where the employer wishes to assess a new employee's competence in a particular type of work, or general suitability for permanent employment, without making an up-front long-term commitment.

- Temporary contracts are relatively easy to terminate provided they have been properly set up and the temporary nature of the employment contract properly documented.

There are, however, certain disadvantages:

- There will inevitably be a lack of continuity resulting from the hiring of a succession of temporary employees.

- It may be difficult to recruit people with suitable experience because of the lack of long-term job security.

- Temporary employees may not have the same level of commitment to the organisation as permanent staff.

- It may be difficult to motivate temporary employees in the absence of any long-term career development opportunities.

The Features of a Fixed–Term Contract   [4.6]

The *Fixed-Term Employees (Prevention of Less Favourable Treatment) Regulations 2002* introduced for the first time into UK law a definition of fixed-term contract (see **4.39** below). A fixed-term contract is defined as a contract of employment that terminates in one of the following circumstances:

- on the expiry of a specific term, i.e. the date on which the contract is to expire is agreed in advance;

- on the completion of a particular task – see **4.24** below;

- on the occurrence or non-occurrence of any other specific event – see **4.26** below.

Historically in UK law, it was only the first of these, i.e. a contract for which the termination date was agreed in advance, that constituted a fixed-term contract. With the advent of the Regulations, however, the definition of fixed-term contract has been broadened out to include other types of temporary contract.

The Duration of a Fixed–Term Contract   [4.7]

The duration of a fixed-term contract can be any length of time agreed between the employer and employee. It is also open to the employer to extend or renew the fixed-term contract on its expiry (see **4.9** below). One provision to note, however, is that the *Employment Rights Act 1996, s 86(4)* stipulates that if an individual is employed on a fixed-term contract for one month or less, but despite this continues to work for the employer for a period of three months or more, the contract is deemed to be for an indefinite period, i.e. a permanent contract.

123

Model Clause Confirming a Contract is for a Fixed-Term [4.8]

The following is an example of a clause that can be used to confirm that a contract is for a fixed-term:

'This contract of employment is for a fixed term of (*number of weeks/ months*). The contract will commence on (*start date*) and finish on (*termination date*).

(*Optional clause*). The Company reserves the right to terminate the contract at any time prior to the expiry of the fixed-term by giving you a minimum of (*number of weeks, for example two weeks*) notice in writing. This could occur for operational reasons, or for any other reason that the Company deems appropriate.

(*Optional clause*) You may terminate this contract at any time prior to the expiry of the fixed-term by giving the Company a minimum of (*number of weeks or months*) *notice in writing*.

When this contract comes to an end, the Company cannot guarantee to offer you any further employment. At its discretion, however, and depending on whether suitable employment is available, the Company may at that time elect to offer you renewal of your fixed-term contract, or permanent employment.

Other terms of your fixed-term employment are contained in a separate document which is attached to this letter.

Yours sincerely

(Name of manager)'.

Extension or Renewal of a Fixed-Term Contract [4.9]

Where a fixed-term contract is extended or renewed immediately upon its expiry, i.e. with no gap between contracts, the employee's period of service with the company will be continuous. This will be the case irrespective of whether the terms and conditions of the extended or renewed contract are the same as those applicable in the previous fixed-term contract. Equally, employment will be deemed continuous where the start date of the renewed contract occurs within four weeks of the termination of the original contract and the new contract is confirmed prior to the termination of the original contract. In these circumstances, the employee will not be deemed to have been dismissed, and there will be no entitlement to redundancy pay.

Model Letters Extending and Renewing Fixed-Term Contracts [4.10]

The following model letters can be used to confirm to employees engaged on fixed-term contracts that the employer wishes to extend or renew the contract for a further fixed-term.

Letter 1 – Extension of the same fixed-term contract on the same terms

'Dear (name of employee)

As you know, your current fixed-term contract is due to expire on (*date*). The Company would, however, like to extend this contract, as the need for the work you are contracted to do is continuing. We would therefore like to ask you to agree to vary the termination date of your fixed-term contract and set a new termination date of (*date*).

All the terms of your current fixed-term contract will continue without change for the duration of the extension to this contract, including the notice clause(s) contained in the original contract.

When this contract comes to an end, the Company cannot guarantee to offer you any further employment. At its discretion, however, and depending on whether suitable employment is available, the Company may at that time elect to offer you renewal of your fixed-term contract, or permanent employment.

Would you please sign a copy of this letter and return it to the undersigned to indicate your acceptance of the extension to your contract.

Yours sincerely

(Name of manager).

I accept the offer of an extension to my fixed-term contract and agree to the new termination date of (*date*).

Name of employee   Date

Signed'

Letter 2 – Renewal of a fixed-term contract on different terms

'Dear (name of employee)

As you know, your current fixed-term contract is due to expire on (*date*). The Company would, however, like to offer you a renewal of this contract. Specifically we would like to offer you another fixed-term contract to work for this Company as a (*job title*) for a further (*number of weeks/months*) commencing on (start date, i.e. the date after the current contract expires) and finishing on (termination date). If you accept this fixed-term contract, it will run continuously with your current contract, affording you continuity of service.

The detailed terms and conditions of this current fixed-term contract are contained in a separate document which is attached to this letter.

(Optional clause). The Company reserves the right to terminate the contract at any time prior to the expiry of the fixed-term by giving you a minimum of (*number of weeks, for example two weeks*) notice in writing. This could occur for operational reasons, or for any other reason that the Company deems appropriate.

When this contract comes to an end, the Company cannot guarantee to offer you any further employment. At its discretion, however, and depending on whether suitable employment is available, the Company may at that time elect to offer you renewal of your fixed-term contract, or permanent employment.

Would you please sign a copy of this letter and return it to the undersigned to indicate your acceptance of the renewal of your contract.

Yours sincerely

(*Name of manager*).

I accept the offer of a renewal of my fixed-term contract as detailed in this letter and accompanying document specifying its terms and conditions.

Name of employee   Date

Signed'

Continuity of Employment [4.11]

Where an individual works on a series of fixed-term contracts that are not consecutive, continuity of employment is usually lost unless the gap between two contracts was less than one calendar week. There are, however, certain circumstances defined in the *Employment Rights Act 1996, s 212(3)* in which continuity of employment can be asserted even though the employee's contract has been terminated for a temporary period of more than a week, provided the contract has subsequently been revived or renewed (whether on the same terms and conditions or not). The Act stipulates that breaks between periods of employment that are due to a temporary cessation of work, or that occur as a result of an arrangement or custom, will count as periods of continuous employment even though no contract is in force during such breaks. In these circumstances, the employee's period of continuous employment is not broken, and the period of the gap between the earlier and the later contract is deemed to form part of their continuous service with the employer.

The Implications of Successive Fixed-term Contracts [4.12]

If, therefore, an employee regularly works for the same employer through a series of fixed-term contracts with gaps between them, the employee may be able to argue that the gaps between contracts were temporary cessations of work and that their continuity of employment is thus preserved throughout the whole period going back to the start of the first contract. If this assertion is challenged, a court or tribunal to whom the matter was referred would adopt an objective approach and review the individual's total employment history, considering the length of the periods of work in relation to the length of the gaps between them. Irrespective of the length of the period of a gap, if it is short in relation to the periods of work that precede and follow it, it may legitimately be viewed as a temporary cessation of work. Similarly, if there has been a series of gaps which, when added together, constitute a relatively short period of time in comparison to the employee's overall period of service, a court or tribunal would be likely to rule that the employee's continuity of employment had been maintained. Furthermore, if there is evidence of an 'arrangement' between the employer and the employee made prior to the completion of an earlier fixed-term contract that the employee would be re-employed in the near future, continuity of employment will be preserved.

A typical example of continuity being preserved in such circumstances would be a teacher engaged on a series of fixed-term contracts, each one lasting for the duration of the academic year. In a case such as this, no contract of employment would be in force during the period of the summer vacation. Case law, however, demonstrates conclusively that the gap between fixed-term contracts in these circumstances is viewed as a temporary cessation of work, allowing the teacher to maintain continuity of employment despite the gaps between contracts.

Full details of continuity of employment in respect of fixed-term employees is contained **CHAPTER 6**.

Termination of Fixed-Term Contracts [4.13]
Expiry Without Renewal of a Fixed-term Contract [4.14]

Curiously, UK law regards the expiry of a fixed-term contract without renewal as a dismissal (*section 95(1)(b)* of the *Employment Rights Act 1996*). This is despite the fact that the nature of a fixed-term contract requires the employer and employee to have agreed in advance that the contract will terminate on a specified date.

Fairness of Termination of a Fixed-term Contract [4.15]

Normally a dismissal on the expiry of a fixed-term contract will be fair on the grounds of 'some other substantial reason' (*Employment Rights Act 1996, s 98(1)(b)* or on grounds of redundancy (see **4.18** below). This does not, however, preclude the employee from taking a claim to an employment tribunal asserting that the dismissal was unfair, although the employee must have worked continuously for the employer for a minimum period of one year in order to be eligible to bring such a claim. If this occurs, the employer would have to be able to demonstrate to the tribunal's satisfaction what the reason for the dismissal was, that it was a substantial (and not trivial) reason, and that they acted reasonably in dismissing the employee for this reason.

Unfair dismissal could be argued successfully if the circumstances of the termination were that the employer was in a position to renew or extend the employee's contract, but failed to do so. This set of circumstances would suggest that the principal reason for the employee's dismissal was not the expiry of the fixed-term contract, but in fact some other reason.

In particular, if the employer allows the employee's fixed-term contract to expire without renewal and then engages another person on a new temporary contract to perform the same work, this will suggest that the reason for the first employee's dismissal is something other than the expiry of the fixed-term contract. Matters could be complicated further if the replacement employee was of the opposite sex or a different racial group to the original employee. This set of circumstances could give rise to a claim for unlawful sex or race discrimination for which there is no minimum period of qualifying service. For example, in the case of *BBC Scotland v Souster [2001] IRLR 150*, the Court of Session had to address whether an Englishman who had been employed on successive contracts as a radio presenter between 1995 and 1997 had been the victim of race discrimination when his employer decided not to renew his contract but instead to appoint a Scottish woman to the same job.

Employers should therefore remain acutely aware of the dangers inherent in *not* renewing a fixed-term employee's contract if continuing work is available.

Generally dismissal on the expiry of a fixed-term contract will be fair provided that:

- The fixed-term contract was set up for a genuine purpose.
- The purpose of the contract and the reason for it being for a fixed-term was known to the employee.
- The underlying purpose of the contract had ceased to be applicable when the employee was dismissed.

Prior to the expiry of an employee's fixed-term contract, the employer should:

- Review whether there is any alternative work available that the employee cold be offered either by renewing their fixed-term contract or offering them work on a permanent basis.
- Discuss any available options with the employee a few weeks before their fixed-term contract is due to come to an end.
- Take all reasonable steps to offer the employee further work if it is available.
- Even though the date of termination will have been agreed in advance, give the employee written notice of at least one week. Where the employee has worked for two years or more, notice should be no less than one week for each complete year worked, in line with the statutory requirements contained in *section 86* of the *Employment Rights Act 1996*.

The employee is in any event entitled (under *section 92* of the *Employment Rights Act 1996*) to request written reasons for dismissal. Upon receipt of such a request, the employer is obliged to comply with it within fourteen days.

Model Clause Giving Notice of Termination of a Fixed-term Contract [4.16]

The following model could be used as part of a letter giving formal notice of termination to an employee whose fixed-term contract is set to expire on a pre-agreed date:

'As previously agreed, your employment with this Company is on the basis of a fixed term contract and it was agreed that your contract would terminate on (*pre-agreed termination date*).

The Company hereby gives you (*number of weeks, which should be not less than one week's notice for each completed year of continuous service*) weeks notice with effect from the date of this letter to confirm that your contract will terminate. Thus your employment will come to an end at midnight on (*date of termination*) and all pay and company benefits will cease on this date.

We regret we are unable to offer you further employment at this time as the need for the type of work you were engaged to perform has diminished (*or the underlying purpose of your contract has ceased to be applicable*). We have reviewed our ongoing needs for people with your experience and skills and regret that no suitable alternative work is available.

We will notify you separately of the details of all payments due to you on the termination of your contract.'

Expiry of Contracts of Apprenticeship [4.17]

One exception to the rule that the expiry of a fixed-term contract constitutes a dismissal in law is the circumstance of a contract for apprenticeship coming to an end. In this case, there will be no dismissal. This principle was confirmed in *North East Coast Shiprepairers Ltd v Secretary of State for Employment [1978] IRLR 149*, a case in which an apprentice fitter was not offered employment following the completion of his apprenticeship with the company. The EAT held that the contract of apprenticeship was a one-off contract that was incapable of being renewed. Thus, the non-employment of the journeyman following the completion of his apprenticeship was simply a failure to employ following the termination of a contract of a completely different nature, and this did not amount to a dismissal in law.

Redundancy Rights upon Termination of a Fixed-term Contract [4.18]

Employees who have worked for the same employer on a continuous basis for a minimum period of two years, and whose contracts are terminated by the employer by reason of redundancy, are entitled to receive a statutory redundancy payment. It does not matter whether the employee's period of employment has been on a single open-ended contract (or so-called 'permanent' contract), on a fixed-term contract or on a series of continuous fixed-term contracts. The fact that an employee has been engaged on a series of short-term contracts does not deprive them of any statutory employment protection rights, provided the contracts are continuous with each other.

The EAT confirmed in the case of *Pfaffinger v City of Liverpool Community College [1996] IRLR 508* that the expiry of a fixed-term contract constitutes a dismissal by reason of redundancy. The EAT also confirmed in this case that employees engaged on a series of fixed-term contracts will become entitled to a statutory redundancy payment each time the contract under which they are engaged expires without renewal, provided they have accrued two years' continuous service at that point in time and provided they have not, prior to the expiry of the previous contract, accepted an offer of re-engagement to commence within four weeks of their termination date.

Thus, an individual whose fixed-term contract expires without renewal within four weeks will be regarded as redundant, and may be entitled to a statutory redundancy payment. In order to qualify for a statutory redundancy payment, an individual must:

- Have been employed on a contract of employment (and not on a contract for service – see **CHAPTER 1** at **1.2**).

- Have gained a minimum of two years' continuous service with the employer.

- Be under the age of 65 at the time of the redundancy (or under the employer's normal retirement age if that is lower than 65).

- Not have accepted (before the termination of the original contract) renewal of their contract or the offer of a new contract (with the same employer or an associated employer) to commence within four weeks of the expiry of the original contract.

The next paragraph will be numbered **4.20**.

Early Termination of a Fixed-term Contract [4.20]

Because a fixed-term contract is set up with obligations on both parties to maintain the contract throughout the period of the agreed fixed-term, this creates a contractual right for the employee to be allowed to continue in employment for the whole of the defined period. This means that early termination of the contract would constitute a breach of contract.

Early Termination by the Employer [4.21]

If, therefore, the employer terminates a fixed-term contract before the agreed termination date (without the consent of the employee), the employee would be able to bring a claim for breach of contract and damages equivalent to the salary and other benefits due for the outstanding period of the contract. The only exception to this would be if the employee had committed an act of gross misconduct entitling the employer to terminate the contract immediately without notice.

In calculating damages due to the employee in the event of an early termination in breach of contract, the court or tribunal would review whether the employee had found, or could reasonably have found, alternative employment within the period during which the fixed-term contract would have run but for the employer's breach of contract. Where the employee had found alternative employment, or where the court or tribunal judged that they could reasonably have found other work, any damages awarded would be reduced accordingly.

There is no minimum period of qualifying service for a breach of contract claim which can be brought either to an employment tribunal or an ordinary civil court.

The employee would also be able to bring a claim for unfair dismissal to an employment tribunal in the event of early termination of the fixed-term contract, subject to their having a minimum of one year's continuous service as at the date their employment came to an end. To defend such a claim successfully, the employer would have to ensure that the reason for the employee's dismissal before the agreed expiry date fell under one of the potentially fair reasons defined in the *Employment Rights Act 1996, s 98(2)* (i.e. capability, conduct, redundancy or legal restriction) and that they acted reasonably in dismissing the employee for this reason.

Early Termination by the Employee [4.22]

If the employee terminates the contract before the expiry of the agreed fixed-term, this too would constitute a breach of contract. However, unless the employer can prove that they suffered a quantifiable loss as a direct result of the employee's early departure, any claim against the departed employee for breach of contract, although technically possible, would normally be impracticable and unlikely to lead to any award of damages.

A more promising course of action for the employer to take in the event of an employee's breach of contract in leaving early would be to seek an injunction to stop them from going to work for a competitor during the outstanding period that the fixed-term contract should have run.

The Effect of Notice Clauses in a Fixed-term Contract [4.23]

There is no reason why an employer cannot insert notice provisions into a fixed-term contract allowing for early termination. It may, on the face of it, seem inconsistent to describe a contract of employment as fixed-term, and by the same token structure it so that it can be terminated early. However, the Court of Appeal has held (in *Dixon v BBC [1979] ICR 281*) that the existence of notice clauses in a fixed-term contract allowing for early termination does not necessarily prevent the contract from being a fixed-term contract.

Consequently, since the inclusion of a clause allowing the employer to terminate a fixed-term contract early would clearly give the employer flexibility in the event of their requirements changing, this seems a sensible course of action to take. The inclusion of such a notice clause would remove the possibility of the employee bringing a breach of contract claim in the event of early termination on the part of the employer (but would not prevent a claim for unfair dismissal if the employee had worked for the employer for one year or more – see **4.15** above).

Equally, the facility for the employee to terminate the contract early could be allowed for in the contract, although it is difficult to imagine any motive for the employer to want to include such a clause.

Contracts for Performance [4.24]

Another type of fixed-term contract is a contract for performance. This type of contract can be entered into where the employer has a specific task to be performed or project to be completed. Examples could include a building to be constructed, a new computer system to be set up or a piece of research to be completed. Although a contract for performance has no set termination date, it is designed to terminate automatically when the specific task or project comes to an end. This is described in law as the contract being 'discharged by performance'.

When setting up a contract for performance, the employer should make sure that:

- There is a genuine business need for the contract to terminate on the completion of a specific task or project (as opposed to a desire to limit the length of an individual's employment for other reasons).

- It is clearly stated in writing that the contract will terminate when the specific task or project is completed.

- The employee has signed to indicate their understanding and acceptance of this fact.

- The task or project on which the individual is engaged is clearly defined and described in such a way that it will be clear when completion has been achieved.

The employer may of course include notice clauses in a contract for performance to allow for termination before the completion of the defined task or project. Early termination would, however, run the risk of the individual bringing an unfair dismissal claim to tribunal, provided they had worked for a minimum period of one year at the date of their termination.

Model Clause Indicating that a Contract will end on the Completion of a Job or Project [4.25]

The following clause could be inserted into a contract for performance to make it clear to the employee that the contract will expire automatically on the completion of the job or project for which they have been appointed:

'Your appointment as *(job title)* is a temporary appointment for the duration of a specific task *(or project)*. The task/project in question involves *(describe the task or project)* and is expected to last for approximately *(approximate number of weeks or months)*. In accepting this appointment, you agree that when this task *(or project)* is complete, your contract of employment will expire automatically.

Would you please sign below to indicate that you have understood and accepted the terms of this temporary appointment.'

Contracts that Continue Until the Happening of a Future Event [4.26]

Another common type of fixed-term contract is one that comes to an end upon the occurrence (or non-occurrence) of a specific event. In the past, the expiry of this type of contract was not regarded as a dismissal in law, but the implementation of the *Fixed-Term Employees (Prevention of Less Favourable Treatment) Regulations 2002* changed this so as to bring the treatment of such a contract into line with that of fixed-term contracts.

Common Examples [4.27]

The most common examples of contracts that end on the happening of a future event are:

- Contracts that depend on the continuing provision of external funding (see **4.29** below).

- Contracts that will end on the return to work of an employee who is absent from work (see **4.30** below).

Key Case [4.28]

The distinction can be complex, as was evident in the case of *Wiltshire County Council v NATFHE & anor [1980] IRLR 198*:

> ### *Wiltshire County Council v NATFHE & anor [1980] IRLR 198*
>
> #### *Facts*
>
> The Council had engaged a part-time teacher to teach at one of their colleges for the duration of the academic year. The arrangements were that the employee would work fluctuating hours depending on the number of students attending her classes, and would be paid only for the hours she worked. It was accepted that if the College Principal decided that a particular course was not sufficiently well attended, the course in question could be stopped before the end of the academic year. When the employee's contract was not renewed, she claimed unfair dismissal, and as a preliminary matter the Court of Appeal had to

assess whether the contract had been a fixed-term contract for the whole of the academic session or a contract for an uncertain duration that would terminate on the happening of an future event, i.e. if the demand for the courses she taught ran out.

Findings

The Court of Appeal upheld the original employment tribunal's decision that the employee's contract was in fact a fixed-term contract. This was because the evidence pointed to the conclusion that the employee had been engaged to work up to the last day of the academic session, irrespective of whether her teaching work might dry up earlier. The Court of Appeal pointed out, however, that any similar case would have to be assessed on its own merits, and if the evidence suggested that an employee had been engaged under a contract of uncertain duration in which employment would cease when the work came to an end, such an arrangement would not amount to a fixed-term contract.

Since the implementation of the *Fixed-Term Employees (Prevention of Less Favourable Treatment) Regulations 2002*, a contract that is set up to expire on the occurrence or non-occurrence of a specific event is regarded as a fixed-term contract in law. The distinctions drawn by the Court of Appeal in the above case are therefore of interest purely for historical purposes.

Contracts that Depend on the Continuing Provision of External Funding [4.29]

The termination of a contract that is dependent on the continuing provision of external funding was not, in the past, regarded as a dismissal in law (although the implementation of the *Fixed-Term Employees (Protection of Employment) Regulations 2002* changed the status of such contracts such that they are now viewed in the same way as fixed-term contracts – see **4.34** below). In the case of *Brown & ors v Knowsley Borough Council [1986] IRLR 102*, which occurred before the law changed in this respect, the employee had been engaged on a contract that said:

'The appointment will last only as long as sufficient funds are provided either by the Manpower Services Commission or by other firms/ sponsors to fund it'.

The EAT judged that the wording of the contract meant it was a contract terminable upon the happening of a future event, namely the discontinuance of external funding. Thus the contract had terminated automatically without a dismissal having taken place.

Contracts that end on the return to work of an employee who is absent from work [4.30]

If an employee is engaged to cover for another employee's absence, this will not be a fixed-term contract unless the termination date is specifically set out in the contract and agreed in advance. This may well be possible in the event that the purpose of the original employee's absence is annual leave, a period of agreed sabbatical leave (see **CHAPTER 6** at **6.23**) or parental leave.

Often, however, it will not be known exactly how long the absent employee will remain away from work. For example the precise duration of a period of absence on account of sickness or maternity leave will not normally be known at the outset. Thus a temporary contract set up to cover such periods of absence will not be a fixed-term contract because it will not be possible to specify the precise termination date with any accuracy, nor will it be a contract for performance because there is no specific job or project to be completed.

Despite this, the termination of employment of a temporary worker engaged for an indefinite period to cover another employee's absence will constitute a dismissal in law because the contract will fall under the new definition of 'fixed-term contract' contained in the *Fixed-Term Employees (Prevention of Less Favourable Treatment) Regulations 2002.*

Temporary Contracts to Cover Maternity Leave and Suspensions on Medical Grounds [4.31]

Special statutory provisions exist (in the *Employment Rights Act 1996, s 106*) for appointments made to cover absences due to maternity leave or to cover another employee's medical suspension.

In these circumstances, the employer must inform the temporary employee in writing that their employment will come to an end on the return to work of the absent employee. Provided this is done correctly and properly documented, the dismissal of the temporary replacement employee on the other employee's return to work will be fair.

Model Clause Indicating that a Contract will end on the Return to Work of an Employee on Maternity Leave [4.32]

The following wording could be inserted into a temporary contract to make it clear to the employee that the contract will terminate on the return to work of the employee whom they have been engaged to replace:

'Your employment as (*job title*) is a temporary appointment for the purpose of providing cover for (*name of employee who is to be replaced*) who will be absent from work on maternity leave. The contract will commence on (*start date*) and will terminate on the return to work of (*name of employee who is to be replaced*). We cannot confirm at this point in time exactly how long the employee's maternity leave will last, but it will not be more than (*number of weeks*). It is a condition of this contract that you agree that when (*name of employee who is to be replaced*) returns to work, your contract of employment will be terminated.

The Company will give you written notice of the date on which your contract will terminate of not less than one week (*or longer, but not less*)

(*Optional clause*). The Company reserves the right to terminate your contract at any time prior to the return to work of (*name of employee who is to be replaced*) by giving you a minimum of one week's notice in writing. This could occur for operational reasons, or for any other reason that the Company deems appropriate.

The terms and conditions of your temporary employment are contained in a separate document which is attached to this letter.

When your contract comes to an end, the Company cannot guarantee to offer you any further employment. At its discretion, however, and depending on whether suitable employment is available, the Company may at that time elect to offer you another temporary contract, or permanent employment.

Would you please sign below to indicate that you have understood and accepted the terms of this temporary appointment.'

Fixed-Term Contracts and Pregnant Workers [4.33]

As stated earlier, employees engaged on temporary contracts in general enjoy the same statutory employment protection rights as permanent staff, subject to the need to gain a minimum period of service to qualify for certain rights.

One right that requires no minimum period of qualifying service is the right to take ordinary maternity leave of up to 18 weeks (set to be increased to 26 weeks in April 2003). All employees who are pregnant, both full and part-time, have this right.

Employees who are pregnant also enjoy considerable protection under UK sex discrimination legislation. It was established in the case of *Webb v EMO Air Cargo (UK) Ltd ECJ [1995] ICR 1021* that the dismissal of a woman on grounds related to pregnancy will be discriminatory on grounds of gender without the need for a comparison with a male employee in comparable circumstances. The *Webb* case concerned the dismissal of an employee who had been hired primarily to replace another employee during the first employee's maternity leave. The ECJ stated that the fact the employee would be unavailable for work during a particularly important period of time for the employer was irrelevant.

In another case (*Caruana v Manchester Airport plc [1996] IRLR 378*) it was held by the EAT that if an employer takes a decision not to renew an employee's fixed-term contract because of her future unavailability on account of pregnancy, this will amount to unlawful sex discrimination. This approach was ratified by the ECJ in the Spanish case of *Jiménez Melgar v Ayuntamiento de Los Barrios [2001] IRLR 848* in which the ECJ ruled that the *EC Pregnant Workers Directive* and the *Equal Treatment Directive* both cover pregnant women who work on fixed-term contracts and that the non-renewal of a fixed-term contract motivated by the worker's pregnancy would constitute direct sex discrimination under the *Equal Treatment Directive*.

In another recent case, *Tele Danmark A/S v Handels- og Kontorfunktionaerernes Forbund i Danmark (HK)*, acting on behalf of *Brandt-Nielsen ECJ [2001] IRLR 853*, the ECJ took the law in this area one step further. The Tele Danmark case concerned a woman who was recruited in June to work on a six-month fixed-term contract starting in July. At the time of her recruitment she was pregnant, but she declined to inform the employer of this fact. Her baby was due in November. When the employer later found out about the pregnancy, the employee was dismissed on the grounds that she would be unable to fulfil a substantial part of the fixed-term contract. The employee claimed sex discrimination.

The ECJ ruled that the employee's dismissal on the grounds of her unavailability to work caused by her pregnancy was direct sex discrimination and the fact the contract was for a fixed-term was irrelevant. They held further that there was no duty on a prospective employee (for either permanent or temporary work) to disclose to their future employer that they are pregnant, as the employer is, in any event, not permitted to take the pregnancy into account when determining who should be employed. The employer's contention that the employee's failure to inform them of her pregnancy at the time she was recruited amounted to a breach of the implied duty of good faith was therefore rejected.

Neither the ECJ nor the UK courts has to date made any ruling on what the position would be in law if a potential contract was for a fixed term and an employee's pregnancy meant that her maternity leave would be for the whole of that period.

It can be seen from the case law that where the timing of an employee's impending maternity leave is such that she will be unavailable to work during part of a forthcoming fixed-term contract, a refusal to employ her will constitute unlawful sex discrimination. Similarly, if a woman is already employed on a fixed-term contract and she is refused renewal of that contract on account of her pregnancy or forthcoming absence on maternity leave, then this too will be unlawful sex discrimination.

Employers should therefore ensure that if a prospective candidate for temporary employment or an employee already engaged on a fixed-term contract is pregnant, the fact of the pregnancy should be disregarded when decisions have to be taken as to whether to offer employment or continued employment.

The EC Fixed-Term Work Directive and its Implementation into UK LAW   [4.34]

The *EC Fixed-Term Work Directive* (Directive No 99/70) was implemented into UK legislation on 1 October 2002. Originally it was set to be implemented by July 2001, but implementation was delayed by the Government due to 'special difficulties' identified during the initial period of consultation.

The Directive defines a fixed-term contract worker as:

'a person having an employment contract or relationship entered into directly between an employer and a worker where the end of the employment contract or relationship is determined by objective conditions such as reaching a specific date, completing a specific task, or the occurrence of a specific event'.

It can be seen from the above definition that the Directive covers people engaged on fixed-term contracts, those employed on a contract for performance and employees working on contracts that are set to terminate on the occurrence of a future event. This at least allows employers who engage temporary staff to escape from the often complex question of whether or not a temporary contract constitutes a fixed-term contract since, at least for the purposes of compliance with the Directive, the differences are now irrelevant.

The *Fixed-Term Work Directive* does not apply to workers supplied on a temporary basis by employment agencies to their clients. There is, however, a separate proposal that temporary agency workers will be the subject of a similar Directive (see **CHAPTER 5** at **5.23**).

The Objectives of the Fixed-Term Work Directive [4.35]

The underlying purpose of the *Fixed-Term Work Directive* was stated as a two-part objective:

1. To improve the quality of fixed-term work by ensuring the application of the principle of non-discrimination. This means that employees engaged on fixed-term contracts are entitled not to be treated less favourably than comparable permanent workers on account of their fixed-term employment status unless there is an objective reason to justify such treatment (the same principle as exists in the *Part-Time Workers (Prevention of Less Favourable Treatment) Regulations 2000 (SI 2000 No 1551)* – see **CHAPTER 3** at **3.6**).

2. To establish a framework to prevent abuse arising from the use of successive fixed-term employment contracts or relationships. In order to prevent abuse of fixed-term contracts, the Directive required member states to introduce one or more of the following measures in order to limit the scope for using a series of successive fixed-term contracts to employ the same person:

   - A limitation on the maximum total duration of successive fixed-term contracts or relationships.

   - A limitation on the number of renewals of fixed-term contracts or relationships.

   - A requirement for employers to provide objective reasons to justify the renewal of a fixed-term contract or relationship (i.e. justify why it is not practicable to employ the person on a permanent contract).

Further provisions in the Directive concern the rights of fixed-term workers to receive information from their employer about permanent job vacancies, and to be given better access to training opportunities.

The Fixed-Term Employees (Prevention of Less Favourable Treatment) Regulations [4.36]

The *Fixed-Term Employees (Prevention of Less Favourable Treatment) Regulations 2002 (SI 2002 No 2034)* were implemented on 1 October 2002.

Scope of the Regulations [4.37]

The Regulations apply to Great Britain, but similar Regulations apply in Northern Ireland.

The draft Regulations are designed to cover only employees, i.e. those engaged by their employer on a contract of employment. Apprentices, people engaged on government supported training programmes and people undergoing work experience of up to one year as part of a higher education course are not covered. The armed forces are also exempt.

The fact that the Regulations cover only employees, and not other workers, contrasts with the *Part-Time Workers (Prevention of Less Favourable Treatment) Regulations 2000*, implemented in July 2000, which expressly cover not only employees but other workers, for example contractors and consultants who provide their services personally to the employer.

The Regulations do not apply to employees who are assigned on a fixed-term basis by an employment agency or employment business to work for one of their clients (see **CHAPTER 5** for a full discussion on temporary staff from employment agencies). This is line with the *Fixed-Term Work Directive*.

Remedies [4.38]

The remedy for an employee whose rights under the Regulations have been breached is to bring a complaint to an employment tribunal. There is no minimum period of qualifying service for an employee to be entitled to bring such a claim, and no age limits. Furthermore, any employee dismissed for attempting to assert their rights under the Regulations can claim unfair dismissal irrespective of their length of service and such a dismissal will be automatically unfair.

Definition of a Fixed-term Contract [4.39]

The definition of a fixed-term contract in the Regulations, *Reg 1(2)* is:

'A contract of employment:

(a) which terminates on the expiry of a specific term; or

(b) which terminates automatically on the completion of a particular task; or

(c) which terminates upon the occurrence or non–occurrence of any other specific event other than the attainment by the employee of any normal and bona fide retiring age in the establishment for an employee holding the position held by him.

Thus workers who are engaged on fixed-term contracts, contracts for performance and contracts that are set up to terminate on the occurrence (or non–occurrence) of a future event (other than retirement) are all classed as fixed-term contracts. The Regulations also amend the *Employment Rights Act 1996, section 95(1)(b)* which states that the expiry of a fixed term contract without renewal constitutes a dismissal in law. As a result of this change, the expiry of any of these types of contracts without renewal will be deemed to be a dismissal in law. This clarifies and simplifies the previous confusing position that whilst the termination of a fixed-term contract was a dismissal in law, the expiry of a contract for performance was not.

The Non-discrimination Principle [4.40]

The key underlying ethic of the Regulations is the non-discrimination principle, i.e. an employee engaged on a fixed-term contract has the right not to be treated less favourably in an overall sense than a comparable permanent employee on the grounds of their fixed–term status, unless such treatment can be justified on objective grounds. In determining whether a fixed-term employee has been treated less favourably than someone working on a permanent contract, the pro-rata principle it to be applied. Similar principles are inherent in the *Part-Time Workers (Prevention of Less Favourable Treatment) Regulations 2000 (SI 2000 No 1551)* which were designed to prevent discrimination against part-time workers in comparison to full-time workers performing similar work (see **CHAPTER 3** at **3.5**).

The right not to suffer discrimination on account of fixed-term status (contained in *Reg 3* covers:

- the terms of the employee's contract; *and*

- the right not to be subjected to any other detriment by any act, or deliberate failure to act, on the part of the employer.

Thus not only do the Regulations apply to employees' contractual terms but they also make it unlawful for an employer to subject a fixed-term employee to any other type of unfavourable treatment on grounds of their fixed-term status (unless there is objective justification for so doing). This means in effect that a wide range of treatment that may not form part of the employee's contractual terms is covered, for example criteria for promotion, appraisal, access to training and general treatment at work.

Regulation 3(2) specifically states that the non–discrimination principle will apply to fixed-term employees in relation to any length of service requirements applied by the employer relating to any particular condition of service, the opportunity to receive training and the opportunity to secure permanent employment. This means that fixed-term employees must be treated equally in comparison to permanent employees with the same length of service with regard to these benefits and opportunities.

When comparing the terms and conditions of a fixed-term employee with those of a comparable permanent employee, it may be justifiable to treat the fixed-term employee less favourably in respect of one particular aspect of their contract provided some other aspect of the contract is more favourable, thus balancing out the less favourable term. This is because Regulation 4 provides that less favourable treatment in respect of a particular contractual term can potentially be justified in circumstances where the fixed-term employee's total package is not less favourable than that of the appropriate comparator. Thus, where challenges are brought under the Regulations, the primary task of the courts and tribunals will be to assess the value of the complete package of the fixed-term employee in comparison with their chosen comparator, rather than focussing on an item–by–item comparison.

The Comparator   [4.41]

In order to assess whether discrimination is taking place, there needs to be a comparison between the treatment of an employee engaged on a fixed-term contract (as defined in the Regulations) and another employee who:

- Is employed by the same employer.

- Is employed on a permanent (i.e. open-ended) contract.

- Is engaged in the same or broadly similar work taking into account (where relevant) whether the fixed-term employee and the permanent employee have similar levels of qualifications, skills and experience.

- Works at or is based at the same workplace, or, where there are no equivalent permanent employees at the same workplace, works for the same employer at a different workplace.

If there is no equivalent permanent employee within the organisation, the fixed-term employee will not be able to seek a remedy under the Regulations. Furthermore, the Regulations do not allow for hypothetical comparisons to be made.

The Right for Fixed-term Employees to Receive a Written Statement of Reasons for Less Favourable Treatment [4.42]

The Regulations provide that fixed-term employees who believe they have been less favourably treated on grounds of their fixed-term status are entitled to request a written statement of the reasons for the less favourable treatment from their employer, and that the employer must comply with such a request within 21 days. The employee's request must be in writing. This right does not apply in the event of the dismissal of the fixed-term employee on expiry of their contract because in these circumstances the employee is in any event entitled under the *Employment Rights Act 1996, s 92* to receive (upon request) a written statement of reasons for dismissal.

The Right to Receive Information about Available Vacancies [4.43]

The Regulations (*Reg 3(6-7)* contain provisions that entitle employees engaged on fixed-term contracts to receive information from their employer about any suitable available vacancy that arises in the establishment. *Reg 3(7)* states that the requirement to inform will only be satisfied 'if the vacancy is contained in an advertisement which the employee has a reasonable opportunity of reading in the course of his employment or the employee is given reasonable notification of the vacancy in some other way'.

Prevention of abuse of fixed-term contracts [4.44]

Measures for implementing the second main principle contained in the *EC Fixed-Term Work Directive*, i.e. measures to prevent abuse of fixed-term contracts, are contained in *Reg 8* of the Regulations.

The Government chose to deal with this matter by imposing a restriction on the renewal of fixed-term contracts in the form of a cut-off date after four years. Thus an employee who has been engaged on a fixed-term contract or a series of continuous fixed-term contracts for four years or more, and whose contract is then extended or renewed, will automatically be entitled to have their new contract treated as a permanent contract unless the employer can objectively justify the employee's continuing engagement on a fixed-term basis.

In these circumstances, the employee would be entitled under *Reg 9* to request a written statement from their employer confirming that their contract is now a permanent contract, and to receive such a written statement within 21 days of the request being made.

This provision does not, however, act to limit the initial length of an employee's fixed-term contract, as the Regulations are directed only at preventing abuse through the use of successive fixed-term contracts.

This provision was not made fully retrospective. *Regulation 8(4)* specifies that any period of continuous employment falling before 10 July 2002 (the latest date by which the Regulations should have been implemented) can be disregarded.

The Regulations allow employers to modify these provisions by way of a collective agreement or valid workforce agreement. Modifications could be an increase or decrease to the four-year time limit. An agreement of this nature would also be able to specify the number of permitted renewals and define acceptable grounds for extending or renewing a fixed-term contract.

Waiver of Redundancy Pay Rights [4.45]

One other important feature of the Regulations was that they removed the facility for employers to include waiver clauses in fixed-term contracts in respect of the employee's right to claim statutory redundancy pay on expiry of their contract. The Regulations repealed the statutory provisions that used to permit such waiver clauses where the fixed-term contract was for two years or more.

This provision was not, however, made retrospective. This means that any waiver clause properly set up prior to the date the Regulations were implemented can remain in force for the duration of that contract. It will not, however, be open to the employer to include the waiver clause in any further extension or renewal to the fixed-term contract.

The Terms and Conditions of Fixed–Term Workers[4.46]

Since the *Fixed-Term Employees Regulations* were implemented into UK law, it is unlawful for employers to offer fixed-term employees less favourable terms of employment than comparable permanent employees unless there is an objective reason that justifies less favourable treatment.

Pay and Pensions [4.47]

Following the adoption of the *EC Fixed-Term Work Directive*, the UK Government formed the view that the Directive did not cover pay and pensions benefits. However, following a period of consultation which produced concrete evidence of pay and pensions discrimination against fixed-term employees in the UK, they announced that they intended to legislate to prevent such discrimination as well as transposing the provisions of the Directive into UK law.

Annual Holiday Entitlement [4.48]

When the *Working Time Regulations 1998 (SI 1998 No 1833)* were implemented in late 1998, the entitlement to paid annual holiday leave was subject to a 13-week qualifying period of service. This meant that where a worker was engaged for a period of less than 13 weeks, they did not accrue any entitlement to statutory paid holiday leave. The 13-week qualifying period for entitlement to statutory holidays was, however, repealed in 2001 following a decision made by the ECJ (in the case of *R v Secretary of State for Trade and Industry, ex-parte Broadcasting, Entertainment, Cinematographic and Theatre Union Case C-173/99 Times Law Reports 28.06.01*) who ruled that it was incompatible with the *EC Working Time Directive* and hence unlawful. The amending legislation, the *Working Time (Amendment) Regulations 2001 (SI 2001 No 3256)*, came into effect on 25 October 2001.

As a result, all workers, irrespective of their length of service, are entitled to four weeks' paid annual holiday in any complete holiday year, and holidays start to accrue from the first day of employment. 'Worker' for this purpose includes not only employees but also contract staff and others who work on a contract for service (see chapter 1 for a full discussion on employment status). This means that temporary workers, including those engaged on fixed-term contracts of any length, are entitled to four weeks holiday each year, or a pro-rata portion of the four-week entitlement in the event that employment lasts for less than a year.

Taking Holiday During the First Year of Employment   [4.49]

The amending Regulations introduced a change to the way entitlement to take annual holiday is to be calculated during the first year of a worker's employment. Workers are entitled to take holidays on the basis of accrual at the rate of one twelfth of the annual entitlement for each month of employment. For this purpose, holidays must be allowed to accrue in advance, i.e. leave accrues on the first day of each month.

General Administration of Holidays   [4.50]

There are further provisions in the *Working Time Regulations, Reg 13(9)* that regulate the way employers administer annual holidays. The Regulations expressly state that:

- holidays must be taken during the holiday year in respect of which they are due, i.e. not carried forward to a new holiday year; *and*

- employers are not permitted to 'buy out' a worker's holiday entitlement by making a payment in lieu except if a worker's employment is terminated during the course of a holiday year with outstanding holidays due. In this case, payment for any holidays that have been accrued but not taken must be made to the worker.

Employers are also permitted under the *Working Time Regulations 1998, Reg 15* to have some input to the timing of an employee's annual holidays. The employer is entitled to refuse to grant holiday on specified dates, or conversely, to require the worker to take all or part of their annual holiday entitlement on particular days, provided proper notice is given as defined in the Regulations.

The collective effect of these provisions is that, in respect of employees engaged on short-term contracts for 48 weeks or less in the same holiday year, it is open to the employer to require the employee to work for the duration of the contract without taking holiday and then pay for the leave when the contract terminates, provided the employee leaves at that point and does not immediately start work with the same employer on another contract. For temporary employment contracts that are to last longer than

48 weeks, paid holidays must be granted during the first year of the individual's employment.

This matter is further complicated by the fact that employers may have designated their holiday year to run (for example) from 1 April until 31 March and the individual's fixed-term contract may therefore span two holiday years. In these circumstances, the principles in the preceding paragraph could not be applied as they stand because each holiday year must be treated separately. Essentially, unless the length of the employee's contract is less than the outstanding portion of the current holiday year, some paid holiday will have to be granted by the employer during the current holiday year otherwise they will be in breach of the *Working Time Regulations 1998*.

Practical Example   **[4.51]**

The following is an example:

An employee is engaged on a nine-month fixed-term contract to run from 1 October 2002 until 30 June 2003. The employer in question operates a holiday year that runs from 1 January to 31 December.

Since the employee's engagement spans two holiday years, their entitlement to statutory paid annual holiday must be calculated separately for each of the two part-years. During 2002, the employee will have worked for three months, i.e. a quarter of the year creating an entitlement of one week's holiday (i.e. a quarter of four weeks). This week's holiday must be granted (on a paid basis) for before 31 December 2002.

In relation to the period of the contract during 2003, i.e. a period of six months, the employee's holiday entitlement will be two weeks. The employer may require the employee not to take holidays during that period and instead make a payment in lieu of the two weeks' holiday when the contract terminates at the end of June. Alternatively, the employer and employee may agree between them that the employee will take some or all of the two weeks' paid leave during the currency of the contract.

Policy on Holiday Entitlement for Short-term Temporary Workers
[4.52]

The following text could either be used to form a policy in its own right, or could be incorporated into a general policy on holiday entitlement:

'Holiday entitlement for temporary employees is in line with the following provisions:

Holiday year

The Company's holiday year runs from 1 January to 31 December (*or other arrangement*) each year. All employees of the Company are entitled to four weeks' paid holiday during each complete holiday year, during which they will be paid their normal salary exclusive of overtime (commission/bonus) payments.

Where a temporary employee's employment spans two holiday years (or parts thereof), holiday entitlement will be calculated separately for each year or part-year.

First part-year of employment

During the employee's first part-year of employment, entitlement to paid holiday will be calculated on a pro-rata basis in proportion to the amount of the holiday year remaining when the employee's employment commenced.

Subject to agreement on the timing and length of annual leave, temporary employees will be entitled to take leave during the first year or part-year of their employment on the basis of accrual at the rate of one twelfth of the four-week annual entitlement for each month of employment. For this purpose, leave accrues in advance, i.e. it accrues on the first day of each month.

Year during which employment terminates

When a temporary employee's contract comes to an end, entitlement for the year in which employment terminates will be calculated on a pro-rata basis in proportion to the amount of the holiday year the employee has worked. Where leave has been accrued but not taken by the time employment terminates, the outstanding holiday entitlement will be paid to the employee along with final salary. Such payment is taxable and subject to national insurance deductions.

If at the time employment terminates an employee has taken holiday in excess of that which has been earned, the Company reserves the right to deduct the equivalent amount of money (at a rate equivalent to the employee's normal basic salary) from their final salary payment.

Timing of holidays

The Company does not permit employees to carry over holidays from one year to the next as this is prohibited by the *Working Time Regulations*. All holidays must therefore be taken during the year in which they are earned.

All employees are required to obtain their line manager's agreement before taking any holidays. No employee should commit themselves to any holiday plans before receiving approval for their holiday dates.'

Conclusion [4.53]

This chapter has explored the features and implications of temporary contracts, in particular fixed-term contracts, the rights of employees who are engaged on temporary contracts, and the legal implications involved when such contracts terminate without renewal.

There are many reasons why employers may wish to engage employees on fixed-term contracts rather than permanent contracts, but they must be aware of the statutory employment protection rights of temporary employees and the implementation of the *Fixed-Term Employees (Prevention of Less Favourable Treatment) Regulations 2002*.

Employees engaged on a succession of temporary contracts without gaps between them will gain continuity of service even where the terms and conditions of the successive contracts are different. In certain circumstances employment under a series of fixed-term contracts with gaps between them can be deemed to be continuous, depending on the reasons for the gaps and their duration.

A further provision for employers to contend with is that the expiry of a fixed-term contract without renewal constitutes a dismissal in UK law, and an individual thus dismissed will often be entitled to a statutory redundancy payment.

Questions and Answers [4.54]

Question

Is it the case that temporary employees have fewer statutory employment protection rights than people engaged on permanent contracts?

Answer

In general, individuals employed on a temporary basis enjoy the same statutory employment protection rights as employees engaged on permanent contracts, provided they are directly employed by the organisation for whom they work. However, since many statutory employment rights are dependent on the individual obtaining a defined minimum period of continuous service, temporary employees engaged on a single contract may not work long enough to become eligible for certain statutory employment benefits.

Question

When a temporary employee is recruited, is it necessary to specify how long the contract will last?

Answer

There is a statutory duty on all employers to provide temporary employees (both full and part-time) whose contract is to continue for more than one month, with a written statement designating (amongst other things) the period for which their employment is expected to continue. If the length of the person's employment is uncertain, then this fact should be stated together with an approximate indication of the expected length of the contract. If the contract is to be for a fixed-term, the written statement must specify the date when it is to end.

Question

What exactly is a fixed-term contract as opposed to any other type of temporary contract?

Answer

A fixed-term contract is defined as a contract of employment that terminates in one of the following circumstances:

- on the expiry of a specific term, i.e. the date on which the contract is to expire is agreed in advance;
- on the completion of a particular task;
- on the occurrence or non-occurrence of any other specific event.

Question

If an employee works on a series of successive fixed-term contracts that are each on different terms and conditions, what effect does this have on the employee's continuity of service with the employer?

Answer

Where a fixed-term contract is extended or renewed immediately upon its expiry, or if it is agreed before the first contract ends that a new contract will start within four weeks, the employee's continuity of service will be maintained. This will be the case irrespective of whether the terms and conditions of the new contract are the same as those that applied in the previous fixed-term contract.

Question

If an employee works on a series of fixed-term contracts for the same employer with gaps between them, how does that affect the employee's continuity of service?

Answer

There are certain circumstances defined in the *Employment Rights Act* in which continuity of employment can be asserted even though the employee's contract has been terminated for a temporary period, provided the contract has subsequently been revived or renewed (whether on the same terms and conditions or not). The Act stipulates that breaks between periods of employment that are due to a temporary cessation of work, or that occur as a result of an arrangement or custom, will count as periods of continuous employment even though no contract is in force during such breaks. In these circumstances, the employee's period of continuous employment is not broken, and the period of the gap between the earlier and the later contract is deemed to form part of their continuous service with the employer.

Question

When a fixed-term contract expires on the agreed termination date, can the employee bring any legal claim against the employer if further employment is not offered?

Answer

Despite the fact that the nature of a fixed-term contract requires the employer and employee to have agreed in advance that the contract will terminate on a specified date, on the completion of a task or on the occurrence or non-occurrence of a specific event, UK law regards the expiry of a fixed-term contract without renewal as a dismissal. Thus an employee who has a minimum of one year's continuous service would be eligible to bring a claim of unfair dismissal to an employment tribunal on expiry of a fixed-term contract without renewal. Normally, however, a dismissal on the expiry of a fixed-term contract will be fair on the grounds of 'some other substantial reason' provided the expiry of the contract is the principal reason for the dismissal. If, however, the employer was in a position to renew or extend the employee's contract, but declined to do so, the employee's claim for unfair dismissal may succeed. This is because such circumstances would suggest that the reason for the employee's dismissal might not be the expiry of the fixed-term contract, but in fact some other reason.

Question

How can an employer make sure that when an employee's fixed-term contract expires, their dismissal is fair?

Answer

Generally, dismissal on the expiry of a fixed-term contract will be fair provided that the fixed-term contract was set up for a genuine purpose, that purpose was known to the employee and the underlying purpose had ceased to be applicable when the employee was dismissed.

Question

If an employer declines to offer employment to an apprentice whose contract of apprenticeship has come to an end, does this constitute a dismissal?

Answer

The EAT has held that a contract of apprenticeship is a one-off contract that is incapable of being renewed, and that the non-employment of an individual following the completion of their apprenticeship does not amount to a dismissal in law.

Question

What, if any, are the redundancy rights of an employee who has been engaged on a fixed-term contract that expires without renewal?

Answer

The EAT has confirmed that the expiry of a fixed-term contract without renewal constitutes a dismissal by reason of redundancy. It follows that an employee whose fixed-term contract comes to an end will be entitled to a statutory redundancy payment provided they have accrued two years' continuous service at that point in time, and provided they have not, prior to the expiry of their fixed-term contract, accepted an offer of re-engagement to commence within four weeks of their termination date.

Question

If an employer elects to terminate a fixed-term contract before it has run its full term, what legal repercussions might there be?

Answer

Early termination of a fixed-term contract imposed on the employee without their agreement would constitute a breach of contract unless there is a notice clause in the contract that expressly allows the employer to terminate early. The employee would be able to bring a claim for damages equivalent to the salary and other benefits due for the outstanding period of the fixed-term contract. There is no minimum period of service required for such a breach of contract claim. The employee would also be able to bring a claim for unfair dismissal to an employment tribunal in the event of early termination of the fixed-term contract, subject to their having a minimum of one year's continuous service as at the date their employment came to an end.

Question

Can an employer sue an employee who leaves their job prior to the agreed termination date of a fixed-term contract?

Answer

Yes, in theory, because this is likely to constitute a breach of contract on the part of the employee. However, unless the employer can prove that they suffered a quantifiable loss as a direct result of the employee's early departure, any claim against the departed employee for damages for breach of contract would be unlikely to succeed.

Question

Can an employer design a fixed-term contract to contain notice clauses allowing for early termination?

Answer

Yes, there is no reason why an employer cannot insert notice provisions into a fixed-term contract allowing for early termination. The Court of Appeal has held that the existence of notice clauses in a fixed-term contract allowing for early termination does not necessarily prevent the contract from being a fixed-term contract.

Question

What is a contract for performance?

Answer

A contract for performance is a temporary contract designed to terminate automatically when the specific task or project for which the employee is engaged comes to an end. This is described in law as the contract being 'discharged by performance'. Following the implementation of the *Fixed-Term Employees (Prevention of Less Favourable Treatment) Regulations 2002*, the expiry of such a contract without renewal is regarded as a dismissal in law.

Question

If an employee is recruited to cover for another employee who is absent from work on maternity leave, can the replacement employee be fairly dismissed once the original employee returns to work?

Answer

Yes, special statutory provisions exist for appointments made to cover absences due to maternity leave. In these circumstances, the employer must inform the temporary employee in writing that their employment will come to an end on the return to work of the absent employee. Provided this is done correctly and properly documented, the dismissal of the temporary replacement employee on the other employee's return to work will be fair.

Question

What are the implications for employers of the implementation into UK law of the *EC Fixed-Term Work Directive*?

Answer

The Directive had two key aims, firstly to improve the quality of fixed-term work by ensuring the application of the principle of non-discrimination. This means broadly that employees engaged on fixed-term contracts are entitled not to be treated less favourably than comparable permanent employees unless there is an objective reason

157

that justifies such treatment. The second key aim of the Directive was to establish a framework to prevent abuse arising from the use of successive fixed-term employment contracts by introducing limitations as to their use.

Question

What does the principle of non-discrimination mean in practice for employees engaged on fixed-term contracts?

Answer

Since the *Fixed-Term Employees (Prevention of Less Favourable Treatment) Regulations 2002* were implemented, an employee engaged on a fixed-term contract has the right not to be treated less favourably than a comparable permanent employee on the grounds of their fixed-term status, unless such treatment can be justified by the employer on objective grounds. This means that the terms and conditions of employment applicable to a fixed-term employee must be at least as favourable in an overall sense as a permanent employee performing the same or similar work in the same workplace, and that the fixed-term employee has the right not to suffer any detriment on account of their fixed-term status.

Question

What entitlement to statutory annual holidays does a temporary employee have?

Answer

All workers, irrespective of their length of service, are entitled to four weeks' paid annual holiday in any complete holiday year, with holiday accruing from the first day of employment. Where employment lasts for less than a year, the worker must be granted a pro-rata portion of the four-week entitlement. Holidays must not be carried forward to a new holiday year, and employers are not permitted to 'buy out' a worker's holiday entitlement by making a payment in lieu except if the person's employment terminates during the course of a holiday year. Thus, if a temporary worker's employment is to last beyond the end of the employer's holiday year, the worker must be permitted to take the appropriate pro-rata amount of paid holidays during that year.

5. Temporary Staff From Employment Agencies

Introduction [5.1]

There has been a rapid growth in the last decade in the use by employers of temporary agency workers. According to a survey commissioned by the DTI in 1999, over half a million people in the UK were supplied to employers through employment bureaux.

There are many advantages in engaging agency workers, for example:

- Their use allows employers flexibility in dealing with short-term staffing needs.
- Staff can often be made available at very short notice.
- Staff shortages created by holidays, sickness absence and maternity leave can be easily and conveniently covered.
- The administration of the temporary worker is handled by the agency.
- The employer can take on additional staff without the usual formalities.
- The contract can usually be terminated at very short notice.

Employment Agencies and Employment Businesses [5.2]

Although the term 'employment agency' is widely used, the correct term for an organisation that engages staff and then supplies them on a temporary basis to other organisations is 'employment business'. Under the *Employment Agencies Act 1973, s 13(2)* an 'employment agency' is defined as an organisation that provides 'services (whether by the provision of information or otherwise) for the purpose of finding workers employment with employers or of supplying employers with workers for employment by them'. Thus an 'employment agency' is an organisation that finds and selects permanent employees for their clients, i.e. one-off transactions after which the agency has no further connection with the person they have placed in employment.

159

By contrast, an 'employment business' is defined in *section 13(3)* of the same Act as an organisation that supplies 'persons in the employment of the person carrying on the business, to act for, and under the control of, other persons in any capacity'. Thus the employment business (which may also be known as a 'contractor') has an ongoing relationship with both the client company to whom they have supplied the temporary worker, and with the worker themselves. A tripartite working arrangement is set up under which the employment business enters into a contract with their client for the supply of staff, and the worker has a contract with the employment business under which the employment business provides the worker with work. The contract with the worker may be for a short or long duration, and may be open-ended or for a fixed-term. Normally the worker is paid by the employment business. The net result of this type of arrangement is that there is no direct contract between the worker and the organisation for whom they perform the work.

Many organisations operate as both an employment agency and an employment business. The term 'employment bureau' can also be used as a generic term covering both employment agencies and employment businesses. However, as this book is concerned only with the management of temporary staff, and not the placement of permanent staff, the popular terms 'employment agency' and 'agency worker' have been used for convenience to denote organisations that hire temporary workers out to their clients, and individuals who are engaged in this way.

The term 'agency worker' is used generally to describe someone who works through an employment agency for one or more of the agency's clients. An employment agency may be a generalist agency supplying people with a variety of backgrounds, or may specialise in, for example, accounting staff, engineering personnel or qualified nurses. It is particularly common in the UK for clerical staff, carers, engineers, nurses, au pairs and drivers to be supplied on a temporary basis by employment agencies.

The Employment Status of Agency Workers [5.3]

The employment status of agency workers has caused problems of interpretation over a period of many years. A tribunal may hold that a worker has a contract of employment with the agency through whom they work, with the client company for whom they provide their services, or that they are self-employed. If a contract exists, then complex arguments may be brought to tribunal about whether it constitutes a contract of employment or a contract for services. This is partly because there is no employment law that dictates what the status of an agency worker should be for the purposes of statutory employment protection legislation.

Furthermore, in most cases to date, the courts have focused only on the particular case in hand rather than providing definitive clarification of the rights of agency workers.

By contrast, employment agencies are obliged under the *Income and Corporation Taxes Act 1988, s 134* to treat the workers they supply to their clients as their employees for the purposes of income tax and national insurance. Accordingly agencies must deduct tax and national insurance from their workers' pay. It is important to note, however, that this obligation has no relevance to the worker's employment status.

The subject of employment status is covered comprehensively in chapter 1. This section focuses on case law that has specifically addressed the question of employment status in relation to agency workers and the general principles emanating from this case law.

Agency Workers as Employees of the Agency [5.4]

The existence of a contract is fundamental to the assertion of many statutory employment protection rights. Because agency workers generally have a contract of some sort with the agency through whom they provide their services and rarely have a contract with the client company for whom they actually work, courts and tribunals have traditionally taken the view that it is the agency, and not the client company, who is to be regarded as the person's employer. However, the determination of whether the contract between the agency and the individual is a contract of employment or a contract for services (see **CHAPTER 1** for a full explanation of the distinction) can be a complex one. If the individual is classed as an employee of the agency, i.e. someone working under a contract of employment, they will be able to assert the full range of statutory employment protection rights, including for example the right to claim unfair dismissal after one year's continuous service. If they are classed as a 'worker', i.e. someone engaged under a contract for services, they will have fewer rights. In some cases, it may even be held that the agency worker is self-employed.

Key Case [5.5]

One example of a case where an agency worker was classed as an employee of the agency through whom he worked was that of *Iles v Ross Newton Associates Ltd t/a Ross Newton Recruitment EAT 568/99:*

161

Iles v Ross Newton Associates Ltd t/a Ross Newton Recruitment EAT 568/99

Facts

Mr Iles was engaged by an employment agency to work for one of their customers, an assignment that ultimately lasted for three years. Two sets of documents were issued to Mr Iles by the agency, the first detailing standard terms appertaining to his general engagement with the agency and the second outlining the terms applicable to the specific assignment with the customer. The standard terms referred to the contract as a contract of service (i.e. a contract of employment), but, inconsistently, decreed that he was not an employee of the agency. When his assignment was terminated on grounds of redundancy, he lodged a claim for redundancy pay against the agency. Since only employees and not other workers are eligible to claim statutory redundancy pay, the tribunal first addressed the question of Mr Iles' employment status.

Findings

The EAT overturned the original employment tribunal's decision that Mr Iles was not an employee of the employment agency. Their decision was based on several factors, in particular the findings that Mr Iles was in practice obliged to abide by certain terms and conditions relating to where and how he was to carry out his work, and obliged to obey any reasonable requests and instructions issued by the agency. The EAT concluded that these obligations were incorporated into the standard contract governing Mr Iles' general engagement with the agency and that they were consistent with the argument that Mr Iles was an employee of the agency rather than (as the agency asserted) an independent contractor. The clause in the contract that stated Mr Iles was not an employee of the agency was inoperable under the *Employment Rights Act, s 203 (1)(a)* which states that any provision that purports to exclude or limit an individual's rights under the Act will be void.

Model Clause Governing the Employment Status of an Agency Worker [5.6]

The following clause could be used by an employment agency to make it clear to a worker that the contract between them is not a contract of employment:

'These terms constitute a contract for services between *(name of employment agency)* and *(name of worker)* and will not give rise to a contract of employment. There is no mutuality of obligation whatsoever between you and *(name of employment agency))*. *(Name of employment agency)* is not obliged to offer you ongoing temporary work, or any minimum amount of work, nor are you obliged to accept any offer of work made by *(name of employment agency)*.'

Global and Specific Contracts [5.7]

Agency workers engaged by employment agencies for the purpose of supply to the agency's clients are often subject to two different sets of terms and conditions. The first will be standard terms governing the relationship between the agency and the individual generally, whilst the second will relate to the individual assignment to work for a specific employer for a fixed or open-ended temporary period.

One trend has been for employment tribunals and courts to draw a distinction between an agency worker's specific engagement to perform work for one particular client for a one-off temporary period, and the worker's general or global relationship with the agency. For example, in *McMeechan v Secretary of State for Employment [1997] IRLR 353*, the Court of Appeal judged that the claimant, who had been engaged by the agency for a series of temporary contracts for various companies, had been an employee of the agency on the last occasion that he was engaged to work through them. This conclusion was reached because the Court judged that the factors pointing towards an employer-employee relationship outweighed the factors that pointed to the opposite conclusion. The Court further held that the existence of a one-off employment contract did not mean that the individual had a global contract of employment spanning periods during which he was not working. In other words, whilst each specific engagement could potentially give rise to a contract of employment between the individual and the agency, the absence of an overriding mutual obligation on the agency to offer the individual future assignments and on the individual to accept any assignment that was offered, meant that there could be no general or global employment contract. As the Court put it:

'There is the general engagement on the one hand, under which sporadic tasks are performed by the one party at the behest of the other, and the specific engagement on the other hand which begins and ends with the performance of any one task. Each engagement is capable, according to its context, of giving rise to a contract of employment.'

The topic of global contracts is explored further in **CHAPTER 7** at **7.5**.

The *McMeechan* case does not mean that every agency worker has a contract of employment with the agency through whom they work. The classification of Mr McMeechan as an employee during one of his assignments was established taking into account the specific facts of the individual case. Other cases have reached different conclusions, for example in the case of *Knights v Anglian Industrial Services EAT 640/96*, the EAT held that Mr Knight's contract with the employment agency was *not* a contract of employment due primarily to a lack of mutuality of obligation and lack of control by the agency over the individual's day-to-day work, two key factors used generally by courts and tribunals who are asked to rule on an individual's employment status.

A contract 'of its own kind' [5.8]

Case law from earlier years tended to view an agency worker as having a contract 'of its own kind' which meant in effect that the worker was neither employed by the agency or the client, nor self-employed. One example was the case of *Ironmonger v Movefield Ltd t/a Deering Appointments [1988] IRLR 461* in which the EAT ruled that an individual who supplied his services through an employment agency fell between the definitions of employed and self-employed.

Key Case [5.9]

A more recent case, that of *Montgomery v Johnson Underwood Ltd [2001] IRLR 269* demonstrates the dilemma that agency workers face when trying to assert their employment rights.

Montgomery v Johnson Underwood Ltd [2001] IRLR 269

Facts

Ms Montgomery was engaged through an employment agency to work as receptionist/telephonist for one of their clients, an engagement that lasted over two years. Her written terms stated that she was self-employed and that the agency had no direct control over her work. Nevertheless they had the authority to dismiss her if her work did not reach the required standard. When the client became unhappy at Ms Montgomery's personal use of their telephone system, they asked the agency to terminate the engagement. Ms Montgomery brought a claim

---

for unfair dismissal to tribunal initially naming the agency as her employer but subsequently adding the client.

Findings

An employment tribunal, at a preliminary hearing, weighed up all the factors of the case and held that Ms Montgomery had been an employee of the employment agency and not an employee of the client company for whom she performed the work. The EAT upheld both parts of the tribunal's decision.

The Court of Appeal, however, overturned the part of the decision that held that Ms Montgomery had a contract of employment with the agency, by which time it was too late for her to appeal the other part of the decision, i.e. that she was not an employee of the client. The Court of Appeal's decision in this regard was based principally on their view that there was an insufficient degree of control over Ms Montgomery's work by the agency. The fact that the agency had the right to terminate the engagement in the event of unsatisfactory performance did not generate a sufficient degree of control to point towards the existence of an employment contract.

The Court of Appeal in this case did not rule that an agency worker can never be the employee of the employment agency through whom they work, but re-asserted the well established principle that the existence of an employment contract depends on there being an 'irreducible minimum' of legal requirements between the parties, i.e. a reasonable degree of mutuality of obligation between the employer and the individual and some sufficient framework of control over the person's work.

Agency Workers as Employees of the Client Company for Whom they Work [5.10]

An agency worker who wishes to assert statutory employment protection rights against the client company for whom they work tends to face an uphill struggle in court, principally because there will normally be no direct contractual relationship between the worker and the agency's client. The EAT has recently held (in *Hewlett Packard Ltd v O'Murphy* [2002] IRLR 4 – see **CHAPTER 8** at **8.10**) that an individual who worked through his own limited company which in turn formed a contract with an employment agency could not be an employee of the client company to whom he was assigned by the agency because there was no direct contract between him and the client.

Confusingly, other case law demonstrates that an agency worker can sometimes be deemed to be the employee of the organisation for whom they work, even though no direct contract exists between the two parties.

Key Cases   [5.11]

One recent case that reached this conclusion was *Motorola Ltd v (1) Davidson (2) Melville Craig Group Ltd [2001] IRLR 4*:

Motorola Ltd v (1) Davidson (2) Melville Craig Group Ltd [2001] IRLR 4

Facts

Mr Davidson worked through Melville Craig Group, an employment agency, providing services for one of their clients. His terms and conditions stated that he was a temporary worker engaged under a contract for services, i.e. the agency did not regard him as their employee. Mr Davidson worked for Motorola for over two years when his assignment was terminated by them following a disciplinary hearing. When he brought a claim for unfair dismissal against Motorola, the claim was challenged on the basis that there had not been a sufficient degree of control over Mr Davidson to give rise to an employer-employee relationship.

Findings

The EAT considered the evidence relating to control over Mr Davidson and held that Motorola, as the hirer, did in fact have effective control. The evidence was that Mr Davidson had worked under Motorola's management's instructions, used their tools, worn their uniform, been obliged to consult over holidays and been in a position to raise grievances with a supervisor employed by them. It was also Motorola's management who had initially suspended Mr Davidson, subjected him to their disciplinary procedure and subsequently terminated his assignment. Furthermore, the evidence suggested that when Mr Davidson was hired, Motorola had laid down very specific requirements in relation to the sort of workers they wanted and could have vetoed

---

his assignment to them. On the basis of this level of control, the EAT held that Mr Davidson's employment status was equivalent to an employment contract. This was despite the fact that in theory the Melville Craig Group, as the agency, could have removed Mr Davidson from Motorola at any time and assigned him elsewhere.

The EAT in this case was not asked to consider any of the other factors that contribute towards the question of whether a worker can be regarded as an employee – see **CHAPTER 1** at **1.8** for more details.

The opposite conclusion was reached in the case of *Costain Building & Civil Engineering Ltd v (1) Smith (2) Chanton Group plc EAT 141/99*:

Costain Building & Civil Engineering Ltd v (1) Smith (2) Chanton Group plc EAT 141/99

Facts

Mr Smith, an experienced engineer, asserted that he had been an employee of Costain, the company to which he had been assigned by Chanton, an agency that supplied labour to building contractors. This was despite the fact that no discussions about Mr Smith's employment status had taken place, Mr Smith had described himself as 'nominally self-employed' and he was on the books of a number of different agencies.

Once in the job, Mr Smith raised a number of health and safety issues, and was subsequently appointed as union safety representative for the site. A few weeks later, Costain informed Chanton that they no longer wanted Mr Smith to work on their site. Mr Smith claimed that this amounted to an automatically unfair dismissal on the grounds that he had undertaken the function of health and safety representative (*Employment Rights Act 1996, s 100 (1)(b)*, a provision that requires the individual to show employee status.

Findings

The EAT found that a contract had been set up between Chanton and Costain for the provision of Mr Smith's services at their building site, but that there was no contract between Mr Smith and Costain directly. The evidence suggested that although Costain had asked Chanton to supply them with an engineer, the person supplied did not specifically have to be Mr Smith. Furthermore the working arrangements contained little that indicated an employer-employee relationship between Mr Smith and Costain. The EAT thus rejected the argument that Mr Smith had been an employee of Costain.

Another case that ruled against the argument that an agency worker was employed by the client company was that of *Serco Ltd v Blair & ors EAT 345/98:*

Serco Ltd v Blair & ors EAT 345/98

Facts

Mr Blair and a colleague were placed by an employment agency with Serco, one of their clients. The contractual arrangements followed the standard arrangements with Mr Blair having a contract with the agency, and the agency having a separate contract with their client for the provision of labour. The client paid the agency for their services, and the agency paid Mr Blair for his work. Once in the job, Mr Blair worked under Serco's instructions, used their pagers and mobile phones, was obliged to wear their uniform and drove a van supplied by them. When the assignment was terminated some two years later by the agency on the instructions of Serco, Mr Blair complained of unfair dismissal citing the client as his employer. Serco for their part disputed that Mr Blair had ever been their employee.

Findings

The EAT overturned the original employment tribunal's decision that Mr Blair had been Serco's employee. They expressed the view that there could be no legal relationship as between an individual and an employer where the contractual arrangements governing the working relationship were made with an employment agency as the intermediary. Even if a legal relationship existed, it could not be classed as a contract of employment because employment contracts must be of a personal nature and cannot be created as a result of third party intervention. They further held that Serco did not exercise a sufficient degree of control over Mr Blair, but instead it was the agency that had ultimate control over whether to terminate the engagement. Although not required to do so, the EAT also expressed the view that Mr Blair was not an employee of the agency either, but was in fact self-employed.

Model Letter to an Employment Agency Regarding the Employment Status of a Temporary Worker [5.12]

The following model letter could be used (or adapted) by companies that use employment agencies for the supply of temporary staff to clarify the employment status of a temporary worker assigned to them by the agency:

'Dear (name of manager in employment agency)

We have recently agreed with your company that (name of temporary agency worker) will be assigned to us for a temporary period (alternative clause: for a period of six weeks/six months, etc) commencing on (worker's start date).

Would you please confirm in writing that the terms of engagement between yourselves and *(name of worker)* constitute a contract of employment, i.e. that you regard him/her as your employee, rather than a worker engaged under a contract for services. We would like to make it clear that *(name of worker)* will not be employed by this company as a result of the contractual arrangements set up between this company and *(name of employment agency)*.

Yours sincerely'

It should, of course, be borne in mind that no written documentation can override a worker's rights, and if the working relationship between the worker and the client company to whom the employment agency has assigned them turns out in practice to contain features which closely resemble those of an employment contract, then a court or tribunal may rule that the individual is the employee of the client company, as in the *Motorola* case above (see **5.11**). Nevertheless, clear documentation indicating that a worker is not employed by the company for whom they work will assist the company to defend any such claim at a later date.

General Principles of Employment Status [5.13]

The principle that follows from case law generally is that when an employer (or hirer) contracts with an agency for the supply of a temporary worker, an employment contract may exist between the hirer and the worker, or alternatively between the agency and the worker, depending on all the facts of the particular case. The outcome of a challenge to the individual's status as an employee will depend on the following factors:

- Whether the agency has undertaken to send, or has been asked to send, a specific person for the assignment with the client company.

- Whether the agency has the authority to terminate the individual worker's assignment and supply a replacement instead.

- The contractual arrangements – where the individual's contract is with the employment agency and the hirer has no direct contract with the worker, it is less likely that the worker could be regarded as an employee of the hirer.

- The specific wording of the worker's contract.

- The degree of control and direction exercised over the worker by the hirer on a day-to-day basis.

- The degree of control exercised over the worker's assignment by the agency.

- Whether it can be said that there is a reasonable degree of mutuality of obligation between the hirer and the individual, or alternatively between the agency and the individual.

- Whether or not the worker is subject to any or all of the terms and benefits applicable to the hirer's permanent staff.

- Whether the individual is subject to the hirer's normal disciplinary rules and procedures and grievance procedures.

- How the individual is regarded and treated generally by the hirer, e.g. whether they are integrated into the team.

- How long the engagement has lasted.

- Whether, in the event of termination of the contract, the hirer would terminate the worker's engagement directly or whether they would ask the agency to remove the worker.

- Whether the hirer, the agency or the worker has supplied any tools or equipment necessary for the worker to perform the job.

Agency Workers' Employment Rights [5.14]

Whether an agency worker is employed under a contract of employment or engaged on a contract for services, they will have certain rights and entitlements in relation to their engagement with the employment agency. The most important of these are rights under the *National Minimum Wage Act 1998* and the *Working Time Regulations 1998 (SI 1998 No 1833)*.

Under the *National Minimum Wage Act 1998, s 1(2)*, temporary agency workers, in line with other categories of workers, are entitled to be paid at a rate not less than the national minimum wage in force at the time. At the time of writing, the adult rate is £4.10 per hour, and is set to rise to £4.20 per hour in October 2002. There is no length of service requirement for a worker to qualify.

Similarly, there is no minimum length of service needed to qualify for the right to four weeks paid annual holiday (or a pro-rata portion of four weeks' holiday in the event that a complete holiday year is not worked) under the *Working Time Regulations 1998, s 13*. Further information about temporary staff's entitlement to paid holidays is provided in **CHAPTER 7** at **7.18**.

Where a worker is engaged by an employment agency on a temporary basis and assigned to one of their client companies, the responsibility for ensuring that the workers' rights are maintained lies with whichever organisation pays the worker's remuneration. In most cases that will be the employment agency and not the client. Organisations that hire temporary staff through employment agencies should, however, understand that employment agencies are obliged to afford temporary workers their rights in terms of pay, hours and holidays, and demonstrate a willingness to cooperate in order that they can properly fulfil their obligations.

Temporary agency workers also have the right not to be suffer sex, race or disability discrimination as against the employment agency through whom they work and as against the client company for whom they perform their services (see **5.15** below).

Agency Workers' Protection against Sex, Race and Disability Discrimination [5.15]

Over and above rights detailed in **5.14** above, agency workers have certain rights as a result of their working relationship with the agency's client, i.e. the company for whom they work. Specifically, agency workers have the right not to suffer sex, race or disability discrimination even where it has been agreed or established that the agency worker is not the employee of the client company for whom they actually work. This is because contract workers are expressly protected against unlawful discrimination in the UK's anti-discrimination legislation. A 'contract worker' is described in the *Sex Discrimination Act 1975, s 9(1)*, and the *Race Relations Act 1976, s 7(1)* as an individual who performs work for a 'principal' but is 'employed not by the principal but by another person who supplies them under a contract made with the principal'. Similar provisions exist in the *Disability Discrimination*

171

Act 1995, s 12. Thus the right not to suffer unlawful discrimination applies to all workers who provide their services personally and does not depend on the existence of a contract of employment or a contract for services.

Two cases which addressed this issue were *Abbey Life Assurance Co Ltd v Tansell [2000] IRLR 387* (disability discrimination) and *Patefield v Belfast City Council [2000] IRLR 664* (sex discrimination). The *Abbey Life* case concerned a computer consultant who had set up his own limited company through which he entered into a contract with an employment agency to provide services to one of the agency's clients. When he was diagnosed as having diabetes, the client refused to continue to engage him and he claimed disability discrimination. The Court of Appeal held that the client was a 'principal' for the purposes of *section 12* of the *Disability Discrimination Act 1995* despite the existence of two intermediary companies instead of one. The client could thus be held liable for their discriminatory treatment of the individual.

Key Case [5.16]

The *Patefield* case is examined below:

Patefield v Belfast City Council [2000] IRLR 664

Facts

Ms Patefield worked through an employment agency on a long-term temporary assignment as a clerical officer for Belfast City Council. When she became pregnant, she wished to return to her job after maternity leave and so asked the Council if they would hold her job open for her. Because neither party regarded the working arrangements as a contract of employment, it was accepted that Ms Patefield did not have the statutory right to return to work, as this right depends on the individual having employee status. In line with this, the Council told Ms Patefield that they could not confirm that they would be in a position to take her back after her maternity leave.

Subsequently the Council moved a permanent employee into Ms Patefield's office to replace her during her maternity leave. Later, when Ms Patefield was ready to return to work, the Council said they could not re-employ her because this permanent employee was undertaking her duties. Although the Council offered her another post, she refused it because the terms and conditions were less favourable than those that she previously enjoyed. She argued before a tribunal that her treatment amounted to direct sex discrimination.

Findings

The Northern Ireland Court of Appeal ruled that the Council had directly discriminated against Ms Patefield on the grounds of sex when they replaced her with a permanent employee. This was despite the fact that they could have lawfully replaced her at any time when she was in post, in line with the contractual arrangements in place with the employment agency. Replacing Ms Patefield with a permanent employee when they knew she wished to return to work after maternity leave caused her a detriment under the *Sex Discrimination (Northern Ireland) Order 1976, Article 12(2)(d)*, since that action had the effect of removing the possibility that she could return to her job. Parallel provisions exist in the *Sex Discrimination Act 1975, s 9(2)(d)*.

An important element in this case was the clear evidence that, had Ms Patefield not been absent on maternity leave, she would have continued in her post indefinitely. It followed that the Council's refusal to allow her to continue in her job after maternity leave amounted to direct sex discrimination simply because no man could have become unavailable for work as a result of pregnancy. Ms Patefield had been treated less favourably than any man would have been treated.

A general outline of the statutory rights of employees, workers and the self-employed is provided in **CHAPTER 1** at **1.34**.

Regulations Governing the Conduct of Employment Agencies and Employment Businesses [5.17]

The provision of personnel by employment agencies and employment businesses is regulated by the *Employment Agencies Act 1973*. Under this Act, the Secretary of State was authorised to make regulations which would:

'...secure the proper conduct of employment agencies and employment businesses and to protect the interests of persons availing themselves of the services of such agencies and businesses'.

Such Regulations were issued in the form of the *Conduct of Employment Agencies and Employment Businesses Regulations 1976*. Certain sectors are excluded from these Regulations, notably nursing agencies which are covered instead by the *Nurses Agencies Act 1957*. Special provisions apply to the entertainment and modelling industries.

Proposed changes to the Conduct of Employment Agencies and Employment Businesses Regulations [5.18]

At the time of writing, the *Conduct of Employment Agencies and Employment Businesses Regulations 1976* are being reviewed with a view to replacing them with new Regulations. Consultation on the final version of the *Conduct of Employment Agencies and Employment Businesses Regulations 2002* (EAA) began in July 2002 and it is likely that the Regulations will eventually come into effect in 2003.

The revised Regulations will impose a core of common standards and are likely to introduce changes impacting on:

- The obligation on employment agencies to provide clear contractual documentation to their temporary workers (see **5.21** below).

- Rules governing the charging of services by employment agencies, including limitations on the practice of requiring 'temp to perm fees'.

- The outlawing of terms in a worker's contract that seek to prevent or restrict the worker from taking up permanent employment with the hirer.

- The responsibility of employment agencies to take appropriate steps to ensure the personnel they supply are suitable.

- The responsibility of employment agencies to check potential workers' qualifications and experience.

- The protection of workers from having their personal details circulated indiscriminately by employment agencies.

- The promotion of competition and flexibility generally.

Definition of Temporary Worker [5.19]

The draft Regulations (*Reg 2*) define a temporary worker as follows:

'A work-seeker who is introduced or supplied to a hirer by a bureau –

(a) other than on the basis that the work-seeker will be the hirer's employee, as defined in *section 230(1)* (of the *Employment Rights Act 1996); or*

174

(b) on the basis that his remuneration will be paid to him directly or indirectly by or on behalf of a bureau or any person connected with a bureau.'

The Rights of Hiring Organisations in Relation to Employment Agency Temps [5.20]

The draft Regulations place responsibility on employment agencies to notify the hiring organisation to whom they intend to supply personnel of certain matters, including:

- The basis on which the business is to be transacted.

- The fees to be charged.

- The procedure to be followed if a worker supplied by the agency proves to be unsatisfactory.

- The basis on which the agency has hired the worker (see **5.21** below).

These provisions must be in writing and must be provided to the hiring organisation before the provision of any services commences.

The Contractual Relationship between an Employment Agency and the Temporary Workers [5.21]

Reg 7 of the draft Regulations states that the supply of temporary personnel to a hiring company must be set up on the basis that there is a contractual relationship between the employment agency and the worker. Unfortunately, however, the draft Regulations themselves do not go so far as to stipulate what the contractual relationship should be, i.e. whether it should be a contract of employment or a contract for services. Nevertheless the revised Regulations will require employment agencies to make it clear to their clients the contractual basis upon which they (the agency) are engaging a temporary worker. Any organisation that is hiring temporary staff through an employment agency will therefore be legally entitled to receive unambiguous documentation stating who is engaging whom and on what basis.

This means that although there will be a clear legal obligation on employment agencies to clarify the contractual relationship they have with each worker, it will ultimately be up to the employment agency to define that contractual relationship, leaving it open for individuals to challenge their employment status as is the case currently.

The Rights of Agency Workers [5.22]

Employment agencies will also be obliged under the revised Regulations to provide their workers with clear information about their employment rights and to set down in writing the contractual terms that will apply, including:

- Whether the worker will be employed under a contract of employment or engaged on a contract for services.

- Details of the terms and conditions of the contract of employment or contract for services.

- Details concerning remuneration and annual leave entitlement.

- A commitment that the employment agency will pay the worker in respect of work done irrespective of whether the hiring organisation pays the agency.

- The length of notice that the worker is required to give and entitled to receive on termination.

Once the revised Regulations are implemented, it should be easier for a temporary worker to assert certain employment rights because they will be able to establish that they have some sort of contractual relationship with the agency through whom they work. In theory, this could make it less likely that a temporary agency worker would be regarded as an employee of the client company to whom they were assigned.

It will clearly be in the interests of organisations that regularly hire temporary staff through employment agencies to ensure that the contract they have with the agency includes a clear statement regarding the employment status of the temporary workers, i.e. the nature of the contract set up between the agency and the worker. It would be particularly advantageous to the hiring organisation if the agency's contract with the temporary worker stated that the person was engaged by the employment agency on a contract of employment. If the documentation stipulates that a particular worker is an employee of the employment agency, the hiring organisation would, logically, be much less likely to face a claim from the temporary worker asserting that a contract of employment or contract for services existed with them.

Future EC Law Protecting the Rights of Agency Workers [5.23]

As yet, the supply of temporary workers by employment agencies to their clients is not governed by European law, nor are agency workers' rights covered by any EC Directive.

The position with regard to agency workers' rights is, however, set to change in the future. In the preamble to the *EC Fixed-Term Work Directive* (see **CHAPTER 4** at **4.34**), there is a statement that 'It is the intention of the parties (i.e. the European Social Partners) to consider the need for a similar agreement relating to temporary agency work'. Since then the European Commission has published a draft Directive covering the rights of temporary agency workers. Under the Directive, temporary agency workers would be granted the right not to suffer less favourable treatment than comparable employees engaged directly by the organisation in which they were placed, unless such treatment could be objectively justified. The UK will therefore be obliged at some time in the future to implement legislation making it unlawful for employers to discriminate against agency workers in terms of pay and conditions except if the particular circumstances justify less favourable treatment. The exact format and content of future UK legislation is of course not yet known, as there will have to be a lengthy process of negotiation (and possible amendments) before the text of the Directive is finalised. It is likely, however, that there will be a minimum period of service that the temporary agency worker would have to serve with the same organisation before becoming eligible for protection against discrimination. The draft Directive has proposed a period of assignment of six weeks after which the right not to suffer discrimination would come into effect.

Conclusion [5.24]

The rights and entitlements of agency workers has, for a number of years, been confused. In particular, the employment status of an agency worker can cause difficulties of interpretation, and case law demonstrates that an agency worker may be an employee of the agency, an employee of the client company for whom they work, or self-employed. The determination of an individual case will depend on all the facts and the precise nature of the working relationship between the worker and the agency/client.

This chapter has examined both statute and case law as it appertains to the employment of agency workers as well as describing the forthcoming changes to the law which will come into effect when revisions to the

Conduct of Employment Agencies and Employment Businesses Regulations 1976 are implemented in the near future.

Questions and Answers [5.25]

Question

When a temporary worker is engaged through an employment agency, who is deemed in law to be the worker's employer?

Answer

There is no employment law that dictates what the employment status of an agency worker should be. The employment status of agency workers has caused courts and tribunals problems of interpretation over the years, and essentially each case is determined on its own merits, depending on a number of factors inherent in the working relationships. A tribunal may hold that a worker has a contract of employment with the agency through whom they work, with the client company for whom they provide their services, or that they are self-employed.

Question

If an employment agency deducts tax and national insurance from their temporary workers' pay, does this mean that the workers are the agency's employees?

Answer

No. Employment agencies are obliged under the *Income and Corporation Taxes Act 1988, s 134* to deduct tax and national insurance from their workers' pay This legal obligation has no direct or binding relevance to a worker's employment status.

Question

Where an agency worker has a contract with the employment agency through whom they work, how easy is it for them to assert that it constitutes a contract of employment as opposed to a contract for services?

Answer

The determination of whether a contract between an employment agency and an individual is a contract of employment or a contract for services can be complex. An agency worker may be deemed to be an employee of the agency if, for example, they are obliged by the agency to abide by certain terms and conditions relating to where and how they carry out their work and to obey reasonable instructions issued by the agency. Other relevant factors would include the length of time the individual had worked for the agency and whether the agency provided any necessary working tools and equipment. Each case would be analysed on its own merits. However, even if it can be shown that a worker is employed by the employment agency for the duration of specific client assignment, this does not mean that they have a global contract of employment with the agency spanning periods during which they are not working. Unless there is an overriding mutual obligation on the agency to offer the individual future assignments and on the individual to accept any assignment that is offered, it is unlikely that there can be a continuous employment contract.

Question

Can an agency worker ever be deemed to be the employee of the client company who has hired them on a temporary basis through an employment agency?

Answer

It is possible, although relatively uncommon, for a temporary agency worker to be deemed to be the employee of the client company for whom they work, largely because no direct contract exists between the two parties. However, in *Motorola Ltd v (1) Davidson (2) Melville Craig Group Ltd [2001] IRLR 4* an agency worker was deemed to be the employee of the client company on the basis of the level of control exercised over the individual's work by the client employer's management. Other cases have, however, reached the opposite conclusion.

Question

What statutory employment protection rights does an agency worker have in respect of their working relationship with an employment agency?

Answer

If an agency worker can demonstrate that they are an employee of the employment agency, they will have the full range of statutory employment protection rights. If, on the other hand, their contract with the agency is a contract for services (and not a contract of employment), they will have fewer rights. Whatever the nature of the contract, they will always have rights under the *National Minimum Wage Act 1998* and the *Working Time Regulations 1998 (SI 1998 No 1833)*, and also the right not to suffer unlawful sex, race and disability discrimination.

Question

In respect of a temporary agency worker, who is responsible for ensuring the person is paid at least the national minimum wage and afforded their statutory entitlement to paid annual leave?

Answer

Where a worker is engaged by an employment agency on a temporary basis and assigned to one of the agency's clients, the responsibility for ensuring that the worker's rights are met lies with whichever organisation pays the worker their remuneration. In most cases that will be the employment agency and not the client company.

Question

Can a temporary agency worker potentially bring a claim to tribunal alleging unlawful discrimination on the part of the client company who has hired them through an employment agency?

Answer

Agency workers have the right not to suffer sex, race or disability discrimination even where it has been agreed or established that the agency worker is not the employee of the client company for whom they actually work. This is because 'contract workers' are expressly protected against unlawful discrimination in the UK's anti-discrimination legislation. Effectively, the right not to suffer unlawful discrimination applies to all workers who provide their services personally and does not depend on the existence of a contract of employment or a contract for services.

Question

What changes are on the horizon in relation the regulation of the hiring of temporary staff and the rights of agency workers?

Answer

At the time of writing, the *Conduct of Employment Agencies and Employment Businesses Regulations 1976* are being reviewed with a view to replacing them with new Regulations. Consultation was completed in March 2001, but the implementation of the revised Regulations was delayed. In addition, a future EC Directive will make it unlawful for employers to discriminate against agency workers in terms of pay and conditions except if the particular circumstances justify less favourable treatment.

Question

How will the new Regulations benefit organisations that hire temporary staff from employment agencies?

Answer

The draft Regulations place responsibility on employment agencies to make it clear to their clients the contractual basis upon which they (the agency) are engaging a temporary worker. There will also be obligations on the agency to notify the hiring organisation to whom they intend to supply personnel of certain other matters, including the basis on which the business is to be transacted, the fees to be charged and the procedure to be followed if a worker supplied by the agency proves to be unsatisfactory.

Question

How will agency workers benefit from the new Regulations?

Answer

The revised Regulations will compel employment agencies to set up a written contract with each of their workers and to specify whether it is a contract of employment or a contract for services. There will also be an obligation to specify the terms of the contract in writing, including details of remuneration and annual leave entitlement, notice periods, and a commitment that the employment agency will pay the worker in respect of work done irrespective of whether the hiring organisation pays the agency.

6. Continuity of Employment

Introduction [6.1]

Where individuals are employed on a temporary or fixed-term basis, their statutory employment rights are in principle the same as those of permanent employees. There is no fixed description or legal definition of a 'temporary employee'. However, since many statutory employment rights are dependent on the individual obtaining a defined minimum period of continuous service, temporary employees engaged on a single contract may not work long enough to become eligible for certain statutory employment benefits. For example the right to claim unfair dismissal requires a minimum qualifying period of service of one year except in a range of special circumstances. The length of an employee's continuous service is thus a very important concept.

This chapter aims to explain the concept of continuity of employment and the effect on continuity of certain types of gaps between periods of employment.

The Meaning of Continuous Employment [6.2]

Continuous employment is a statutory concept and the length of an employee's continuous service always falls to be calculated according to the rules laid down in statute, namely those specified in the *Employment Rights Act 1996, ss 210–219*. This means that it is not open to an employer and employee to reach a private agreement on the employee's length of service for statutory purposes, a principle that was upheld by the EAT in the case of *Carrington v Harwich Dock Co Ltd [1998] IRLR 567*. Equally it is not open to an employer to deny an employee continuity of employment in circumstances where statute confers the right upon them to benefit from continuity, for example an agreement that an employee should resign and be re-engaged a short time later in a new position will not act to remove the employee's right to claim continuous employment back to their original start date with the company.

In terms of the employee's contractual rights, however, (as opposed to their statutory rights), it is open to the employer and employee to reach agreement on any term or benefit in any way they choose. This will not, however, affect the employee's statutory rights. The principle behind this is enshrined in the *Employment Rights Act, s 203* which lays down that any provision in a contract of employment that excludes or limits the operation of any provision of the Act will be void. Thus statute always takes precedence over anything set out in a contract of employment.

The criteria for service to be continuous during any specified period of time are that:

1. The employee must have been employed on a contract of employment by the same employer, or an associated employer, for the period of time in question.

2. The contract of employment must have remained in force during every week of the particular period.

3. The contract must have continued without a break in employment of more than one calendar week (except in special circumstances – see **6.12** below).

A contract of employment will subsist irrespective of whether the employee is working full or part-time during any particular week. The number of hours worked under the contract in any particular week is thus irrelevant to the concept of continuity of employment (see **6.6** below).

Where an employee works on a succession of temporary or fixed-term contracts (with the same employer) without gaps between them, continuity of service will be maintained. This will be so even where the successive fixed-term contracts are on different terms and conditions.

Additionally, in certain circumstances, employees who work on temporary or fixed-term contracts with gaps between them can also maintain continuity of service. These circumstances are defined in the *Employment Rights Act 1996, s 212(3)*, which states that certain types of breaks between periods of employment will count as periods of continuous employment even though no contract is in force during the breaks. These provisions are explored in **6.12** below.

However, temporary or fixed-term employees who are engaged on a periodic basis with frequent spells of non-employment in between periods of employment may not gain sufficient continuity of service to qualify for certain statutory employment rights unless they can show that the gaps between contracts fell within the exceptions defined in the Act.

The *Employment Rights Act 1996, s 210(5)* stipulates that in the event of a dispute in a court or employment tribunal over whether an employee's service is continuous, a presumption will be made in favour of the employee, i.e. it will be assumed in the absence of evidence to the contrary that the employee's length of service was continuous.

Once continuity is broken as a result of a gap of more than a week between contracts, an employee who has returned to work for the same employer will have to start building up continuity again from scratch, irrespective of the length of the previous period of employment.

Statutory Rights that are Based on Length of Service [6.3]

Individuals who are engaged on a contract of employment enjoy a wide range of statutory employment rights. Some of these rights are effective from the first day of employment, whilst others are dependent on the employee working for a defined minimum period of time.

Statutory Rights Available from the First Day of Employment [6.4]

Statutory employment rights to which employees are entitled from the first day of their employment include:

- Rights in relation to pay, for example the right to receive the national minimum wage, the right to received itemised pay statements, the right not to have unauthorised deductions made from their pay and the right to receive statutory sick pay for up to 28 weeks during periods of absence from work due to personal sickness (unless the contract is for three months or less in which case no entitlement to statutory sick pay kicks in).

- Rights in relation to the contract of employment, i.e. the right not to suffer a breach of any of the express or implied terms of the employment contract and the right to have the contract transferred from the employee's current employer to a new employer in the event of a relevant business transfer under the *Transfer of Undertakings (Protection of Employment) Regulations 1981.*

- The right for men and women to receive equal pay for work that is judged to be 'like work', work rated as equivalent under a job evaluation scheme, or for work of equal value.

- The right not to be discriminated against on the grounds of sex, race or disability (it should be noted that job applicants also enjoy protection against discrimination on these grounds throughout the process of recruitment).

185

- The right not to be treated unfavourably on account of part-time status and the right for part-time workers to receive a written statement of reasons for less favourable treatment on request.

- The right not to be treated unfavourably on account of fixed-term status and the right of employees employed on fixed-term contracts to receive a written statement of reasons for less favourable treatment on request.

- Rights under the *Working Time Regulations 1998 (SI 1981 No 1833)*, namely the right to limit working hours to an average of no more than 48 hours per week, the right to take certain minimum rest breaks and the right to take a minimum of four weeks paid annual leave.

- Certain pregnancy/maternity rights including the right to be offered alternative work or (if none is available) be suspended on full pay for health and safety reasons whilst pregnant, and the right to take up to eighteen weeks maternity leave.

- The right to be accompanied by a colleague or trade union official at disciplinary or grievance hearings.

- Rights in relation to termination of employment, including the right to statutory minimum periods of notice upon termination of employment and the right to claim automatically unfair dismissal in certain defined circumstances.

- Certain trade union rights and health and safety rights, e.g. the right to belong, or not to belong, to a trade union of the individual's choice and to take part in trade union activities at an appropriate time and the right not to suffer a detriment in relation to health and safety.

- The right to be granted time off work for public duties, ante-natal care, to care for dependants and for certain other defined purposes.

- Rights under health and safety legislation, including the right to a safe workplace and a safe system of work.

Statutory Rights that Require a Minimum Period of Continuous Service [6.5]

The following represents a summary of statutory employment rights that are dependent on length of service:

Statutory employment right	Length of service required to qualify for the right
The right to a written statement of the key terms and conditions of employment	One month
The right to receive medical suspension pay	One month
The right to guaranteed pay where an employee is laid off or placed on short time	One month
The right to statutory maternity pay	Six months, calculated as at 15 weeks before the employee's baby is due
The right to take unpaid additional maternity leave	One year. This is to be reduced to six months in April 2003.
The right to take 13 weeks' unpaid parental leave in respect of each child under five years of age	One year
The right not to be unfairly dismissed	One year
The right to a written statement detailing the reasons for dismissal on request	One year
The right to a statutory redundancy payment	Two years
The right to paid time off work whilst under notice of redundancy in order to look for a new job	Two years

Continuity of Employment for Part-Time Employees [6.6]

Where an employee works part-time and the working pattern involves a regular pattern of days and/or hours, the employee will normally retain continuity of employment irrespective of the number of days worked or the number of days not worked, provided it is clear that the contract of employment subsists during any weeks when no work is done.

Whether or not the contract of employment continues in force during any weeks when no work is done will depend principally on whether there is an obligation on the employer to continue to provide work on the defined pattern, and an obligation on the employee to continue to perform the work. If, therefore, the employee's work pattern is regular and the working arrangements are such that both the employer and the employee expect the arrangements to continue, then it is likely that the employee's continuity of employment will be preserved during weeks when no work is done.

Case law demonstrates that mutuality of obligation is an essential element if a contract of employment is to exist. For example, in the case of *Nethermere (St. Neots) Ltd v Taverna and Gardiner [1984] IRLR 240*, the Court of Appeal stated that a contract of employment could exist only if there was a minimum of obligations on both sides. **CHAPTER 1** at **1.10** provides a detailed analysis of the concept of mutuality of obligation in relation to employment status.

In contrast, if there are frequent complete weeks (consisting of a Sunday to a Saturday inclusive) during which a part-time employee does no work, it may be argued that no contract is in force during these weeks, and that continuity is thus broken. This is likely to be the case when someone is engaged on a casual basis and where their working hours are undefined and/or irregular. In these circumstances it is unlikely that the individual will gain continuity of employment through the gaps between periods of employment as there will (arguably) be no mutuality of obligation upon which to assert the existence of a continuing contract of employment.

Employers should, however, be wary of assuming that part-time employees who work irregular patterns do not have continuity of employment.

Working Alternate Weeks [6.7]

An example of a part-time worker whose employment pattern involves gaps of a week or more could be someone who works alternate weeks, i.e. they work (full-time or part-time) for one week, but do not work at all during the following week. If the individual's employment contract makes it clear that this is the pattern of work under which the person is employed, they would in all likelihood still be considered to be employed during the week when they were not physically working. An example of a legal challenge in these circumstances occurred in the case of *Colley v Corkindale [1995] ICR 965* in which the EAT held that a contract of employment under which an employee was engaged to work five and a half hours every second Friday subsisted through the weeks when the employee did not work. The key factor leading to this decision was that there was a clear obligation for the employee to work the defined hours.

By contrast, where an individual is engaged to work on a casual basis (i.e. where there is no express or implied obligation on the part of the employer to offer work and no obligation on the part of the individual to accept work when it is offered), it is unlikely that the person would gain continuity of employment through any gaps between working assignments, unless the gaps were never longer than a calendar week.

Model Contractual Clause Indicating that an Employee is Engaged to Work Alternate Weeks [6.8]

The following type of clause could be used to confirm the contractual arrangements of an employee whose working pattern is to involve working alternate weeks:

'Your normal days and hours of work are as follows: you will work every second week on Thursday, Friday and Saturday, each day from 10.00 am to 3.15 pm. These hours are to include an unpaid break of 15 minutes each day on which you work. Thus your normal working hours average out at seven and a half hours a week. Your contract of employment will remain in force both during the weeks you work, and the weeks you do not work.'

Gaps between Contracts of Employment and Their Effect on Continuity [6.9]

According to the *Employment Rights Act 1996, s 210(2)*, continuous employment is calculated in completed calendar months and years. Thus an employee whose contract starts to run on 1 July 2002 will have accrued one year's continuous service on 30 June 2003 (assuming there is no break in employment between these two dates).

By contrast, the assessment of whether an individual's employment has remained continuous over a period of time falls to be determined on a week-by-week basis. The *Employment Rights Act 1996, s 212(1)* expressly states that any week during which a contract of employment is in force (whether the employee has worked full-time or part-time) will count in computing the employee's period of employment. *Section 210(4)* of the Act states that continuity will be broken if there is a week that does not count in computing length of service. It is important to note, however, that a week for this purpose is defined as a period running from a Sunday to a Saturday. For example, a break in employment from the Tuesday of one week until the Thursday of the following week would not constitute a break in continuity because it does not include a continuous period from a Sunday to a Saturday inclusive.

If there has been a gap between contracts of less than a calendar week, the issue of what the employee was doing during the gap makes no difference to the employee's continuity of service once they have re-commenced work for the employer. Even if the employee has worked for another employer during the gap, this will not disturb their continuity of employment in these circumstances.

Gaps During Which the Contract of Employment Remains in Force [6.10]

Certain periods of absence from work do not have any effect on continuity of employment because the employee's contract of employment is deemed to continue in force during their absence. Such periods of absence include:

- Sickness absence. It is usual for an employee's contract of employment to remain in force during all periods of sickness absence, but see **6.12** below for further information.

- Maternity leave. Furthermore, once an employee has returned to work from maternity leave, all the weeks during which she was on maternity leave must be counted as continuous service for the purpose of calculating her overall length of service in the future.

- Parental leave, although periods of parental leave need not be counted towards the employee's total period of continuous service (see **6.11** below);

- Statutory and contractual holiday absence.

Gaps That do not Break Continuity but do not Count Towards Continuous Service [6.11]

There are some situations in which an employee may be absent from work for one or more continuous weeks which, following the employee's return to work, will not count towards their total length of employment, but at the same time will not break their continuity of employment. The following situations fall into this category:

1. Where the employee is absent from work on account of parental leave. Contracts of employment remain in force during parental leave (albeit in a limited way), but, once the employee has returned

to work, their period of parental leave need not be counted for the purpose of continuity of employment. It follows that when, at a later date, an employer is assessing an employee's length of service for the purpose of statutory employment rights, they may exclude any period of time during which the employee was absent from work on parental leave. The practical outcome of this is that the employee's periods of employment before and after their parental leave are joined together as if they were continuous with each other.

2. Where the employee is absent from work because they are taking part in a strike or because of a lock-out. These provisions are contained in the *Employment Rights Act 1996, s 216(1-3)*. The correct method of calculating the overall length of service of an employee who has had a period of absence due to a strike or lock-out is to 'postpone' the employee's start-date by the number of calendar days (not working days) equivalent to the number of days they were on strike.

3. The *Employment Rights Act 1996, s 217* provides that in certain limited circumstances where an employee is absent from work because they have been called up for military service, their continuity of employment will be preserved.

4. Where the employee is employed overseas for a temporary period, although overseas service is relevant only for the purposes of calculating length of service in relation to entitlement to statutory redundancy pay. Thus, service overseas must be deducted from the employee's total length of service for the purpose of calculating statutory redundancy pay, but such service does not otherwise affect the employee's continuity of employment. It follows that temporary overseas service will not affect an employee's statutory rights in any other way, unless the employee moves permanently away from the UK and works wholly outside Great Britain.

Gaps During Which the Contract of Employment does not Remain in Force [6.12]

There are other defined circumstances in which continuity of employment can be asserted even though the employee's contract has been terminated for a temporary period of more than a week, provided the contract has subsequently been revived or renewed. These circumstances are defined in the *Employment Rights Act 1996, s 212(3)* which states that certain types of breaks between periods of employment will count as periods of continuous employment even though no contract is in force during the breaks. In these circumstances the period of the gap between the earlier and the later engagement is deemed to form part of the employee's period of continuous employment. The relevant provisions are summarised here and explored further from **6.13** onwards.

- The *Employment Rights Act 1996, ss 212(3)(a)* and *(4)* states that for a period of up to 26 weeks during which an employee is absent from work in consequence of sickness or injury, continuity of employment will be preserved. However, it is more usual for the employee's contract of employment to remain in force during periods of sickness absence, rendering the application of this statutory provision on continuity unnecessary.

- Under the *Employment Rights Act 1996, s 212(3)(b)*, continuity of employment will be preserved where the employee is absent from work on account of a temporary cessation of work (see **6.13** below).

- Where the employee is absent from work as a result of an arrangement, or in circumstances which are customary in the particular industry, continuity will be maintained (*Employment Rights Act 1996, s 212(3)(c)* (see **6.20** below).

- According to the *Employment Rights Act 1996, s 219*, an employee who has been dismissed and subsequently reinstated or re-engaged as a result of a successful unfair dismissal claim, or following conciliation or arbitration through ACAS, is entitled to enjoy continuity of employment back to their original start date. This means that all the weeks that fell between the date of the employee's dismissal and the date of their reinstatement (or re-engagement) will count towards their continuous service, and they will be entitled to receive all their back-pay.

It is important to bear in mind that any weeks during which the employee's contract is not in force but during which continuity is nevertheless preserved as a consequence of the legislative provisions, will count towards the calculation of the employee's total period of continuous employment. Thus, once the employee has resumed working under the contract, it is as if the period of the gap has never occurred. If, at some time in the future, the employer is calculating the employee's length of service, the gaps must be disregarded, i.e. counted as if the employee had been working normally.

Temporary Cessations of Work [6.13]

The *Employment Rights Act 1996, s 212(3)(b)* states that any week during which an employee is absent from work on account of a temporary cessation of work will count in computing the employee's period of continuous employment.

Definition of Temporary Cessation of Work

Key Case **[6.14]**

There is no definition of what constitutes a temporary cessation of work in statute, but the House or Lords has held in the leading case of *Fitzgerald v Hall, Russell & Co Ltd [1969] 3 All ER 1140* that it means a period during which an employee would have been at work but for the fact that the employer could not find any work for the employee to do.

Fitzgerald v Hall, Russell & Co Ltd [1969] 3 All ER 1140

Facts

Mr Fitzgerald worked as a welder for a firm of shipbuilders. When there was a shortage of welding work, some of the welders, including Mr Fitzgerald, were dismissed by reason of redundancy. Some eight weeks later, Mr Fitzgerald was re-employed. When, several years later, he was made redundant again, there was a dispute over his length of service. Mr Fitzgerald claimed that his length of service should be regarded as going back to his original start date with the company, whilst the employer asserted that the eight-week period of non-employment broke his continuity, particularly since (they argued) there had been no *cessation* of work, but merely a *diminution* in the amount of work available.

Findings

The House of Lords held that there had in fact been a temporary cessation of work, and that Mr Fitzgerald's continuity of employment was thus preserved.

A temporary cessation of work could occur for many reasons, for example:

- A down-turn in the employee's business due to market conditions.

- A lessening of the employer's work at the end of a particular season or peak period.

- The loss of a major contract.

- A gap in time between the completion of one contract and the start of another.

- A temporary shutdown.

The law does not place any limit on the length of a temporary cessation of work in relation to an employee's right to have continuity of employment preserved, although it would normally be a period measurable in weeks rather than months. The only rules are that:

- There must be a cessation of work (and not just a redistribution of the same amount of work amongst fewer employees).

- The cessation of work must be genuinely temporary (although it does not matter whether the parties knew whether the break would be permanent or temporary at the time it began – instead the tribunal or court will look back, take all relevant factors into account and adopt an objective approach).

- The reason for the employee's absence from work must be the temporary cessation of work, and not some other reason.

- The reason for the employee's re-employment must be that the amount of work has returned to its pre-existing level.

Regular Gaps between Periods of Employment [6.15]

If an employee works for the same employer on a regular basis, but their periods of employment are regularly punctuated with periods of non-employment, it can be difficult to ascertain whether the periods of non-employment can be classed as temporary cessations of work, thus allowing the employee to preserve their continuity of employment. In these circumstances, a court or tribunal to whom the matter was referred would adopt an objective approach and review the individual's total employment history, considering the length of the periods of work in relation to the length of the gaps between them. Irrespective of the length of the period of a gap, if it is short in relation to the periods of work which precede and follow it, it may legitimately be viewed as a temporary cessation of work. Similarly, if there has been a series of gaps which, when added together, constitute a relatively short period of time in comparison to the employee's overall length of service, a court or tribunal is likely to rule that the employee's continuity of employment has been maintained.

In *Sillars v Charrington Fuels Ltd [1989] IRLR 152*, the Court of Appeal held that a temporary cessation of work had to be interpreted as meaning a relatively short period of time in comparison to the period actually worked.

In this case, the employee had over a number of years worked from October until around May, a pattern that involved between 21 and 32 weeks working over the year. The Court of Appeal took the view that, since the employee had only ever been employed for approximately half a year at a time, the gaps could not legitimately be viewed as temporary cessations of work.

The Effect of Temporary Cessations of Work on Employees Engaged on Fixed-term Contracts [6.16]

The statutory provisions governing continuity of employment following a temporary cessation of work can in certain circumstances benefit employees engaged on a series of fixed-term contracts.

A typical example of this would be a teacher engaged on a series of fixed-term contracts, each one lasting for the duration of the academic year. In these circumstances, no contract of employment would be in force during the period of the summer vacation.

Case law demonstrates conclusively that the gap between fixed-term contracts in these circumstances will be viewed as a temporary cessation of work. The leading case on this matter is *Ford v Warwickshire County Council [1983] IRLR 126*, a case concerning a teacher who had been employed for eight years under a succession of fixed-term contracts that expired at the end of each academic year. The House of Lords held that the statutory provisions governing temporary cessations of work apply to the expiry of a fixed-term contract in the same way as they do to the termination of an open-ended contract, provided the individual is subsequently re-employed. In the *Ford* case, the simple analysis was that:

- There was a period of time during which no contract of employment was in force.

- The reason for this was that there was no work for the employee to do (because the school was closed during the summer holidays).

- The employee was therefore absent due to a temporary cessation of work.

The House of Lords ruled also that the fact that an employee's absences from work are foreseen, agreed and regular does not prevent the absences from being attributable to temporary cessations of work.

The Effect of a Redundancy Payment on Continuity [6.17]

Employees who have worked for the same employer on a continuous basis for a minimum period of two years, and who are dismissed by reason of redundancy, are entitled to receive a statutory redundancy payment. It does not matter whether the employee's period of employment has been on a single open-ended contract (or so-called 'permanent' contract), on a fixed-term contract or on a series of continuous fixed-term contracts. This is because, under the *Employment Rights Act 1996, s 136(1)(b)*, the expiry of a fixed-term contract is regarded in law as a dismissal.

The statutory definition of a redundancy is contained in the *Employment Rights Act 1996, s 139(1)*. Essentially, a redundancy situation arises where the requirements of a business for employees to carry out work of a particular kind have ceased or diminished. The word 'ceased' in this context can include a temporary cessation of work as well as a permanent stoppage, and similarly 'diminished' requirements for employees to perform the work may be either permanent or temporary. Thus, when an employee's contract is terminated by dint of a temporary cessation of work, this gives rise to a redundancy entitlement.

There is, however, one exception to the provision that termination of an employee's contract due to a temporary cessation of work constitutes a dismissal by reason of redundancy. This is where the employee is offered a new contract (whether permanent or temporary) prior to the termination of the original contract, and the new contract is to take effect within four weeks of the expiry of the original contract. In these circumstances the employee is not regarded in law as having been dismissed, and there is therefore no redundancy.

Because the definition of redundancy can include circumstances in which there is a temporary cessation of work, an employee laid off as a result of a temporary cessation of work will be entitled to a statutory redundancy payment (subject to their having at least two years' qualifying service). It was confirmed in the case of *Pfaffinger v City of Liverpool Community College [1996] IRLR 508* that employees engaged on a series of fixed-term contracts will become entitled to a statutory redundancy payment each time the contract under which they are engaged expires without renewal, provided they have accrued two years' continuous service at that point in time. The gaps between the contracts that were due to a temporary cessation of work did not break the employee's continuity of employment.

The *Pfaffinger* case concerned a part-time lecturer who had been employed for thirteen years on a series of fixed-term contracts, each one lasting for a single academic term. When a dispute arose one year and Ms Pfaffinger elected not to return to work after the summer vacation, she brought a case to tribunal claiming entitlement to statutory redundancy pay based on the whole thirteen years of her employment. The EAT confirmed that, because the gaps between contracts were due to temporary cessations of work, Ms Pfaffinger's total service was continuous. They further held that each time one of Ms Pfaffinger's fixed-term contracts had expired on account of a temporary cessation of work, this constituted a redundancy dismissal, entitling her potentially to a statutory redundancy payment. It was confirmed that her entitlement to redundancy pay was unaffected by her return to work under a new contract the next academic term because no offer of re-engagement had been made before the expiry of the previous contract. Ms Pfaffinger was therefore entitled to a statutory redundancy payment based on the whole of the period of her employment, since she had not previously claimed, or been paid, any redundancy pay.

It is important to note that entitlement to a statutory redundancy payment and entitlement to have employment regarded as continuous are two separate matters in statute. The receipt of a redundancy payment will have no effect on the question of whether the person's employment can be regarded as continuous in the event that they are re-employed at a later date once the employer's work has picked up again.

No Double Payments [6.18]

The *Employment Rights Act 1996, s 214(2)* makes it clear, however, that an employee is not entitled to receive statutory redundancy pay twice for the same period of employment. This means that, for the purposes of entitlement to redundancy pay only, the employee's continuity of employment will be broken each time they receive a statutory redundancy payment. The employee will only become eligible for redundancy pay again once they have gained a further two years continuous service, even though, for other purposes (notably the right to claim unfair dismissal), the length of their continuous employment may be regarded as going back to the date of commencement of their first contract.

Another important point to note is that the statutory provision under which employees are ineligible to receive statutory redundancy pay twice for the same period of employment applies only to statutory redundancy payments made when the employee's dismissal is genuinely due to redundancy, and not to any other type of termination payment, for example an ex-gratia payment that the employer may have elected to make. A payment labelled as a redundancy payment which is in reality an ex-gratia termination payment will not act to disentitle the employee to claim a future statutory redundancy payment for the whole of the period of their continuous employment with the employer. This is so irrespective of the amount of the ex-gratia payment.

Model Letter Informing Employees of a Temporary Cessation of Work [6.19]

The following letter could be used as a model to inform employees that there has been a temporary down-turn in the employer's business necessitating the termination of their contract.

'Dear (employee's name),

As you know, the amount of work this company has available for people with your skills has recently diminished as a result of (*reason, for example the loss or completion of a contract*). We therefore have no option but to give you notice that your current contract of employment will terminate on (*state date, ensuring the employee receives the statutory and/or contractual notice period to which they are entitled*).

We anticipate, however, that this downturn in the company's business will be temporary and that we may be able to offer you re-employment in the future on the same type of contract. Although we cannot guarantee any offer of re-employment, we will contact you as soon as we are in a position to calculate our future requirements for additional staffing.

In the meantime, you will be paid all wages due to you on your termination date, together with any accrued holiday pay. Details of the amounts involved will be notified to you separately.

(*Alternative clauses*) As you have not worked for the company for two years or more, you will not be entitled to a statutory redundancy payment on the termination of your current contract.

(*or*)

As you have gained (*number of years*) complete years of continuous service, you are entitled to a statutory redundancy payment on termination, details of which will be notified to you separately.

(*or*)

As you have gained *(state number of years)* complete years of continuous service since your last statutory redundancy payment (which was paid to you on *(date)*, you are entitled to a statutory redundancy payment on termination of this contract, details of which will be notified to you separately.

If you have any queries on the above, please do not hesitate to contact the undersigned.

Yours sincerely

(Name of manager)'.

Absences Through Custom or Arrangement [6.20]

Another of the circumstances in which continuity of employment will be preserved despite a gap between two periods of employment is when the employee's absence from work is by arrangement or custom. The *Employment Rights Act 1996, s 212(3)(c)* states that any week during which an employee is absent from work by arrangement or custom will count in computing the employee's period of continuous employment. This provision will only apply, however, where an employee's absence is not governed by their contract of employment. If the absence is provided for in the contract, continuity will be preserved in any event because of the continued existence of the contract.

There is no stated maximum period of time during which an employee may be absent by arrangement or custom and still maintain continuity of employment.

Absence as a result of an arrangement [6.21]

An absence on account of an 'arrangement' for the purposes of the *Employment Rights Act 1996, s 212(3)(c)* could occur in a number of different circumstances, examples of which are:

- Where employees are engaged on the basis of seasonal work, for example workers who are employed in hotels during the summer months, laid off when the hotel closes for a short period during the winter and re-engaged at the beginning of the following season (see **CHAPTER 7** at **7.14** for information about seasonal workers). For example, in *Tongue Hotel Co Ltd v Mackay [1983] EAT 416/83*, the EAT held that a waitress who had worked throughout the summer

199

season in a hotel in the north of Scotland had continuity of employment despite the fact that she had been paid off at the end of the summer season. There was sufficient evidence for the tribunal to conclude that, despite the termination of the employee's contract, the hotel's management had regarded her as continuing in their employment until the beginning of the following season at which time she was re-engaged on a full-time basis.

- Where an employer and an employee agree jointly that the employee will take a period of extended leave, for example sabbatical leave, and that their job will be held open for them. So long as this arrangement is made prior to the commencement of the period of leave, continuity of employment will be preserved. For example, in Curr v Marks & Spencer, the employee had taken a period of sabbatical leave between 1990 and 1994. The 'arrangement' had been made in accordance with her employer's policy. The EAT held ultimately (when in 1999 the employee was made redundant and claimed redundancy pay based on her total period of employment back to 1973) that her continuity of service was maintained through the period of sabbatical leave.

- Where employees' contracts of employment are governed by a trade union agreement that makes it clear that in certain defined circumstances, gaps between periods of employment up to a specified duration will not be treated as breaking continuity.

For a private arrangement to be effective in preserving an employee's continuity of employment throughout a period of absence, the arrangement must have been entered into in advance of the absence. If an agreement is reached after an employee's return to work following a break in service that the employee's service will be regarded as continuous as from the beginning of their first period of employment, this will not act to preserve the employee's continuity of employment for statutory purposes. For example, in *Murphy v A Birrell & Sons Ltd [1978] IRLR 458*, it was held that where an employee resigns from their employment, apparently permanently, but is subsequently re-employed, an agreement reached at that time that the employee's service will be regarded as continuous will be void and unenforceable.

An agreement made after the employee's return to work may of course give rise to *contractual* obligations on the part of the employer, but cannot alter the statutory provisions which take precedence over anything agreed in contract.

Model Letter Confirming an Agreed Period of Unpaid Absence
[6.22]

The following model letter can be used when an agreement is being set up with an employee for them to take an agreed period of unpaid absence. The wording of this model letter assumes that the employer has a definite intention to re-employ the individual after the period of absence.

'Dear *(name of employee)*,

Following our recent discussions, I would like to confirm the following agreed arrangements in relation to your forthcoming period of leave.

We have agreed that you will take a period of unpaid leave commencing on *(date)* and lasting *(number of weeks or months)*. Your current contract of employment will therefore terminate on *(date)* and you will be paid all outstanding wages/salary, holiday pay and any other amounts due to you at that time. Details of these amounts will be notified to you in due course.

We have also agreed that the company will re-employ you after your period of leave, commencing on or around *(date)*, but in any event no later than *(date)*. If you do not re-commence employment by this latter date, the company will no longer be under any obligation to re-employ you.

During the period of your leave, you will not be paid any salary or wages, nor will you be entitled to any benefits from the company. *(Optional clause)* We have agreed, however, that during your period of leave you will *(state any activities that have been agreed, for example that the employee should undertake a specified course of study)*.

Would you please arrange to make contact with the undersigned approximately *(two weeks, one month, or other timescale)* prior to the date we have pledged to re-employ you, so that we can discuss and agree the final arrangements for your re-employment.

We cannot guarantee to offer you re-employment in the same job as your current contract, but will undertake to re-employ you in a position that will make appropriate use of your skills and experience and at a level of seniority similar to that of your current position. The precise terms and conditions applicable on your re-employment will be notified to you at the time of our discussions, and will not be less favourable to you than the terms and conditions of your current contract. However, this does not preclude any mutual agreement being reached for you to be re-employed on different terms.

I wish you success during your period of leave, and look forward to being in contact with you around *(approximate date)*. Would you please sign and date one copy of this letter and return it to the undersigned.

Yours sincerely

(Name of manager).

I have read and understood this letter, and agree to its terms.

Name of employee .... Date ....

Employee's signature ....

Sabbatical Leave [6.23]

Sabbatical leave is a period of leave or career break (paid or unpaid) granted to employees for one of a range of defined purposes, for example so that the employee can undertake a full-time course of study, or for family reasons. The employer may elect to pay the employee full or part salary during sabbatical leave, or may stipulate that all periods of sabbatical leave will be unpaid. If pay is maintained during the employee's absence, the employer would be entitled to set down conditions that the employee must meet, for example that the leave must be used for a purpose that will benefit the business or that the employee will produce written reports of their activities during the period of leave.

Model Policy on Sabbatical Leave [6.24]

The following model policy could be adopted (or adapted to suit) by organisations that wish to offer their employees the opportunity to take periods of sabbatical leave. It is assumed, for the purposes of this model policy, that the organisation granting sabbatical leave would intend the employee's employment to continue during the period of leave on account of the provisions in the *Employment Rights Act 1996, s 212(3)(c)* (see **6.21** above).

Policy

It is the Company's policy to offer its employees the opportunity to take a period of sabbatical leave of up to *(maximum length of time)*. In order to qualify for sabbatical leave, the employee must have a minimum of *(number of years, for example three)* years continuous service with the company. No more than one period of sabbatical leave will be granted to any one employee during any period of *(number of years, for example ten)* years.

Both full and part-time employees are eligible to apply for sabbatical leave. The timing of sabbatical leave and the number of weeks or months of leave granted is, however, at the Company's complete discretion.

Periods of sabbatical leave will normally be granted only on an unpaid basis. The Company may, however, at its discretion, agree to pay the employee full or part salary during sabbatical leave in circumstances where it can be shown that the activities the employee intends to undertake during sabbatical leave will be of direct benefit to the Company, as well as to the employee.

Sabbatical leave may be granted in the following circumstances:

- Where the employee intends to undertake a full-time course of study at a recognised college or university. Where this course of study is directly relevant to the employee's career with the Company, sabbatical leave may be granted on a paid basis, although this is not guaranteed.

- Where the employee intends to carry out research that is likely to be relevant to the Company's activities. In these circumstances, sabbatical leave may be granted on a paid basis, although this is not guaranteed.

- Where the employee intends to undertake specific activities that will broaden their experience and skills.

- Where the employee intends to carry out voluntary unpaid work that will be of benefit to the community, or to a recognised charitable organisation.

- Where the employee wishes to undertake a period of overseas travel, for example for the purpose of visiting family.

- Where the employee wishes to take time away from work in order to fulfil their childcare responsibilities.

- Where the employee can demonstrate to the Company's satisfaction that they will use the period of leave in another appropriate way.

Conditions applicable to the granting of sabbatical leave

1. Employees who are absent on sabbatical leave will remain under contract to the Company and will continue to accrue continuous service.

2. During sabbatical leave, the employee will not normally be permitted to undertake paid employment with any other organisation unless this is agreed in advance with the Company.

3. Employees on sabbatical leave must keep in regular contact with the Company. This must be done by sending a summary of activities at least once a month by letter or e-mail.

4. Employees who by agreement undertake a period of sabbatical leave will be notified in writing of which terms and conditions of their employment will continue, and which will be suspended, during the period of their absence.

5. Employees must give at least (*number of weeks, for example four*) weeks notice of their intended date of return from sabbatical leave if this has not been agreed in advance.

6. On an employee's return from sabbatical leave, the Company cannot guarantee employment in the same job as the employee previously held, although every reasonable effort will be made to reinstate the employee in the position they held prior to their absence. Where the Company does not offer the employee the same job, suitable alternative employment will be offered on terms and conditions that are not less favourable to the employee than those applicable when sabbatical leave commenced.

7. Where a period of sabbatical leave is granted on a paid basis, the employee will be required to work for the Company after sabbatical leave for a period of at least (*number of years, for example one*) year(s). Any employee who fails to comply with this condition will be required to repay to the Company all amounts of money paid to them by way of salary and expenses during the period of sabbatical leave.

Absence as a Result of a Custom [6.25]

If there is a well-established custom in a particular organisation, or within a particular industry as a whole, that employees who are paid off for a limited period of time and then re-engaged will retain continuity of service, this practice may be sufficient to guarantee the employees continuity of employment each time there is such a break in employment. The effect of the consistent adoption of such a custom is that its application will have evolved into a term that is implied into employees' contracts of employment. This is based on the rationale that the custom is so well-known that it is understood to be an entitlement right from the start of the employment relationship.

Entitlement to Statutory Maternity Pay [6.26]

In order to qualify for statutory maternity pay, a temporary worker must be an employee engaged on a contract of employment as opposed to an independent contractor working on a contract for services. Furthermore, the employee must have had a minimum of six months continuous employment as at the fifteenth week before her expected week of childbirth (known as the 'qualifying week'). In most circumstances, for the purposes of calculating a pregnant employee's continuous service for SMP purposes, periods of absence during which no contract of employment was in force as a result of a temporary cessation of work or an arrangement or custom will count towards the employee's period of continuous employment only *after* the employee has returned to work.

Special provisions exist, however, in the *Statutory Maternity Pay (General) Regulations 1986, Reg 11(3A)* that benefit employees whose employment is temporary and spasmodic but nevertheless regular, for example employees engaged on regular fixed-term contracts and seasonal employees. The Regulations provide that continuity of service can, provided certain criteria are fulfilled, be preserved for SMP purposes even if the employee's qualifying week falls in a period when no work is available and even if she does not return to work for the employer.

The special provisions apply to female employees engaged on spasmodic work who are absent from work in the qualifying week on account of pregnancy. Provided the conditions in *Reg 11(3A)* are met, an employee in these circumstances will still qualify for SMP. These conditions are that in the pregnant employee's employment, it must be customary for the employer to:

- offer a temporary employee work for fixed periods of 26 consecutive weeks or less; *and*

- offer such work for such periods on two or more occasions in a year (for periods that do not overlap); *and*

205

- offer the available work to those employees who had worked for the employer during the last or a recent period of this type of employment.

Conclusion [6.27]

The length of an employee's continuous employment is very important for several reasons, in particular because many statutory employment rights are dependent on the individual obtaining a defined minimum period of continuous service. Thus temporary or fixed-term employees engaged on a single contract may not work long enough to become eligible for certain statutory employment benefits. Part-time employees accrue continuous service in the same way as full-time employees provided their contract of employment subsists without gaps of more than one calendar week.

It is important for employers to have an overall understanding of the law on continuity of employment which governs the circumstances in which an employee's service is to be regarded as continuous, and when it is not.

Certain periods of absence from work do not have any effect on continuity of employment because the employee's contract of employment is deemed to continue in force during their absence. Other types of absence, defined in statute, may not break continuity even though the contract of employment has been terminated. These include absence on account of a temporary cessation of work, and absence as a result of an arrangement or custom within the particular organisation or industry.

Questions and Answers [6.28]

Question

What factors impinge on the calculation of an employee's continuous service?

Answer

Continuous employment is a statutory concept and the length of an employee's continuous service always falls to be calculated according to the rules laid down in statute, namely those specified in the *Employment Rights Act 1996, ss 210–219*. This means that it is not open to an employer and employee to reach a private agreement on the employee's length of service for statutory purposes. Equally it is not open to an employer to deny an employee continuity of employment in circumstances where statute confers the right upon them to benefit from continuity.

Question

Are all an employee's statutory employment rights dependent on their gaining a defined minimum period of continuous service?

Answer

No. Individuals who are engaged on a contract of employment enjoy a wide range of statutory employment rights from the first day of their employment. Certain rights are, however, dependent on the employee working for a defined minimum period of time, for example the right to claim unfair dismissal depends, with some exceptions, on the employee having gained at least one year's continuous service and the right to statutory redundancy pay depends on a minimum of two years' continuous employment.

Question

Where an employee works part-time, how does this affect their continuity of employment?

Answer

Where an employee works part-time and the working pattern involves a regular pattern of days and/or hours, the employee will normally retain continuity of employment irrespective of the number of days worked or the number of days not worked, provided it is clear that the contract of employment subsists during any weeks when no work is done. The number of hours worked under the contract in any particular week is thus irrelevant to the concept of continuity of employment.

Question

How long does a period of non-employment have to be in order for it to break an employee's continuity of service?

Answer

Section *210(4)* of the *Employment Rights Act 1996* states that continuity will be broken if there is a complete week that does not count in computing length of service, i.e. a week during which the employee's contract of employment is not in force. It is important to note, however, that a week for this purpose has been defined as a period running from a Sunday to a Saturday.

Question

If a part-time employee works for their employer on an ad-hoc basis with no regular pattern, are they likely realistically to gain continuity of employment?

Answer

If there are complete weeks during which a part-time employee does no work, it may be argued that no contract is in force during these weeks, and that continuity is thus broken. Whether or not the contract of employment continues in force during any weeks when no work is done will depend principally on whether there is an obligation on the employer to continue to provide work, and an obligation on the employee to continue to perform the work, for example if there is a regular, agreed working pattern which both parties expect to continue. If, however, there is no such mutuality of obligation or agreed regular pattern of working, the individual will not gain continuity of service through the gaps between periods of employment as there will (arguably) be nothing upon which to assert the existence of a continuing contract of employment. This will be the case unless the gaps between periods of employment are never longer than a calendar week.

Question

What effect on an employee's continuity of employment do different types of absence have, for example holiday leave, maternity leave, parental leave and sickness absence?

Answer

Certain periods of absence from work do not have any effect on continuity of employment because the employee's contract of employment is deemed to continue in force during their absence. These include statutory and contractual holiday leave, maternity leave, parental leave and, in most cases, sickness absence.

Question

If an employee is assigned to work overseas for a temporary period of time, what effect does this have on their continuity of employment?

Answer

Where the employee is employed overseas for a temporary period, this does not affect their continuity of employment except in one respect. This is that overseas service is not counted towards the employee's total length of service for the purpose of entitlement to statutory redundancy pay. Temporary overseas service will not affect an employee's statutory rights in any other way, however, unless the employee moves permanently away from the UK and works wholly outside Great Britain.

Question

Are there any circumstances in which an employee's continuity of employment can be preserved despite gaps between periods of employment of longer than one calendar week?

Answer

Yes, there are a limited number of defined circumstances in which continuity of employment can be asserted even though the employee's contract has been terminated for a temporary period of more than a week, provided the contract has subsequently been revived or renewed. These circumstances are defined in the *Employment Rights Act 1996, s 212(3)* which states that certain types of breaks between periods of employment will count as periods of continuous employment even though no contract is in force during the breaks. Two of these circumstances are when the employee's absence is on account of a temporary cessation of work, and when the absence is as a result of an arrangement made between the employer and the employee or a custom in the particular organisation or industry.

Question

What does a 'temporary cessation of work' mean?

Answer

There is no definition of what constitutes a temporary cessation of work in statute, but the House or Lords has held in the leading case of *Fitzgerald v Hall, Russell & Co Ltd [1969] 3 All ER 1140* that it means a period during which an employee would have been at work but for the fact that the employer could not find any work for the employee to do. Examples of circumstances leading to a temporary cessation of work could be the loss of a contract or a temporary shut-down.

Question

How long can a period of absence on account of a temporary cessation of work last before it breaks an employee's continuity of service?

Answer

The law does not place any limit on the length of a temporary cessation of work in relation to an employee's right to have continuity of employment preserved, although it would normally be a period measurable in weeks rather than months. Usually, if a gap between two periods of employment is short in relation to the periods of work which precede and follow it, it may legitimately be viewed as a temporary cessation of work.

Question

Can teachers who work on a series of fixed-term contracts each lasting for the duration of the academic year claim continuity of employment through the periods of the summer vacations during which no contract of employment is in force?

Answer

Yes, case law demonstrates conclusively that the gap between fixed-term contracts in these circumstances will be viewed as a temporary cessation of work. The House of Lords held in the leading case of *Ford v Warwickshire County Council [1983] IRLR 126* that the statutory provisions governing temporary cessations of work apply to the expiry of fixed-term contracts in the same way as they do to the termination of open-ended contracts, provided the individual is subsequently re-employed by the same employer.

Question

Can employees who have been engaged on a series of fixed-term contracts that are deemed to be continuous claim a redundancy payment if they are laid off as a result of a temporary cessation of work?

Answer

Yes, provided that they have at least two years' qualifying service at the time of the termination of their contract, and provided they are not offered a new contract to commence within four weeks. This comes about because the definition of redundancy can include circumstances in which there is a temporary cessation of work. It was confirmed in the case of *Pfaffinger v City of Liverpool Community College [1996] IRLR 508* that employees engaged on a series of fixed-term contracts will become entitled to a statutory redundancy payment each time the contract under which they are engaged expires without renewal, provided they have accrued two years' continuous service at that point in time. However, an employee is not entitled to receive statutory redundancy pay twice for the same period of employment.

Question

Where an employee whose fixed-term contract has expired has been paid a statutory redundancy payment, does this automatically break their continuity of employment?

Answer

The receipt of a redundancy payment will have no effect on the employee's continuity of employment for statutory purposes. In other words if the employee is re-employed by the same employer following a temporary cessation of work, their service will be regarded as continuous back to the date of the commencement of the original contract. However, redundancy pay cannot be paid twice in respect of the same period of employment.

Question

Can an employer and an employee agree together that, following the employee's re-employment after a period of absence, the employee's service will be regarded as continuous?

Answer

The *Employment Rights Act 1996, s 212(3)(c)* states that any week during which an employee is absent from work by arrangement (or custom) will count in computing the employee's period of continuous employment. However, for an 'arrangement' to be effective in preserving an employee's continuity of employment throughout a period of absence, the arrangement must have been entered into in advance of the absence. If an agreement is reached after an employee's return to work that the employee's service will be regarded as continuous as from the beginning of their first period of employment, this will not act to preserve the employee's continuity of employment for statutory purposes. An agreement made after the employee's return to work may, of course, give rise to *contractual* obligations on the part of the employer, but cannot alter the statutory provisions which take precedence over anything agreed in contract.

7. Casual Workers, Students and Seasonal Workers

Introduction [7.1]

Employing staff on a casual or short-term basis is a popular approach amongst employers whose business demands fluctuate at different times of the week or throughout the year. Certain industries, typically tourism, hotels and restaurants, distribution, agriculture and construction employ large numbers of casual and seasonal workers. According to the Labour Force Survey conducted in 2001, about 50 per cent of seasonal and 37 per cent of casual employees work in the distribution and hotel and restaurant sectors.

Casual workers can be a particularly useful source of additional staffing where the employer's levels of work are unpredictable, fluctuating or irregular, or where the need for work to be done is very short-term, for example the need for a hotel to hire extra staff to serve guests at a private function.

The Employment Status of Casual Workers [7.2]

A casual worker is someone who is engaged to work for an employer either on a one-off basis for a short period of time or on an ad-hoc, as required basis, usually with no regular pattern of days or hours. In most cases, the employer will not guarantee the casual worker any minimum amount of work within a given period of time (nor any minimum amount of pay), and the casual worker will be free to either accept work when it is offered, or reject it if they are unable or unwilling to work at the particular time offered. This means that there will no mutuality of obligation in the working relationship (see **CHAPTER 1** at **1.10** for a discussion of mutuality of obligation). Thus non-availability on the part of the casual or the facility for them to refuse to work at a particular time will generally indicate that the working arrangements between employer and casual do not constitute a contract of employment. In most cases therefore, casuals are regarded as independent contractors rather than employees.

The topic of employment status is dealt with fully in **CHAPTER 1**.

The Statutory Rights of Casual Workers [7.3]

Even if a casual worker is engaged full-time for a temporary period, thus creating a higher likelihood that employee status can be asserted, their engagements are often for very short periods, for example a few days or a week or two, thus not allowing them to accrue the length of service necessary to qualify for many statutory employment protection rights (see **CHAPTER 6** at **6.5** for a table of statutory rights that are dependent on a minimum period of length of service). This will be the case unless the casual can argue that there is an overriding 'umbrella' contract that continues in force during periods when they are not working (see **7.5** below).

It is worth noting at this point that all workers, including casuals, are entitled to protection under the UK's discrimination legislation (i.e. the sex, race and disability discrimination laws) irrespective of employment status or length of service. They also have rights under the *Working Time Regulations 1998 (SI 1998 No 1833)* (see **7.18** below) and the right to receive the minimum wage (currently £4.10 per hour for adults, set to rise to £4.20 per hour in October 2002).

Typically, casual workers are paid only for the hours they work, and do not receive any fringe benefits other than those required by statute, notably statutory paid holiday entitlement under the *Working Time Regulations 1998* (see **7.18** below).

Mutuality of Obligation [7.4]

Because of the nature of casual employment, the relationship between employer and worker will not usually contain any mutuality of obligation. This in turn will have the effect that the employment status of a casual worker will not usually be that of employee, i.e. the arrangements under which they are engaged will not constitute a contract of employment. Instead they will be regarded as an independent worker engaged under a contract for services. Courts and tribunals have held reasonably consistently over the last few years that a reasonable degree of mutuality of obligation between the parties is a key factor in determining whether the individual is an employee. In other words, unless there is an obligation on the employer to provide work and a corresponding obligation on the individual to perform the work, a contract of employment cannot be said to exist.

Two of the major cases dealing with this issue were *O'Kelly and others v Trusthouse Forte plc [1983] IRLR 369* and *Clark v Oxfordshire Health Authority EAT 1054/95*. In the *O'Kelly* case, the Court of Appeal upheld an employment tribunal's decision that a casual wine waiter who could be called upon to work as and when he was required was not an employee of the hotel where he worked even though he was regarded as a regular member of staff and given preference over other casual staff. The decision was based on the absence of any obligation on the employer to provide work and a similar absence on the part of the wine waiter to accept work when it was offered.

In the *Clark* case, the Court of Appeal similarly held that a bank nurse retained on the books of a nursing agency whose engagement was on a day-to-day basis with no guarantee of work being made available was not an employee. The Court stated that a contract of employment could not exist in the absence of a mutuality of obligation subsisting throughout periods during which the nurse was not engaged.

The implications of this for the casual worker are that they will be unable to claim a wide range of statutory employment protection rights that are available only to employees. Three of the most important of these are the right to claim unfair dismissal, the right to redundancy pay in the event of a dismissal being on account of redundancy, and the right to take maternity leave and resume working afterwards.

Factors that are relevant in assessing whether a reasonable degree of mutuality of obligation exists between the parties are:

- Whether the individual is free to provide a substitute as opposed to performing the work personally.

- Whether the individual has on occasion refused work when it was offered.

- The overall length of time the individual has worked for the employer and the length of individual periods of engagement.

- Whether the individual has worked for other employers during that time.

- The existence of a notice period in the contract.

- Whether the working hours and patterns are set and regular.

Because casual staff often work on an irregular, variable and often unpredictable ad hoc basis, mutuality of obligation is usually difficult to establish.

215

Umbrella Contracts [7.5]

In order for a casual worker to be able to argue that they are an employee of the organisation for whom they work (and in order to assert continuity of employment), they would have to demonstrate that there was an overriding 'umbrella' or 'global' employment contract that spanned the periods during which they were not working. Courts and tribunals have to date been fairly consistent in their unwillingness to find that a global contract of employment exists between periods of casual engagement.

Nevertheless it may be possible for an individual to argue that a global contract of employment exists if either there is evidence to suggest that the parties have expressly agreed that the individual's work will be on a regular, defined pattern or if a continuing mutuality of obligation can be implied from the circumstances of the case. This could occur if the situation is one in which:

- the working relationship is a long-standing one; *and*
- the working hours and patterns of the casual worker are set and regular; *and*
- the employer relies on the casual worker to work at set times; *and*
- the worker expects to attend work at those set times.

In these circumstances, the status of 'employee' could be argued, thus potentially entitling the person to a wide range of statutory employment rights and benefits.

Often a working arrangement that begins as irregular, non-committal and casual develops through time into one in which the individual works a regular pattern, with the employer relying on the worker to be available at set times of the week and the individual expecting the work to continue on the regular pattern. In these circumstances, it can sometimes be argued that mutuality of obligation has been created as a result of the conduct of the parties and the employee can thus contend that a contract of employment exists. In the case of *Nethermere (St Neots) Ltd v Gardiner & anor [1984] IRLR 240*, the Court of Appeal took the view that expectations that are fulfilled over a period of time may harden into obligations.

The fact that a casual worker's working pattern is set and regular will not, however, on its own be sufficient to establish that there is an overriding contract of employment unless there is also some concrete evidence that some mutuality of obligation exists in an overall sense, i.e. that the obligations between the parties subsist during the periods when the casual is not actually working. This will be the case even in situations where it can be shown that each separate short-term engagement constitutes a contract of employment.

The determination of this issue usually requires an examination of the working periods themselves, their length and regularity (or absence of such), the length of the gaps between them and whether there is any understanding between the parties (express or implied) that the casual worker will resume working after a period during which no work was done, or will always be available on a fixed pattern or arrangement. In practice each case would be examined on its own merits.

Even where it can be argued as a result of other factors inherent in the working relationship that a casual worker is an employee of the organisation when they are actually working, the existence of an umbrella contract can be hard to establish. In the absence of an umbrella contract, the casual employee's working arrangements would in effect be regarded as a series of short-term contracts of employment.

Cases that Address the Employment Status of Casual Workers **[7.6]**

Two cases that addressed the employment status of casual workers were *Carmichael & anor v National Power plc [2000] IRLR 43* and *Scarah & ors v Fish Container Services Ltd, unreported 08.11.94*:

Carmichael & anor v National Power plc [2000] IRLR 43

Facts

The employer wished to engage tour guides to conduct tours around their power stations. Ms Carmichael and a colleague were engaged, with the engagement described as being 'employment on a casual, as required' basis with wages payable (net of tax through the employer's payroll) only for hours worked. There was no indication in writing as to when or with what frequency tour guide work would be available. The documentation did not contain any notice provisions in relation to termination, and the casuals were not entitled to the sickness, holiday or pension benefits that applied to the company's regular employees. Equally, the employer's disciplinary and grievance procedures did not apply to them. Ms Carmichael and her colleague were, however, trained by the employer and required to meet the employer's standards as regards the quality of the tours they conducted. They were also required to wear a uniform.

In practice the two women worked on most occasions when they were asked to do so, but there were instances when they declined to work. For example there was evidence when the matter went to court at a later date that during 1994 Ms Carmichael was unavailable for work on seventeen occasions and her colleague on eight.

When a dispute arose as to whether the casuals were entitled to a written statement of particulars of employment, the employer argued that they were not employees working under a contract of employment and therefore not entitled to receive such a statement. As a preliminary matter, therefore, the employment status of the two individuals had to be determined.

Findings

This case went all the way to the House of Lords who held that no contract of employment existed because there was no mutuality of obligation between the parties. This decision was based on evidence that the company was not obliged to provide any work for the tour guides if no tours were booked, and even when tours were booked, there was no obligation on them to use the services of any particular tour guide. Similarly, the individuals were not obliged to accept offers of work when they were made and there was evidence that they did in practice decline offers of work from time to time without any negative repercussions. The absence of mutuality of obligation was a crucial factor as, without a minimum obligation on each side, there could be no employment contract.

In the case of *Scarah & ors v Fish Container Services Ltd, unreported 08.11.94*, the claimants worked unloading crates of fish as and when they were needed. Work was allocated from day to day depending on how much work was available. The company prepared a recorded telephone message each day stating which workers were required that day, and individuals could telephone the recorded message to find out if they were needed. When the work ceased altogether, they claimed constructive dismissal which in turn required them to establish that their engagement with the employer had been a contract of employment.

The Court of Appeal rejected the contention that there was a global contract of employment because there was an insufficient degree of mutual obligation between the parties. This finding was largely due to the evidence that, even if the company had nominated a particular worker to work on a particular day, the worker was under no obligation to turn up to work.

Checklist [7.7]

Despite the difficulties casual workers often have in establishing employee status, employers should be wary of assuming that their casual workers are not employees. It is advisable for an employer who regularly engages casual workers and who wishes to avoid classing them as employees, to:

- Devise a clearly worded written agreement for each casual worker hired to indicate that there is no mutuality of obligation between the parties (see **7.8** below for an example).

- Keep detailed records of who is engaged and the dates of their engagements.

- Keep a record of occasions when work is offered but refused by the casual worker.

A full discussion of the subject of employment status is provided in **CHAPTER 1**.

Model Clause for Casual Engagement [7.8]

The following text could be used to indicate that a casual worker is not an employee on account of an absence of mutual obligations between the parties:

'You are engaged by this Company as a casual (*job title*) to work on an ad-hoc, as-required basis. The nature of the work is part-time and intermittent (and of no fixed pattern). (*Alternative clause*) You will normally be expected to work on (*days of the week*) from (*start and finish times*) for a period of (*number of weeks*) weeks, but these times may vary from week to week in line with the requirements of the business and there may be weeks when you are not required).

There is no obligation on the Company to offer you any minimum amount of work in any given week or month, and no obligation on you to accept work when it is offered. You are not an employee of this Company.'

Model Contract for Casual Engagement of a Professional on an Ad-hoc Basis [7.9]

The following model contract would be suitable where an employer wishes to engage a professional individual to work on a variable, as-required basis without creating any mutuality of obligation.

'Contract for the provision of services

between

(*Name of company*), having a place of business at (*address*), (hereafter referred to as 'the Company').

and

(*Name of worker*) (hereafter referred to as 'the Worker')

The Contract

These terms constitute a contract for services between the Company and the Worker.

These terms will not give rise to a contract of employment between the Company and the Worker. There is no mutuality of obligation whatsoever between the Company and the Worker. The Company is not obliged to offer the Worker ongoing work, nor is the Worker obliged to accept any offer of work made by the Company.

No variation or alteration to these terms will be valid unless agreed by both the Company and the Worker in writing.

Start Date

This contract will commence on (*date*) and will last for a period of one year.

Duties

The Company engages the Worker to provide (*type of work or service*) as agreed and the Worker will provide such services as required and directed by the Company.

Rate of Pay

The Worker will be paid a fee of (£ – *per hour or per day*). This will be paid monthly in arrears by cheque/BACS (*after deduction of income tax and national insurance*).

Expenses

The Company will reimburse the Worker for all reasonable expenses wholly and exclusively incurred in the performance of duties, provided that the Worker furnishes the Company with a properly completed expense claim form, together with receipts or other evidence of expenses.

Place of Engagement

The Company is based at (*address*). The Worker will, as and when requested by the Company, deliver services at the Company's base or in such other places as may be reasonably required by the Company.

Hours of Work

The Worker will, as and when requested by the Company, deliver services on such dates as may be reasonably required by the Company. There is no fixed pattern of work and no normal hours of work, and the amount of work offered to the Worker will be variable. The Company is not obliged to offer the Worker any minimum amount of work.

Holiday Entitlement

The Company's holiday year runs from 1 January to 31 December. In accordance with the *Working Time Regulations 1998 (SI 1998 No 1833)*, the Worker is entitled to 1.67 days paid leave per calendar month (the monthly equivalent to four weeks paid holiday per calendar year). This entitlement is inclusive of public holidays.

Holidays must be taken in the year in which they are earned, i.e. not carried over to another holiday year.

All holiday dates must be agreed in advance with the Company. The Company reserves the right to nominate specific dates on which the Worker will take annual leave entitlement. In these circumstances the Company will give the Worker notice of not less than two weeks. (*Optional clause:* Holidays must be taken in blocks of not less than one calendar week).

221

Pay in lieu of holidays not taken will not be made except (where appropriate) on termination of this contract. Payment in lieu of holidays accrued but not taken as at the date of termination will be calculated on a pro-rata basis and paid along with the Worker's final fee payment.

The Company reserves the right, upon the termination of this contract for any reason, to deduct from the Worker's final fee payment an amount equivalent to any periods of holiday entitlement which the Worker has taken before the date of the termination of the contract, but not accrued.

Illness

If the Worker is unable to come to work on account of sickness or injury (or for any other reason), he/she must inform (*named person*) of the reason for the absence as soon as possible.

In the event that the Worker is unable to attend work due to sickness or injury, the Company will not be liable to pay either SSP or any fee payment.

Right to carry out other Work

Throughout the course of this contract, the Worker has the right to advertise for, seek and undertake contracts to supply services to other parties.

Confidentiality

The Worker will not at any time during the course of this contract (except insofar as is necessary and proper in the course of the work) or at any time after the termination of the contract, use or disclose to any person any confidential information that is in any way related to the Company's business dealings or clients.

Documentation

All records, documents, drawings and other papers (and all copies thereof) including private notes concerning the Company's business and its clients, and all computer disks containing Company information, must be used only for the purpose of the Company's business and will remain the properly of the Company at all times.

In the event of termination of this contract, the Worker will return to the Company all records, documents, drawings and other papers (and copies thereof), and computer disks, concerning the Company's business and its clients.

Qualifications

In the event that the Worker holds him/herself out as certificated or qualified to a particular level, he/she will provide copies of certificates or evidence of such qualification to the Company on request.

Conduct

It is a condition of this contract that the Worker will not engage in any conduct that is or might be detrimental to the interests of the Company. The Worker will ensure that his/her services are carried out with reasonable care and skill to a standard reasonably required by the Company, and in compliance with the Company's policies, procedures and practices. (*Optional clause:* Due to the specialist nature of the services that the Company provides, the Company will be solely responsible for the procedures under which the work is performed).

Indemnity and Insurance

It is a condition of the contract that the Worker takes out and maintains in force professional indemnity insurance in terms satisfactory to the Company, and that the Worker exhibits the policy to the Company if requested.

Health and Safety

The Worker must comply with the Company's safety policies and practices at all times. The Worker is responsible for taking care of him/herself and other persons who may be affected by his/her acts or omissions.

Data Protection

In relation to the *Data Protection Act 1998*, the Worker agrees to the processing of personal data by the Company for the purposes of calculating fee payments due and maintaining any records that are necessary for the performance of the Contract.

Notice Provisions

The Contract may be terminated by either the Company or the Worker by giving the other party not less than one month's notice in writing.

In the event of serious misconduct, negligence, any failure to meet the Company's standards, or any material breach of contract on the part of the Worker, the Company may terminate the contract immediately without notice, payment in lieu of notice or any other compensation.

Acceptance

I have read and understood this contract for services and agree to accept its terms of engagement.

Signed (Worker's signature)   Date:

Signed on behalf of the Company   Date:

Zero-Hours Contracts – The 'Regular Casual'   [7.10]

A zero-hours contract, sometimes known as a nil-hours contract, is a contract under which a casual worker undertakes to work for an employer on a regular basis without any minimum amount of work being guaranteed. The underlying purpose of a zero-hours contract is to formalise and manage the engagement of regular casuals more effectively. Pay is made only for actual hours worked.

The main difference between this type of contract and a casual contract is that the individual will usually be viewed as an employee of the organisation for whom they work, rather than an independent contractor. This is because the contract is viewed as continuing in force throughout the year even when there is no work available. Thus an overriding or umbrella contract exists during periods when the individual is not working (see also **7.5** above).

Zero-hours contracts can be designed in different ways:

- a contract under which the individual is under an obligation to work whenever the employer demands it (subject to certain times of the year when, for example, the individual may be on holiday); *or*

- a contract under which the individual is obliged to come into work subject to a minimum notice period being given, but otherwise not obliged to work; *or*

- an arrangement under which the individual is free within reason to accept or reject any offer of work (although if this was the arrangement, it would be unlikely that the individual could assert

224

that they were an employee of the organisation due to the lack of mutuality of obligation – see **7.2** above).

A zero-hours contract in its pure form is a very one-sided arrangement in which the employer can elect whether to offer the employee work depending on their requirements whilst at the same time they can demand that the employee to should make themselves available within reason whenever called upon.

The Implications of Zero-Hours Contracts [7.11]

The implications of engaging regular casual workers on zero-hours contracts are therefore that:

● The contract will be a contract of employment and not a contract for services (see **7.2** above).

● The individual will accrue continuity of service whether or not they are actually at work and they will thus gain statutory employment rights.

Some of the benefits to the employer are that:

● A zero-hours contract will give the employer flexibility as to the number of staff they engage during any particular period, as there will be an available pool of workers on whom they can call.

● Where workers are engaged on a zero-hours contract as opposed to engagement on a purely ad-hoc basis, it will be more likely that they will be available to come to work when required.

● If some benefits are offered to workers engaged on zero-hours contracts, this may help the employer to attract and retain a committed pool of workers who are more likely to treat the needs of the employer as a priority.

● Formalising arrangements with casual staff will give the employer a more accurate picture of their worker headcount.

Continuity of Employment [7.12]

As stated, because a zero-hours contract is set up to continue throughout the year irrespective of whether the employee is at work and irrespective of the number of hours worked, the employment relationship will continue during periods in which no work is done. Furthermore, the periods during which the zero-hours contract subsists but no work is being done are likely to be viewed by tribunals as periods of continuous employment. This is because periods when an employee is not working will be deemed to be absences on account of a 'temporary cessation of work' under the *Employment Rights Act 1996, s 212(3)(b)*. Essentially, a temporary cessation of work occurs where an employee's contract is suspended as a result of no work being available, and the employee is re-employed at a later date (see **CHAPTER 6** at **6.13** for a full explanation of the law governing temporary cessations of work).

Model Clauses for a Zero-Hours Contract   [7.13]

The following represents a selection of clauses which employers may wish to adopt for workers engaged on zero-hours contracts:

'The Company does not guarantee to provide you any minimum amount of work in any given week or month of the year. You will be paid only when work is performed at a fixed hourly rate of £ ...'

'The employer will offer you work as and when it is available but cannot guarantee that any minimum amount of work will be offered.'

'The Company reserves the right to terminate your zero-hours contract if, on two or more consecutive occasions, you are unavailable to come to work as requested.'

'It is a condition of this contract that you are available to work upon being given at least 24 hours notice. This will be the case except when a period of leave, for example holiday leave, has been agreed in advance.'

'In the event that you are asked to work and given less than 24 hours notice, you are free to accept or reject the Company's offer of work.'

'You are engaged on a zero-hours contract which means that no specific minimum number of hours, nor pay, is guaranteed in any given period.'

Employing Seasonal Workers   [7.14]

Seasonal workers may be engaged to cover a particularly busy time of the year, or to work on a particular type of work that is known to be short-term. Examples include shop assistants engaged to work during the weeks running up to Christmas, hotel workers engaged in a hotel that is open only for the summer season and workers engaged to harvest potatoes or strawberries (for example) at the time of year the harvest is ready.

Seasonal workers may be engaged on a contract of employment, or may be regarded as self-employed contractors. The nature of the employment relationship will depend on a range of factors described fully in **CHAPTER 1**.

Assuming that the contract is one of employment, rather than a contract for services, it could be one of several types, i.e.:

- A fixed-term contract with specified start and finish dates (see **CHAPTER 4** at **4.6**).

- A temporary contract of no specific fixed duration but with a clear statement that employment is temporary and an indication given as to the approximate length of time that the employer expects to require the person's services.

- A contract for performance, i.e. a contract of employment that is clearly described as one that will expire automatically when the work (for example the harvesting of the potatoes) has been completed (see **CHAPTER 4** at **4.24**).

The Implications of Regular Seasonal Work [7.15]

Where an individual is engaged on a regular basis for seasonal work over a period of several years, it can be argued that the arrangement includes an exchange of mutual promises for future performance. This in turn can give rise to the assertion that there is an umbrella or global employment contract spanning the whole year and that the person's employment is continuous despite the fact that they do not work throughout the whole year.

The question of whether a global contract can be said to exist in such circumstances depends largely on an analysis of all the features of the working arrangements, but in particular the length of the periods of employment in comparison to the length of the periods of non-employment. Where, over a period of time there has been a regular pattern of work, a court or tribunal is more likely to hold that there is an overriding contract of employment. Even if an employee takes up other employment during the off-season, this will not prevent their employment with the first employer from continuing (a principle established in the case of *Thompson v British Channel Ship Repairers and Engineers Ltd [1970] ITR 85*).

For example in the case of a seasonal worker engaged by a hotel to work from March to October each year, the period during which the person is not working is relatively short when compared to the period of employment. By contrast, someone engaged to pick strawberries would be likely to work for only a few weeks of the year and it could not logically be argued that there was any global contract that subsisted during the remainder of the year.

In the case of *Tongue Hotel Co Ltd v Mackay [1983] EAT 416/83*, the EAT held that a waitress who had regularly worked throughout the summer season in a hotel in the north of Scotland retained continuity of employment during the period the hotel was semi-closed for the winter. There was sufficient evidence for the tribunal to conclude that, despite the termination of the employee's contract at the end of the summer season, both parties had understood and expected that the contract would be revived when the hotel opened again for business in the spring. Thus there was an implied mutual promise of future performance and the employee's employment was continuous.

In another case, *Town & Country Prints v Hoare EAT 1408/96*, the employee worked in a shop that closed down during the winter season. When a dispute arose, an employment tribunal addressed the question of whether, despite the fact that the employee had no contract during the closed season, an express or implied arrangement existed between the parties that she would remain on the employer's books throughout the closed season, thus affording her continuity of employment under the *Employment Rights Act 1996, s 212(3)(c)*. The EAT upheld the tribunal's ruling that the employee's continuity of employment was preserved.

Model Clause for a Contract with a Seasonal Worker for Temporary Work [7.16]

The following is a model clause that could be used by an employer who wished to engage someone on a seasonal basis:

'Your employment with the Company is temporary and will last only as long as work is available (*or as long as the business is open for the season, or until a specified date*). It is expected that this will be approximately (*number of weeks or months*). Your employment will therefore be terminated when the season comes to a close. The Company may, at its discretion elect to offer you further employment next season but this cannot be guaranteed.

During the period of this temporary contract, your employment may be terminated at any time for any reason by either party, by giving (*one week's notice/two week's notice*) in writing.'

Employing Students [7.17]

Many students these days need to work throughout the academic year in order to have enough money to fund their studies. Often they will seek part-time employment for most of the year (typically evening or night work) and perhaps full-time employment during the periods of the university or college vacations.

Like seasonal workers, students may be engaged on a contract of employment, or may be regarded as self-employed contractors. The nature of the employment relationship will depend on a range of factors described fully in **CHAPTER 1**. The legal and practical implications of part-time employment are covered in **CHAPTER 3**.

Where the engagement of a student constitutes a contract of employment, the student will accrue continuity of service irrespective of whether they work full or part-time. This will be the case unless there is a gap between two periods of employment (during which the contract of employment is no longer in force) of more than one calendar week. Even in these circumstances, however, continuity of employment can be asserted in certain circumstances if the gap between two periods of employment is due to a temporary cessation of work, or following an arrangement made in advance that the student would be absent from work for a temporary period. These provisions, detailed in the *Employment Rights Act 1996, s 212*, are explained fully in **CHAPTER 6** at **6.13**.

Where a student is employed directly by the employer, they will be entitled to the same statutory benefits as any other employee, subject to the need to have a defined minimum period of continuous service to qualify for certain statutory employment protection rights (see **CHAPTER 6** at **6.5** for a full list).

Working out Annual Holiday Entitlements [7.18]

Under the *Working Time Regulations 1998 (SI 1998 No 1833)*, all workers are entitled to four weeks' paid annual holiday in any complete holiday year. Short-term temporary workers are entitled to a pro-rata portion of the four-week statutory holiday entitlement. There is no minimum length of service requirement to qualify for paid leave and holidays thus start to accrue from the first day of employment. Furthermore, entitlement to paid holidays is available not only to employees, but to other workers including casuals, students and seasonal workers.

During the first year of employment, workers are entitled to take holidays (subject to the agreement of the employer in respect of the dates of any holidays) on the basis of accrual at the rate of one twelfth of the annual entitlement for each month of employment. For this purpose, holidays must be allowed to accrue in advance, i.e. leave accrues on the first day of each month. This means that entitlement to paid leave builds up monthly.

Further provisions in the *Working Time Regulations, Reg 13(9)* stipulate that:

- Holidays must be taken during the holiday year in respect of which they are due, i.e. not carried forward to a new holiday year.

- Employers are not permitted to 'buy out' a worker's holiday entitlement by making a payment in lieu except if a worker's employment is terminated during the course of a holiday year with outstanding holidays due.

- When a temporary worker's period of engagement comes to an end, the employer must make a payment in lieu of any holidays that have been accrued but not taken irrespective of how long the period of employment has lasted.

- When the calculation of holiday pay due to a worker who is leaving results in a figure that includes a fraction of a day, this must be rounded up to the next whole number.

The *Employment Rights Act 1996, s 224* stipulates that where a worker has no normal working hours, the amount of a week's pay (which must be used to calculate the amount of pay due when a worker is on holiday) is the amount of the employee's average weekly remuneration in the period of the previous twelve weeks. Any weeks during which the worker did no work, and therefore received no pay, must be discounted and an earlier week brought into the calculation instead. This provision would be relevant when calculating the amount of holiday pay due to a casual worker.

Employers are permitted under the *Working Time Regulations 1998 (SI 1998 No 1833), Reg 15* to have some input to the timing of an employee's annual holidays. The employer is entitled to refuse to grant holidays on specified dates, or conversely, to require the worker to take all or part of their annual holiday entitlement on particular days, provided proper notice is given as defined in the Regulations.

This means that, in respect of employees engaged on short-term contracts, the employer can elect to require the employee to work for the duration of the contract without taking holiday and then pay for the leave when the contract terminates, provided the employee leaves at that point and does not immediately start work with the same employer on another contract.

Further information about statutory annual leave for temporary workers, together with a model policy on holiday entitlement for short-term temporary workers, is available in **CHAPTER 4**.

Examples of holiday entitlements on termination [7.19]

Statutory entitlement to paid annual leave is four weeks per complete holiday year. Thus casual workers, seasonal workers and students who work for only a few weeks at a time will accrue a pro-rata portion of that holiday entitlement which must then be paid to the worker when their engagement ends (unless they have taken paid holiday during the period of their engagement). Some examples are as follows:

1. A seasonal worker in a hotel or shop starts work on 1 April and works through until 30 September, a period of 26 weeks exactly. The worker takes one week's paid leaving in July by agreement. Holiday entitlement on leaving will be one week.

2. Another seasonal worker begins work on 20 May and works through to 31 August without taking any holidays. This is a period of fifteen continuous weeks. The resulting pro-rata holiday entitlement is 5.77 days (twenty days divided by 52 and multiplied by fifteen), which must be rounded up to the next whole day. Thus the worker would be entitled to be paid an extra six days when they leave.

3. A student works three evenings a week in a hotel throughout the whole year. The employer would be obliged to allow the student to take four weeks' paid holiday during the year (on dates to be agreed). Whilst on holiday, the student would be entitled to receive their normal weekly rate of pay. It would not be permissible to buy out the holiday entitlement.

4. A casual worker is engaged to work over a period of sixteen weeks on an irregular basis, working different numbers of hours each week. When the casual worker's engagement terminates, the amount of holiday due would be 6.15 days (i.e. twenty days divided by 52 and multiplied by sixteen), which in turn must be rounded up to seven days. The seven days pay would be paid at a rate calculated by taking a weekly average of the worker's actual pay over the last twelve weeks of the engagement.

5. A student works for three complete weeks picking potatoes in the autumn. On leaving, the student's holiday entitlement will be 1.15

days (twenty days divided by 52 and multiplied by three), which must be rounded up to two days. Two days pay at the student's normal daily rate must then be paid on termination. If pay has been variable on a day-to-day basis, an average of actual pay must be calculated taking into account the three weeks worked.

Conclusion [7.20]

This chapter has explored the employment status and rights of casual workers, seasonal workers and students. Casual workers often have difficulty establishing that they are employees of the organisation for whom they provide their services due to a lack of mutuality of obligation in the working relationship. Even if employment status can be asserted in respect of a particular engagement, there is the further barrier that casual and seasonal workers may not gain sufficient continuity of employment to qualify for certain key statutory employment protection rights. This will be the case unless the employee can show that there is an 'umbrella contract' spanning periods during which they are not working.

Nevertheless, certain rights do accrue irrespective of employment status or length of service, notably the right to paid annual holidays under the *Working Time Regulations*, the right to the national minimum wage and the right not to suffer unlawful sex, race or disability discrimination.

Questions and Answers [7.21]

Question

What does 'casual work' mean?

Answer

A casual worker is someone who is engaged to work for an employer either on a one-off basis for a short period of time or on an ad-hoc, as required basis, usually with no regular pattern of days or hours. In most cases, the employer will not guarantee the casual worker any minimum amount of work within a given period of time (nor any minimum amount of pay), and the casual worker will be free to either accept work when it is offered, or reject it if they are unable or unwilling to work at the particular time offered.

Question

What are the statutory employment rights of casual workers?

Answer

A casual worker's rights will depend on two factors, firstly whether they are employed directly by the employer for whom they provide their services, and secondly their length of continuous service. Usually, casual workers are not deemed to be employees of the organisation for whom they provide their services but even if employee status can be asserted, the engagements of casual workers are typically for very short periods, thus not allowing them to accrue the length of service necessary to qualify for many statutory employment protection rights.

Question

Are casual workers usually regarded as employees in law?

Answer

Courts and tribunals have held reasonably consistently over the last few years that a reasonable degree of mutuality of obligation between the parties is a key factor in determining whether a casual worker is an employee. Because of the nature of casual employment, the relationship between employer and worker will not usually contain any mutuality of obligation. This in turn will mean that the employment status of a casual worker will not usually be that of employee. Instead they will be regarded as an independent worker engaged under a contract for services.

Question

If a casual worker is an employee in law (and not an independent contractor), do they nevertheless lose out on statutory rights if there are frequent gaps between contracts?

Answer

Even where it can be argued that a casual worker is an employee of the organisation when they are actually working, the existence of an 'umbrella contract' that spans the periods during which they are not working can be hard to establish. In the absence of such an umbrella contract, the casual employee's working arrangements would in effect be regarded as a series of short-term contracts of employment. Since some (but by no means all) statutory rights are dependent on the employee having a defined minimum period of continuous service, the casual could in effect lose out on certain rights.

Question

What is a zero-hours contract?

Answer

A zero-hours contract is a contract under which a casual worker undertakes to work for an employer on a regular basis without any minimum amount of work or pay being guaranteed. The main difference between this type of contract and a casual contract is that the individual will usually be viewed as an employee of the organisation for whom they work, rather than an independent contractor. This is because the contract is viewed as continuing in force throughout the year even when there is no work available.

Question

Where an employer engages the same seasonal workers every year, is there any possibility that these employees could gain continuity of employment despite the fact that they are not employed throughout the whole year?

Answer

Where an individual is engaged on a regular basis for seasonal work over a period of several years, it can sometimes be argued that the arrangement includes an exchange of mutual promises for future performance. This in turn can give rise to the assertion that there is an umbrella or global employment contract spanning the whole year and that the person's employment is continuous despite the fact that they do not work throughout the whole year. The question of whether a global contract can be said to exist in such circumstances depends largely on an analysis of all the features of the working arrangements, but in particular the length of the periods of employment in comparison to the length of the periods of non-employment.

Question

If an employer employs students who work part-time during term times and full-time during the periods of the college or university vacation, what effect do these arrangements have on the student's continuity of employment?

Answer

Where the engagement of a student constitutes a contract of employment, the student will accrue continuity of service irrespective of whether they work full or part-time. This will be the case unless there is a gap between two periods of employment (during which the contract of employment is no longer in force) of more than one calendar week. Even in these circumstances, however, continuity of employment can be asserted in certain circumstances if the gap between two periods of employment is due to a temporary cessation of work, or following an arrangement made in advance that the student would be absent from work for a temporary period.

Question

Where a casual worker has worked for only a few weeks, must the employer pay holiday pay on termination of the worker's engagement?

Answer

Yes, all workers are entitled to paid holidays under the *Working Time Regulations 1998* irrespective of length of service. Thus when a temporary worker's period of employment comes to an end, the employer must make a payment in lieu of any holidays that have been accrued but not taken, irrespective of how long the period of employment has lasted. The amount of leave is pro-rated according to the portion of the holiday year that the casual has worked, then rounded up to the next whole day.

8. Self Employed Workers and Contractors

Introduction [8.1]

In respect of employment protection legislation, there are three 'categories' of people, each of whom are treated differently by the law:

1. Employees engaged directly on a contract of employment.

2. Workers engaged on a contract for services.

3. Self-employed people who are in business on their own account and provide their services to their clients or customers.

The term 'worker' is generally used to describe someone who provides their services personally to an organisation, but is not regarded as an employee of that organisation. A wide range of people (for example contract staff, casual workers and some freelance or self-employed people) can be classed as workers, provided the other party to the contract is not their client or customer. Such workers have fewer statutory employment rights than employees engaged under a contract of employment. Nevertheless, the trend in recent years has been for new legislation to cover all workers, whether employed directly or engaged indirectly.

The third category, that of self-employed entrepreneur/contractor is outside the scope of the definitions of 'employee' and 'worker'. A self-employed person typically performs short-term contract work rather than being engaged over a long period. The person is in business on their own account and the organisation for whom they provide their services is their client or customer, rather than their employer. In many cases they do not receive a salary, but instead submit invoices for payment on the completion of agreed work.

Despite the above general distinctions, some self-employed people can be classed as 'workers' for the purpose of certain employment protection legislation provided the working relationship in question points towards that conclusion. By contrast, the genuinely self-employed entrepreneur will not be viewed as a 'worker' and will therefore not, as a rule, be entitled to any employment protection rights.

One case that addressed this point was *Byrne Brothers (Formwork) Ltd v Baird IRLR 683*, in which the EAT held that four carpenters who worked on assignments for a building contractor – purportedly on a self-employed basis – were 'workers' for the purpose of the right to four weeks' statutory holiday entitlement under the Working Time Regulations. This was because they provided their carpentry services personally and did not run their own individual businesses, as the company contended.

There is one exception to the general principle that self-employed people in business on their own account are not covered by employment protection legislation. All four anti-discrimination laws (the *Sex Discrimination Act 1975*, the *Equal Pay Act 1970*, the *Race Relations Act 1976* and the *Disability Discrimination Act 1995*) avoid the distinction between 'employee' and 'worker' and instead refer to 'employment'. 'Employment' is defined as employment 'under a contract of service or of apprenticeship or a contract personally to execute any work or labour'. This definition is to be found in *section 82(1)* of the *Sex Discrimination Act 1975, section 1(6)* of the *Equal Pay Act 1970* and *section 78(1)* of the *Race Relations Act 1976*. Very similar wording appears in *section 68(1)* of the *Disability Discrimination Act 1995*. Thus individuals who provide their services personally for a client or customer are protected against sex, race and disability discrimination, even though they cannot enjoy other employment protection rights.

A full discussion of employment status and the distinction between employees and workers is contained in **CHAPTER 1**, whilst this chapter concentrates on self-employed people and contractors.

Types of Self-Employment [8.2]

Independent contractors may be people working on any of the following arrangements:

- Individuals who work freelance providing their personal services to one or more organisations, for example self-employed IT specialists or training providers.

- An individual who has set up their own limited company and who works through that company for one or more organisations.

- An individual in either of the above two categories who provides their services through an employment agency (see **CHAPTER 5** for information about temporary staff hired through employment agencies).

- An individual who works for several employers on a casual as required basis (see **CHAPTER 7**).

- An individual who is employed by or contracted to an employer that has a contract to perform work for another employer and who is assigned to work for the second employer for the duration of the particular contract. An example might be a labourer engaged by a sub-contracting firm that is providing labour to the main contractor on a building project.

Clarifying the Individual's Employment Status [8.3]

Even though an employer and an individual contractor agree between themselves that the individual is self-employed, that on its own is not determinative of the person's employment status. In the event of a legal challenge at a later date, an employment tribunal or court will not regard the label the parties have put on the contract as conclusive proof of the individual's employment status, but will instead examine the actual working relationship between the organisation and the individual with a view to judging whether, in reality, it was akin to an employment contract or a contract for services. However, the existence or otherwise of a direct contract between a self-employed individual and the organisation for whom they provide their services will be a crucial factor (see the *Hewlett Packard* case in **8.10** below). Full details of the subject of employment status are provided in **CHAPTER 1**.

Freelance, Self-employed Workers [8.4]

Where an employer elects to engage a freelance, self-employed worker, there are a number of potential implications. Certain implied terms that form part of every employment contract will not be applicable to a contract with a self-employed person, in particular the duty of fidelity and the duty to cooperate.

It is important for employers who engage self-employed contractors or consultants to ensure that the contractual arrangements address the following issues:

- The nature of the task or project to be performed.

- How long the task or project will last and any notice clauses.

- Any quality standards and how they will be judged or measured.

- Working hours, for example whether they are fixed, variable or at the self-employed person's discretion.

239

- Whether tools, equipment and materials will be provided by the freelance worker or by the employer.

- Details of any restrictions to be imposed on the self-employed person regarding their freedom to work for other, perhaps competing, organisations during the course of the contract.

- What company rules and policies will apply to the person, for example health and safety rules, smoking policy, e-mail and internet restrictions, etc.

- Provisions regarding confidentiality, especially if the freelance worker will have access to confidential or sensitive information in the course of their work.

- The provisions that will apply if the person acts in breach of contract.

- Whether the self-employed worker should be required to provide their own professional indemnity insurance.

- Details of how the person should invoice the employer and whether they should do so on a staged basis or once only at the end of the task or project.

Some model contractual clauses are provided in **8.7** below.

Consultants [8.5]

Consultants, i.e. those who specialise in a particular subject and hire out their services to one or more organisations in an advisory or problem-solving capacity (usually on a short-term or ad-hoc basis), are generally regarded as self-employed, independent contractors. Nevertheless it is advisable for employers who hire in consultants to ensure that the contractual relationship is clearly defined in writing, making it clear that the contract is not an employment contract.

Case Law Challenging the Status of Self-employed People [8.6]

The following represents a selection of tribunal decisions in relation to self-employed workers' employment status:

Filcom Ltd v Ross EAT 472/93

In *Filcom Ltd v Ross EAT 472/93*, Mr Ross was one of a group of contract staff working for Filcom Ltd in the telecommunications field,

240

providing his services to the company's clients. Filcom Ltd regarded Mr Ross as a self-employed individual in business on his own account because he held a certificate issued by the Inland Revenue entitling him to be treated as self-employed for income tax and national insurance purposes.

When a dispute arose over pay, the company argued that, because Mr Ross was self-employed, he was not entitled to be regarded as a 'worker' for the purposes of the protection of wages legislation. The EAT, however, held that because the company could not be regarded as Mr Ross' client or customer, he was not in business on his own account. Instead, Mr Ross provided his services personally to Filcom Ltd on a contract for services and he was thus a 'worker' rather than an independent contractor. There were a number of factors that led the tribunal to this conclusion, namely:

- Mr Ross was obliged to accept the rates of pay offered by the company.

- Payment was made weekly in arrears.

- The company provided all the specialised tools and equipment that Mr Ross required to perform his work.

- Mr Ross was, in a general sense, regarded as a member of the company's staff.

- Mr Ross was not free under the contract to provide a substitute for himself if he was unable or unwilling to work on a particular occasion.

- The contract actually referred to the 'provision of services' by Mr Ross.

Lane v Shire Roofing Co (Oxford) Ltd [1995] IRLR 493

In this case, the claimant was a builder/roofer/carpenter who traded as a one-person firm and was categorised as self-employed by the Inland Revenue. He was engaged by Shire Roofing initially to work on a large commercial roofing contract and subsequently to re-roof a porch at a private house. Following an accident at the private house that resulted in serious injuries, Mr Lane brought proceedings to court which required a decision in the first instance as to whether he was an employee, a worker engaged on a contract for services or a self-employed person in business on his own account.

The Court of Appeal held that Mr Lane had in fact been an employee of Shire Roofing Co Ltd and that the company was therefore liable for his injuries. Even though Mr Lane operated his own one–person business and was self–employed for taxation purposes, the working relationship he had with the company was more akin to lump working (see **8.8** below), i.e. he had been employed only for his labour and was not a specialist sub–contractor engaged to perform part of a building contract.

Young & Woods Ltd v West [1980] IRLR 201

When the employer in this case wished to hire sheet-metal workers to work in their factory, they offered Mr West the option of employment as an employee or engagement on self-employed status. Mr West chose the latter on account of the tax advantages in being self-employed, and the employer thus paid his wages without deducting tax at source. The Inland Revenue was fully aware of this arrangement. Nevertheless, Mr West's working conditions were the same as those applicable to the company's ordinary employees.

When his contract was terminated, Mr West brought a claim to tribunal for unfair dismissal and, as a preliminary matter, the tribunal had to determine his true employment status. Ultimately the Court of Appeal upheld the original tribunal's decision that Mr West had been an employee of the company despite the agreement that he would be self-employed. They pointed out that the question of someone's employment status is a question of law and the fact that an agreement has been reached that a particular individual is self-employed is not conclusive. The matter had to be determined taking into account the reality of the working relationship and it was clear that Mr West was not in business on his own account. The fact that the Inland Revenue regarded him as self-employed was a separate matter.

Model Contractual Clauses for use in a Contract with a Self-employed Person [8.7]

Employers who engage self-employed people on short-term projects from time to time may wish to insert some or all of the clauses (as appropriate) into the contract in order to clarify the working relationship:

'The terms of this contract will not give rise to a contract of employment or a contract for services. You are a self-employed individual in business on your account and your engagement with this Company is for the purpose of providing a specific one-off (consultancy) service.'

'The terms of this contract do not create or imply any mutuality of obligation. The Company is not obliged on the completion of this contract to offer you ongoing work or any further work, and you are not obliged to accept any such offer of work made by the Company'.

'The terms of this contract do not bind you to any fixed hours of work provided the agreed work is completed by the agreed deadline date'.

'Whilst engaged on the Company's business, you will ensure that your work is carried out with reasonable care and skill to a standard reasonably required by the Company. However, due to the specialist nature of the work for which you have been engaged, you will be solely responsible for the procedures by which your services are performed'.

It is a condition of this contract that you will not engage in any conduct which is or might be detrimental to the interests of the Company.'

'You will be liable for any loss, damage or injury to any party resulting from any negligent act or omission on your part during the course of this contract. It is a condition of this contract that you take out and maintain in force professional indemnity insurance in terms satisfactory to the Company, and that you exhibit the policy to the Company if requested to do so.'

'In the event that you holds yourself out as certificated or qualified to a particular level, you will provide copies of certificates or evidence of such qualification to the Company on request'.

'In the event that you are unable to personally perform the work for which you are contracted to do, you may provide a substitute for yourself provided the person nominated as a substitute is properly qualified, skilled and experienced in the type of work to be performed'.

'During the course of this contract, you have the right to advertise for, seek and undertake contracts to provide services to other parties. In so doing, however, you must adhere to the Company's terms and conditions regarding confidentiality'.

'You will not at any time during the course of this contract (except insofar as is necessary and proper in the course of the work) or at any time after the termination of the contract, use or disclose to any person any confidential information that is in any way related to the Company's practice, business dealings or clients.'

'Your fees will be paid monthly in arrears on submission of a correctly formatted invoice.'

'Lump Working' [8.8]

Often one firm (a sub-contractor) will be asked by another firm (the main contractor) to provide people to perform work on a contract held by the main contractor, for example where the main contractor on a building site sub-contracts the provision of labour to a sub-contractor. The quaint expression 'lump working' refers to an arrangement whereby workers organise themselves as self-employed suppliers of labour to be hired out on a group contract basis, either directly or through an intermediate sub-contracting employer.

Lump working is prevalent in the construction industry and can take several forms:

1. The workers may be contracted directly by the main employer on a self-employed basis.

2. The workers may be engaged by the sub-contractor on a self-employed basis and sub-contracted to the main employer.

3. The workers may be employed directly by the sub-contractor and sub-contracted to the main employer.

The employment status of such lump workers will depend on the precise nature of the working relationship and the various factors detailed in **CHAPTER 1** at **1.8**.

Individuals Working Through their own Limited Company [8.9]

It is common in certain sectors, particularly in information technology, the offshore oil industry and engineering, to find individuals working through their own limited company (known as a 'personal service company'). Historically such individuals would not usually have been regarded as employees of the client company for whom they provided their services because the contract would be set up as a contract between the client company and the individual's limited company, rather than being a contract between the client company and the individual. However, if the reality of the situation points towards a different conclusion, a tribunal will be entitled to disregard the contractual label that the parties have put on to the relationship.

Indeed, case law in recent years has shown that an individual working through their own personal service company can be regarded as an employee of the client company for whom they are working, depending on all the factors inherent in the working relationship. One example was the case of *Catamaran Cruisers Ltd v Williams & ors [1994] IRLR 386* described in **8.10** below. By contrast, where an employment agency acts as an intermediary between the individual's limited company and the client company, the EAT has held (in *Hewlett Packard Ltd v O'Murphy [2002] IRLR 4* – see **8.10** below) that the individual cannot be an employee of the client company for whom they provide their services on account of the absence of a direct contract between them.

Essentially, the only thing that can be said with any certainty is that the employment status of an individual working through their own limited company is open to challenge, and the outcome of any such challenge will be determined taking into account not only the contractual documentation but also the actual working arrangements between the parties. **CHAPTER 1** provides a detailed analysis of employment status.

Case Law Challenging the Employment Status of Individuals Working Through their own Limited Company [8.10]

The following represents a selection of tribunal decisions in relation to individuals working through their own limited companies:

Winter v Westward Television Ltd EAT 589/77

Mr Winter owned a limited company together with his wife. Following his agreement to work for Westward Television on an exclusive basis, it was arranged that his remuneration would be paid to the limited company rather than to him personally. The EAT subsequently held that Mr Winter was not an employee of the company as the contractual relationship was between two limited companies.

Catamaran Cruisers Ltd v Williams & ors [1994] IRLR 386

In contrast to the *Winter* case above, the outcome in the case of *Catamaran Cruisers Ltd v Williams & ors [1994] IRLR 386* was that an individual working through his own limited company was held to be an employee of the company for whom he provided his services. According to the EAT, the nature of the working relationship was that Mr Williams was obliged to provide his services personally and the terms and conditions of his engagement were the same as those that applied to the company's permanent workforce, including terms relating to sick pay, holiday entitlement and the application of the company's disciplinary procedure. To all intents and purposes, therefore, the relationship was one of employer-employee. The EAT thus ruled that the case fell within the general rule that a relationship of employer-employee cannot be altered simply because the parties put a different label on it.

Hewlett Packard Ltd v O'Murphy [2002] IRLR 4

Mr O'Murphy was an IT specialist who owned and managed a limited company for the sole purpose of contracting out his services to clients. Through the medium of this limited company, he set up a contract with an employment business. The employment business in turn contracted his services as a consultant to their client, Hewlett Packard. The client paid the employment business a fee for the provision of computer specialists and the employment business in turn paid a fee to Mr O'Murphy's limited company.

The outcome of these arrangements was that Mr O'Murphy's limited company's contract was with the employment business and there was no direct contract between him and the client company for whom he provided his services. Despite this, when at a later date the contract was terminated, Mr O'Murphy argued that he had in reality been an employee of Hewlett Packard and was therefore eligible to bring a claim for unfair dismissal to tribunal. As a preliminary matter, therefore, the question of Mr O'Murphy's employment status had to be determined.

The employment tribunal that originally heard the case ruled that in reality Mr O'Murphy had been an employee of Hewlett Packard largely on account of evidence concerning the nature of the working relationship between them.

When the EAT heard the appeal, however, they overturned the tribunal's decision, largely because of the absence of a direct contract between Mr O'Murphy and Hewlett Packard. The EAT found that the contracts that existed were genuine and were not merely a device for concealing a working relationship that was in practice something different.

IR35 Rules – Income Tax and National Insurance Implications [8.11]

In April 2000, the *Finance Act 2000, Schedule 12*, commonly known as the 'IR35' rules, came into effect. The aim of these rules was to eliminate tax and national insurance avoidance by individuals who provide their services through an intermediary company by compelling them to pay tax and national insurance under the system appropriate to employees.

The IR35 provisions apply where an individual worker provides their services to a client company through an intermediary (often their own limited company) in circumstances where, if they had been engaged directly, they would be regarded in law as an employee of the client company. If these are the circumstances, the Inland Revenue will hold under IR35 that the individual must pay income tax and national insurance (including employers' national insurance) on the fees they receive as if they were an employee of their own limited company. IR35 is particularly likely to apply where an individual works full-time for a single client company through their own personal service company. It would not, however, apply where an individual was genuinely self-employed.

Specifically, the IR35 rules apply where:

- The individual works for one employer through a limited company.

- The limited company is owned and controlled by the individual.

- The working arrangements between the individual and the employer are similar in practice to those of an employment contract.

- The individual is obliged to perform services personally for the employer and is not free to provide a substitute.

The IR35 rules apply both where there is one intermediary company (i.e. the individual's own limited company) or more than one. Thus IR35 will apply in circumstances where an individual through their own limited company enters into a contract with an employment agency to perform work for one of the agency's clients. In these circumstances, the agency, as the intermediary company, would be required to deem themselves the employer of the individual for income tax and national insurance purposes despite the fact that their contract was with the individual's limited company and not the individual personally.

The key to establishing whether IR35 applies is to determine whether, but for the use of the intermediary company (or companies), the relationship between the individual and the client company for whom they work would be regarded in law as a contract of employment. This in turn will require an analysis of all the features of the working relationship between the client company and the individual. Whether the key features necessary for the existence of an employer–employee relationship actually exist will be a question of fact for a court or tribunal to decide. One key question is whether the individual is genuinely in business on their own account – if so, then IR35 will in theory not apply.

It is important to note that the application of IR35 does *not* necessarily affect the employment status of the individual for the purposes of statutory employment protection legislation. IR35 has to do with the status of the individual for tax and national insurance purposes only. Nevertheless, it seems logical to conclude that, if the Inland Revenue regards a particular individual as an employee for tax purposes, then an employment tribunal would be likely to reach the same conclusion in relation to employment status. This quite simply is because the tribunal in making their judgement on employment status will have reviewed the same factors as the Inland Revenue use to assess tax status.

A challenge to the legality of the IR35 legislation was taken to court in 2001 by the Professional Contractors Group Ltd (an organisation consisting of some 11,000 members working in service companies) arguing that the legislation was contrary to European Community law or the European Convention on Human Rights. The case failed, however, and both the High Court and the Court of Appeal accepted the justification put forward by the Inland Revenue that the objective and effect of the legislation was to combat tax avoidance and/or reduce decreasing tax revenue.

Checklist [8.12]

Employers who regularly enter into contracts with one-person limited companies may wish to review the contractual arrangements carefully. They may in turn wish to minimise the possibility that the individual might be viewed as their employee. There are certain features of a working relationship that, if genuinely implemented as part of the contract, will reduce the chances of the relationship being viewed as a contract of employment. To increase the chances of achieving this outcome, the employer should incorporate as many as possible of the following points into the contract:

- That the individual has the right to provide a substitute to perform the work if they are unable or unwilling to do so on a particular occasion.

- That there is no mutuality of obligation between the parties, i.e. the employer is not obliged to engage the individual for any minimum number of occasions or amount of time and the individual is not obliged to accept work when it is offered by the employer.

- That the individual will not be integrated into the organisation's team.

- That the individual is expected to work independently, for example the work will not be closely directed or controlled by the company, the individual may determine their own hours of work, the individual may decide on their own methods of work, etc.

- That the individual may perform some or all of the work from home, using their own facilities and equipment.

Provided at least some of the above features genuinely form part of the working relationship, it is unlikely that the individual would be regarded as an employee of the company for whom they work, and equally unlikely that the IR35 rules would apply. In particular, the facility for the individual to provide a substitute at their discretion, is likely to mean that no contract of employment exists, assuming of course that this facility is actually put into practice on occasion.

Conclusion   [8.13]

Independent contractors and people who are genuinely self-employed are regarded in law as being in business on their own account and are not, as a general rule, entitled to employment protection rights. The organisation for whom they provide their services is viewed as their client or customer, rather than their employer. There are also income tax implications as a result of this classification. However, the distinction between someone who is genuinely self-employed and someone who is engaged on a contract for services (a 'worker') is not always clear or obvious. In the event of a dispute, courts and tribunals will examine the actual working relationship between the parties and the label put on the contract will not, on its own, be decisive. Employers should therefore take care when engaging self-employed individuals or contractors that the terms of the engagement are clearly understood and documented.

Questions and Answers [8.14]

Question

For the purpose of employment protection legislation, what is the distinction between a worker engaged on a contract for services and a self-employed individual?

Answer

If an individual is in business on their own account and the organisation for whom they provide their services is in reality their client or customer rather than their employer, they will in general not be covered by employment protection rights. In contrast, a 'worker' engaged on a contract for services is someone who provides their services personally to an employer who is not their client or customer. The distinction between the two can, however, often become blurred and difficult to establish.

Question

If contractual documentation is set up making it clear that the individual is not engaged on a contract of employment or a contract for services, will that be sufficient to protect the employer from legal claims challenging employment status?

Answer

Even though an employer and an individual contractor agree between themselves that the individual is self-employed and document their agreement, that on its own will not be determinative of the person's employment status. In the event of a legal challenge, an employment tribunal or court will not regard the label the parties have put on the contract as conclusive proof of the individual's employment status, but will instead examine the actual working relationship between the organisation and the individual with a view to judging whether, in reality, it was akin to an employment contract or a contract for services.

Question

What are the implications of engaging self-employed workers?

Answer

There are a number of implications, for example certain implied terms that form part of every employment contract will not be applicable to a contract with a self-employed person, in particular the duty of fidelity and the duty to cooperate. Other issues that will have to be addressed include quality standards, who will provide tools, equipment and materials, confidentiality and professional indemnity insurance.

Question

What is 'lump working'?

Answer

'Lump working' refers to an arrangement whereby workers organise themselves as self-employed suppliers of labour to be hired out on a group contract basis, either directly or through an intermediate sub-contracting employer. An example would be where the main contractor on a building site sub-contracts the provision of labour to a sub-contractor.

Question

If an individual is engaged to provide services through their own limited company, does this automatically mean that the person cannot be regarded in law as an employee of the organisation for whom they provide their services?

Answer

The employment status of an individual working through their own limited company can be open to challenge, and the outcome of any such challenge will be determined taking into account not only the contractual documentation but also the actual working arrangements between the parties. Generally, such individuals are not regarded as employees of the client company for whom they provide their services because the contract is usually set up as a contract between the client company and the individual's limited company, rather than being a contract between the client company and the individual. However, if the reality of the situation points towards a different conclusion, a tribunal will be entitled to disregard the contractual label that the parties have put on to the relationship.

Question

What are the IR35 rules and how do they impact on an individual's employment status?

Answer

The IR35 provisions apply where an individual worker provides their services to a client company through an intermediary (often their own limited company) in circumstances where, if they had been engaged directly, they would be regarded in law as an employee of the client company. If these are the circumstances, the Inland Revenue will hold under IR35 that the individual must pay income tax and national insurance (including employers' national insurance) as if they were an employee of their own limited company. It is important to note, however, that IR35 has to do with the status of the individual for tax and national insurance purposes and does not therefore determine the employment status of the individual for the purposes of statutory employment protection legislation.

9. Avoiding Sex Discrimination

Introduction [9.1]

The *Sex Discrimination Act 1975* makes it unlawful to treat a female employee less favourably than a male employee was or would have been treated in comparable circumstances if the reason for the less favourable treatment is linked to gender. The *Equal Pay Act 1970* protects employees from discrimination in relation to employees' pay and other contractual terms. Protection under both Acts applies equally to men, although in practice more women than men are the victims of sex discrimination in the workplace.

Since a much larger proportion of women than men are engaged in part-time work, and a marginally larger proportion of women than men work in temporary jobs, any detrimental treatment of part-time employees, or temporary employees, may constitute indirect sex discrimination against women unless the treatment in question can be objectively justified. The aim of this chapter is to explore the law on sex discrimination as it applies to part-time and temporary workers.

An Overview of the Laws on Sex Discrimination [9.2]

Protection against sex discrimination in employment is afforded by the *Sex Discrimination Act 1975* and by the *Equal Pay Act 1970*. The two Acts together form a comprehensive package providing substantial protection to workers against sex discrimination. The *Sex Discrimination Act* and the *Equal Pay Act* are mutually exclusive, which means that if a complaint is made under one Act it cannot also be made under the other. The distinction is that the *Equal Pay Act* covers inequality of pay and other terms and conditions of employees' contracts of employment, whilst the *Sex Discrimination Act* protects employees from discrimination in areas that are not governed by the terms of the contract. There is no minimum service qualification for protection under either of the two Acts, thus all workers, including temporary and fixed-term workers, are protected against sex discrimination from the first day of their employment.

Protection under the Equal Pay Act 1970 [9.3]

The key purpose of equal pay legislation is to eliminate sex discrimination in pay practices. The *Equal Pay Act* does not address the issue of fair wages in a general sense. Thus employees have no general statutory right to equal pay with other employees where any differences in pay rates are not due to the gender of the individuals. Similarly, a claim for equal pay cannot be made unless the claimant can identify an appropriate comparator of the opposite sex (see **9.8** below). Importantly, however, part-time workers do have a statutory right to the same rate of pay (on a pro-rata basis) as comparable full-time workers under the *Part-Time Workers (Prevention of Less Favourable Treatment) Regulations 2000 (SI 2000 No 1551)* (see **CHAPTER 3** at **3.26**).

'Pay' in the context of equal pay has been defined by Article 141 of the Treaty of Rome as 'any other consideration, in cash or in kind, which the employee receives directly or indirectly from the employer in respect of employment'. Despite its name, the *Equal Pay Act* therefore applies not only to employees' pay, but also to other contractual terms such as occupational sick pay, contractual holiday entitlement, provision of insurance benefit and benefits from occupational pension schemes.

The key element of the *Equal Pay Act 1970* (contained in *section 1[2]*) is that all employees' contracts are deemed to include an equality clause relating to the terms of their contract.

The House of Lords has ruled (in *Hayward v Cammell Laird Shipbuilders Ltd [1988] IRLR 257*) that in relation to claims for equal pay, each term of an employee's contract is to be regarded as a 'distinct provision or part of the contract' that should be compared with a similar provision or part in the comparator's contract. This means that each term of the contract must be viewed individually when comparing a woman's contractual terms with those of a comparable man.

The cumulative effect of these provisions is that employers must not treat an employee less favourably on the grounds of their sex than another employee of the opposite sex with regard to any of the terms contained in their contract of employment, and if they do so, the person who has suffered such discrimination will have the right to pursue a claim for equal pay in relation to each individual term of their contract.

The Comparator in Equal Pay Claims [9.4]

To bring a claim under the *Equal Pay Act*, an employee has to compare their treatment with a colleague of the opposite sex who works in the same employment and who is performing:

- like work (where the duties of the two jobs are the same or broadly similar); *or*

- Work rated as equivalent (in accordance with an objective job evaluation scheme); *or*

- work of equal value (measured in terms of the demands made on the individuals performing the jobs).

If an employee can succeed in showing one of these three elements, the equality clause implied into their contract will operate to entitle them to be placed in the same position as their comparator in relation to the terms of the contract of employment, unless the employer can show that the difference between a woman's and a man's contract was caused by a 'genuine material factor' unrelated to sex. Thus the provisions of the *Equal Pay Act* do not prevent employers from paying a lower (or higher) salary to a particular individual for reasons unrelated to sex. Factors that could be regarded as genuine material factors justifying a difference in contractual terms could include (for example) the length of an employee's relevant experience, a higher level of job performance (properly measured) and different qualifications or skills.

Outcome of a Successful Equal Pay Claim [9.5]

Where an employee succeeds in a claim for equal pay, the employer will be obliged to modify their contract to bring its terms into line with the more advantageous terms of the comparator's contract, and pay up to six years' compensation for past differences. It is not permissible to achieve equal pay the other way around, i.e. by downgrading the comparator's terms in order to bring them into line with those of the complainant.

Checklist for Equal Pay [9.6]

- Monitor the pay rates of men and women at all levels in the organisation so that any discrepancies in rates can be quickly identified and checked.

- Make sure there is an objective reason unrelated to gender whenever two individuals of different sexes are being paid differently for performing essentially the same or similar work.

- Analyse and record the reasons why individuals doing the same job or similar work are being paid different rates of pay or afforded different contractual benefits.

- Review the rates of pay and other contractual benefits of part–time workers and compare these to equivalent full–time workers to ensure there is no less favourable treatment of part–timers on account of their part–time status.

- Review the rates of pay and other contractual benefits of temporary and fixed–term employees to ensure that any differences in the levels of benefits can be objectively justified.

- Record the reasons for any changes to pay or pay patterns, so that these can be objectively justified if the need should arise.

Protection under the Sex Discrimination Act 1975 [9.7]

The *Sex Discrimination Act 1975* covers sex discrimination in relation to the employee's treatment at work generally, for example discrimination in relation to the benefits, facilities and services they are offered by their employer, opportunities for promotion, transfer and training and in relation to disciplinary proceedings and dismissal. There is also a provision in *section 6(2)(b)* that protects workers from 'any other detriment'. This essentially is a catch–all provision that can be applied to a variety of situations, including for example, reduction of wages, demotion, the application of procedures, non–contractual practices and of course harassment.

Protection is also extended under the *Sex Discrimination Act* to discrimination on the grounds of marriage.

The Comparative Approach [9.8]

The *Sex Discrimination Act* is structured to facilitate claims based on a comparison between the treatment of one person and the treatment of another of the opposite sex. Thus a fixed–term or part–time worker who believes they have suffered unfavourable treatment on the grounds of sex must compare their treatment with another worker of the opposite sex in circumstances that are similar. A test that is often used is 'would the person have been treated in the way they were treated *but for* their sex (a principle originating from the case of *James v Eastleigh Borough Council [1990] IRLR 288).*

A part–time or fixed–term worker alleging sex discrimination must be able to demonstrate that the unfavourable treatment they received was on the grounds of their sex, and not for some other reason. A worker's perception of unfairness may be wholly justified (or not) as the case may be, but unless they can show that the unfair treatment in question was rooted in reasons of sex, there will be no remedy under the *Sex Discrimination Act*. In order for discrimination to be shown, however, the person's sex does not have to be the only reason for the unfavourable treatment, so long as it is a substantial or important factor.

The Scope of the Sex Discrimination Act and the Equal Pay Act [9.9]

All workers are protected against sex discrimination, irrespective of their employment status. Hence home-workers, casual staff, agency temps, contractors and some self-employed people are able to rely on the provisions of both the *Sex Discrimination Act* and the *Equal Pay Act* irrespective of whether they are employed under a contract of employment or engaged under a contract for services (the distinction is explained fully in chapter 1). This is because both Acts define 'employment' as: '. . . under a contract of service or of apprenticeship or a contract personally to execute any work or labour'. The *Sex Discrimination Act* also protects job applicants throughout the process of recruitment.

Workers are also protected against sex discrimination irrespective of their age, the number of hours they work, or their length of service. Thus part-time workers and temporary workers enjoy the same statutory protection under the two Acts as permanent, full-time workers.

People Posted to Great Britain [9.10]

Protection against discrimination applies not only to people working in Britain, but also to those who are posted to work in Britain for a temporary period. Unless the employment is wholly outside Britain, the *Sex Discrimination Act* and the *Equal Pay Act* will apply.

People Working on Ships, Aircraft and on Offshore Installations [9.11]

People who work on ships registered in Britain or on aircraft are protected by sex discrimination legislation unless in practice they work wholly outside Great Britain. People working offshore on oil and gas installations within British waters are also protected.

Employers' liability for sex discrimination [9.12]

The *Sex Discrimination Act 1975, s 41[1]* states that employers will be liable for an act of discrimination committed 'in the course of employment.... ... whether or not it was done with the employer's knowledge or approval'. Thus any act of sex discrimination perpetrated by a manager against any worker, including fixed-term and part-time workers, or by one colleague against another, will create liability for the employer whether or not the company's management were aware that a discriminatory act had taken place. In certain circumstances, the individual who perpetrated the act of discrimination can also be held liable.

Eligibility to Complain of Sex Discrimination   [9.13]

Employees and other workers are eligible to bring a complaint of sex discrimination to an employment tribunal irrespective of length of service or age, provided they do so within three calendar months of the discriminatory act complained of. In the case of a series of discriminatory acts, for example an ongoing course of conduct that amounts to sexual harassment, then the tribunal claim must be lodged with the tribunal office no later than the end of the three month period following the latest in the series of incidents.

The Burden of Proof   [9.14]

Applicants to tribunal do not need to prove 'beyond reasonable doubt' that they were subjected to sex discrimination in the workplace. Tribunals operate generally according to the 'balance of probabilities' test, and are entitled to form their own view of whether a particular form of treatment was sufficient to amount to sex discrimination, and, where the facts are disputed, which party's evidence they find more credible.

In October 2001, the Government implemented new Regulations (by amending the *Sex Discrimination Act 1975)* that shifted the burden of proof in cases of sex discrimination from the complainant to the employer. This was necessary in order to conform with an EC Directive (Council Directive 98/52 EC) known as the *Burden of Proof Directive*. This Directive also contained a new and wider definition of indirect sex discrimination (see **9.15** below). Since this change was introduced, the burden of proof in claims of sex discrimination lies with the employer rather than with the employee (as was previously the case).

Since the shifting of the burden of proof to the employer, all an employee has to do to found a potential claim for sex discrimination is to establish facts from which a court or tribunal could conclude that discrimination occurred, i.e. show that they received less favourable treatment than a colleague of the opposite sex in comparable circumstances. It will then be up to the employer, if they are to succeed in refuting the employee's claim, to show that there was no breach of the principle of equal treatment in relation to the employee in question. To do this, the employer must provide concrete evidence that there was an alternative credible reason for the unfavourable treatment of the employee that was unrelated to their sex. If in practice the employer is unable to provide such evidence, the tribunal is bound to conclude that the treatment was based on sex or influenced by sex and hence unlawful. Equally, if the tribunal considers that the evidence put forward by the employer to explain the alleged discriminatory treatment is inadequate or untrue, they will uphold the employee's claim.

This emphasises the need for every employer to take concrete action to prevent sex discrimination from occurring in the workplace. To do this, the employer should:

- Adopt a positive approach to equal opportunities in the workplace.

- Design and implement an equal opportunities policy to promote fair employment practices and fair treatment of all staff, including part-time and temporary workers (see **9.41** below for a model policy).

- Implement an effective and accessible complaints procedure so that any worker with a genuine complaint of sex discrimination has the opportunity to seek a solution.

- Conduct equal opportunities training for all managers and supervisors.

- Scrutinise any conditions or criteria applied by management and any general practices within the organisation to make sure that these do not have a disproportionate adverse impact on women (see next section).

- Most importantly of all, take concrete measures to implement the policy, procedure and training throughout the workplace, and ensure evidence is available to support this.

The Meaning of Indirect Sex Discrimination [9.15]

Discrimination can be direct or indirect. Direct sex discrimination occurs where an individual suffers unfavourable treatment directly on grounds of their sex. This is usually obvious, unlike indirect sex discrimination which tends to be more subtle, less blatant, and often unintentional. Indirect sex discrimination occurs in the following circumstances:

- the employer applies a provision, criterion or practice to all employees equally; *but*

- the provision, criterion or practice places a considerably larger proportion of women than men at a disadvantage (or vice versa, i.e. more men than women are adversely affected); *and*

- the provision, criterion or practice is to the detriment of an individual woman (or man); *and*

- the employer cannot show objective justification for the application of the provision, criterion or practice irrespective of the sex of the person to whom it is applied.

These provisions are explained further below.

Provision, Criterion or Practice [9.16]

The wording 'provision, criterion or practice' was introduced as a change to the *Sex Discrimination Act 1975, s 1(2)* following the implementation of *the EC Burden of Proof Directive* in October 2001. The previous wording in the Act referred to a 'requirement or condition', which suggested that the element giving rise to a complaint of indirect sex discrimination had to be something that formed part of the employee's contractual requirements, or had to be applied as a definite requirement rather than a mere 'practice'. The new wording encompasses 'requirement and condition' but is wider than the original definition.

It is irrelevant whether or not the employer intended the provision, criterion or practice to be discriminatory. Indirect sex discrimination is often, if not prevalently, unintentional, but lack of intent to discriminate is no defence in law.

Considerably larger proportion [9.17]

The essence of indirect sex discrimination is that a provision, although applied equally to both men and women, has a disproportionate adverse impact on one of the sexes as compared to the other. The criterion used in the *Sex Discrimination Act 1975* to assess adverse impact is that there must be a considerably larger proportion of women than men (or men than women) who are placed at a disadvantage as a result of the provision. Employment tribunals have wide discretion in practice to assess the evidence put before them in order to interpret whether or not one of the sexes has realistically suffered a disparate adverse impact as a result of a provision, criterion or practice applied by the employer.

In relation to part-time working, there is a long line of case law from both the UK and Europe that has upheld the general principle that a considerably smaller proportion of women than men can in practice work full-time because of child-minding and domestic responsibilities (see **9.26** below).

The Court of Appeal has held (in *London Underground Ltd v Edwards No 2 [1998] IRLR 364*) that, even where a requirement imposed by an employer places only one employee at a disadvantage, it can still be classed as indirectly discriminatory on grounds of sex. Despite being the only employee who could not comply with her employer's new rostering system involving an early morning start-time, Ms Edwards, a single parent, succeeded in a case of unlawful sex discrimination. The Court of Appeal held that the employer could not justify insisting that the employee should work the new roster. The Court accepted that women are in general more likely than men to be single parents and that a considerably smaller proportion of women would therefore have been able to work the new rosters.

The key principle for employers from this case is that they should be certain that any hours requirement imposed on employees can be objectively justified, both collectively and individually, based on the needs of the business.

Prior to the implementation of the *EC Burden of Proof Directive*, the *Sex Discrimination Act* contained a further condition for a claim of indirect sex discrimination to be upheld. Previously, a woman (or a man) had to show that they could not in practice comply with the particular requirement or condition that they alleged was indirectly discriminatory. The prerequisite for the employee to show that it was impossible in practical terms for them to comply with the requirement no longer forms part of the legislation.

Practical Example [9.18]

Fiona and her husband have two young children under the age of five. Fiona does not wish to work full-time because she feels strongly that she wants to take an active part in the day-to-day care of her children, at least until they are both old enough to go to school. Arranging day-care for her children would be relatively easy because Fiona's mother lives nearby and is always willing to help out, and in any event her personal circumstances are such that she could easily afford to engage a child-minder or send the children to a private nursery.

Fiona has decided she would like to work part-time and has applied for a number of positions for which she is suited in terms of her background and previous work experience. One prospective employer has told Fiona at interview that the job is hers if she wants it. However, having enquired whether she could be employed on a part-time or job-share basis, the prospective employer has simply informed Fiona that unless she is prepared to take up the post on a full-time basis, no job offer would be forthcoming. No reason has been given for the refusal to consider part-time working other than 'this company does not wish to engage part-time staff'.

If Fiona was to bring a claim for indirect sex discrimination to an employment tribunal on the grounds of this employer's unjustified refusal to agree to engage her on a part-time basis, what would be her chances of success?

Prior to the amendments made to the *Sex Discrimination Act* as a result of the implementation of the *EC Burden of Proof Directive*, Fiona would have to have shown (if she was to succeed in a claim for indirect sex discrimination) that it was impossible in practice for her to comply with the requirement to work full-time. In practice it would have been difficult, if not impossible, for someone in Fiona's circumstances to demonstrate that she was unable to work full-time – due to the availability of her mother as a child-minder and the fact that she could easily afford child-care.

Since the *Sex Discrimination Act* was amended in October 2001, however, Fiona would be in a stronger position to argue that a refusal without good reason to agree to permit her to work part-time was unlawful. Under the revised provisions, there is no longer a need for an employee who is placed at a disadvantage by a discriminatory requirement or provision imposed by the employer to show that they could not in practice comply with it. All that has to be shown is that the provision is to the person's detriment. Fiona would in all likelihood not find it difficult to demonstrate that the requirement to work full-time was to her detriment as full-time working would clearly prevent her from spending quality time with her young children and her desire to be employed on a part-time basis has led to her losing the job opportunity.

Fiona would thus have a stronger basis than would have been the case in the past on which to bring a complaint of indirect sex discrimination to tribunal. The employer's refusal to afford her the opportunity to work part-time, unless it could be justified on objective grounds, would be likely to be ruled indirectly discriminatory against her on grounds of sex.

The Pool for Comparison **[9.19]**

When an employment tribunal is tasked with assessing whether or not a particular provision, criterion or practice has a discriminatory impact on women (or men), they have to identify an appropriate 'pool' for the purposes of making a relevant comparison. The establishment of the 'right' pool, and the measurement of disparate impact can often be a complex process.

For example, in relation to a condition that restricts eligibility for a particular company benefit, the pool for comparison would normally incorporate everyone who would be eligible for the benefit if the condition was not applied. The relative proportions of men and women within the pool can then be reviewed in order to establish whether or not the proportion of women who are eligible for the benefit is considerably smaller than the proportion of men who are eligible. To be successful in a case of indirect sex discrimination, the complainant must show that the criterion or condition placed a considerably larger proportion of women than men at a disadvantage (or vice versa) and that it acted to their detriment, i.e. they were ineligible for the benefit on account of the restricting condition.

In any event, courts and tribunals have, over the years, accepted that in general terms a much larger number of women than men work part-time. It follows that any criterion or practice that causes a detriment to part-timers will have a disproportionate adverse impact on women and is likely to be ruled unlawful under sex discrimination legislation unless it can be objectively justified (see **9.21** below).

Detriment **[9.20]**

In order to succeed in a claim of indirect sex discrimination, the complainant must show that they personally suffered a detriment as a direct result of the discriminatory provision, criterion or practice imposed by the employer. A complaint cannot be founded on an assertion that a provision or requirement is theoretically discriminatory on the grounds of sex. For example a requirement imposed by an employer that transfer to a particular job depends (amongst other criteria) on ability to perform heavy lifting would be indirectly discriminatory against women (because fewer women than men in general would be physically capable of performing heavy lifting). If, however, a particular woman is not personally disadvantaged by this criterion, i.e. she is physically capable of performing the lifting duties required for the job and is therefore considered for it, she would have no case.

263

Justification [9.21]

The law on indirect sex discrimination does not mean that employers can never introduce rules, requirements, policies or practices that may adversely affect female (or male) employees. Provided there is an objective factor unrelated to gender that justifies the provision in question, then its application will not be unlawful despite its discriminatory impact. There is no duty on the employer to prove that there was no alternative way to achieve the objective they have put forward by way of justification.

The issue of justifiability is not dealt with in statute, thus the setting of the standard for justification has been left to courts and tribunals to establish. The decisions of courts and tribunals in both the UK and Europe over a period of many years have to a great extent clarified when and under what circumstances an employer may justify a provision that is indirectly discriminatory on grounds of sex. Essentially the employer has to show that the provision was, in a practical sense, necessary in order to achieve a legitimate business aim and appropriate to the achievement of that aim. It will not be enough to show that the measure was based on administrative convenience or management preference.

The following case are examples of rulings that have helped to clarify the circumstances in which an employer may justify a provision that is indirectly discriminatory.

- In *Bilka-Kaufhaus GmbH v Weber von Hartz [1986] IRLR 317*, the European Court of Justice held that, in order to justify a discriminatory provision, the employer must show that the reason for it corresponds to a real need on the part of the business and is appropriate and necessary with a view to achieving that need. The *Bilka-Kaufhaus* case concerned equal pay and was decided in relation to Article 141, but the principles emanating from it have been held to apply equally to claims brought under the *Equal Pay Act* and the *Sex Discrimination Act*.

- In *Hampson v Department of Education and Science [1990] IRLR 302*, the Court of Appeal stated that in assessing justifiability, what was required was 'an objective balance between the discriminatory effect of the condition and the reasonable needs of the party who applies the condition'. Although the *Hampson* case was one of race discrimination, the principles apply equally to complaints of sex discrimination. Thus employers applying provisions that may be indirectly discriminatory should aim to strike an objective balance between the reasonable needs of the business on the one hand, and the discriminatory effect of the requirement on the other. This is often described as the 'principle of proportionality'. Under the principle of proportionality, the disparate impact caused by the criterion or condition that is indirectly discriminatory should be judged in relation to the number of employees affected by it and the degree of detriment caused by its application. This should then be weighed against the employer's genuine business needs.

- In *Greater Manchester Police Authority v Lea [1990] IRLR 372*, the EAT held that, in order to justify objectively a provision that has a disproportionate adverse impact on women (or men as in this case), the employer must be able to show that the application of the provision in question had some relevance to or connection with the needs of the employer. An argument that a rule or provision has been implemented in order to further some social need or reasonable policy, for example to help the less well-off, is unconnected to the needs of the employer and thus insufficient to provide justification.

Factors that are often put forward by way of justification include (for example):

- Market forces and/or skills shortages.

- Geographical differences, for example to justify a London weighting allowance.

- Needs specific to the particular business.

- Business aims such as a desire to, increase profits, provide a better service to customers, reduce absenteeism, etc.

- The nature of the individual's position.

- Differences between individuals in terms of qualifications, skills, experience and job performance.

It is advisable, in light of the law in this area, for employers to carry out regular reviews of their policies, procedures, rules, provisions, practices and any conditions or criteria attached to specific jobs to make sure that either:

- there is no disproportionate adverse impact on women (or men) as a result of the policy, procedure, rule, provision, practice, condition or criterion; *or*

- if there is a disparate impact, the employer can nevertheless objectively justify the need for the policy, procedure, rule, provision, practice, condition or criterion on grounds that are clearly related to the needs of the business or the individual job.

265

Indirect Discrimination against Men [9.22]

Although the evolution of the law on sex discrimination has related mainly to claims brought by women, men are able to rely equally on the provisions contained in the *Sex Discrimination Act 1995, s 1(1)(b)*. However, in relation to part-time working, because most part-timers in the UK are women, it is not possible for a man who works part-time to argue that treatment that places part-timers at a disadvantage is indirectly discriminatory against men. The reality is that the opposite is the case, i.e. detrimental treatment of part-timers is usually discriminatory against women in that it affects more women than men.

However, male part-timers would be able to rely circuitously on the principle that any provisions that discriminate against part-timers are discriminatory on grounds of sex. Once it has been established that a provision, criterion or practice operated by the employer is indirectly discriminatory against female staff, the provision, criterion or practice would have to be disapplied. If the employer chose to disapply the provision only in relation to female employees, then male employees would have an immediate claim for direct (not indirect) sex discrimination.

Practical Example [9.23]

If an employer operated a discriminatory pay practice under the terms of which part-timers were paid on a less favourable basis than full-time staff performing similar work, this would be indirectly discriminatory against women assuming the majority of part-timers in the organisation were women. A male part-timer would not, logically, be able to argue that the pay practice indirectly discriminated against men because men would be the minority sex amongst the part-time staff. This is because the *Sex Discrimination Act 1975, s 1(2)* states that a provision, criterion or practice is indirectly discriminatory where it places a considerably larger proportion of women than men (or men than women) at a disadvantage. In the above scenario, men are the smaller proportion rather than the larger proportion of the part-time staff.

The male part-timer could, however, argue that, if a female colleague in his position has brought, or could bring, a successful equal pay claim citing a full-time male worker as a comparator, he too should be entitled to bring a claim for equal pay, even though he is not under the present regime a member of the disadvantaged sex. Any alternative analysis would lead to the conclusion that the male part-timer would be the victim of direct sex discrimination once his female colleague had established equal pay with a full-time male comparator. Thus the male part-timer can bring what is amusingly known as a 'piggy-back' claim, relying on the right of female part-timers to bring an equal pay claim in these circumstances.

Operating a pay practice in which part-timers are paid on a less favourable basis than full-time staff performing similar work would also be in contravention of the *Part-Time Workers (Prevention of Less Favourable Treatment) Regulations 2000 (SI 2000 No 1551)*. The Regulations are discussed fully in **CHAPTER 3**.

When Less Favourable Treatment of Part-Time or Temporary Workers can Constitute Indirect Sex Discrimination [9.24]

Over and above the legislation affording protection against unfavourable treatment to part-time and fixed-term workers (see **CHAPTERS 3** and **4** respectively), less favourable treatment of part-timers (and possible temporary employees) can constitute indirect sex discrimination against female employees.

Less Favourable Treatment of Part-timers [9.25]

Any condition, requirement, policy, criterion, rule, provision or practice that places part-timers at a disadvantage when compared to full-time staff may be indirectly discriminatory against female staff on grounds of sex if it is likely to have a disproportionate adverse effect on female employees. This is the case simply because the vast majority of part-timers are, in practice, women (approximately 80 per cent at the time of writing). Thus, if in a particular organisation more women than men are employed on a part-time basis, the provision of inferior terms, conditions, benefits, policies, procedures or practices to part-timer workers will have a greater adverse effect on women than on men and will be discriminatory.

Following a reference to the ECJ, the EAT expressly ruled in *Jenkins v Kingsgate (Clothing Productions) Ltd (No 2) [1981] IRLR 388* that a variation in the basic rate of pay between a man and a woman doing equivalent work cannot be justified just because the man works full-time and the woman works part-time, unless the difference can be objectively justified. To justify the difference, the employer would have to show that it was reasonably necessary in order to achieve a legitimate business aim that the employer sought for economic or other reasons. Seeking to save money by employing cheap female labour was not a justification.

Why an Insistence on Full-time Working may be Indirectly Discriminatory against Female Employees [9.26]

Similarly, insisting without justification that a job must be done full-time can amount to indirect sex discrimination against women. The argument is based on the contention that fewer women than men are able to work full-time as a result of family responsibilities, and that a requirement that a particular job must be performed on a full-time basis (rather than part-time or on a job-share basis) thus places women at a disadvantage. Unless the employer can objectively justify the requirement for the employee in question to work full-time on objective business grounds, the result will be indirect sex discrimination, entitling the person affected to take a complaint to an employment tribunal and claim compensation.

Another point to bear in mind is that, if the employer has agreed to permit one or more female employees to work part-time or on a job-share basis, refusing to grant the same entitlement or opportunity to a male employee in similar circumstances could be directly discriminatory against the male employee in question. The same rights and entitlements must be made available on an equal basis to both male and female staff, if a claim for sex discrimination is to be avoided.

Less Favourable Treatment of Temporary Workers [9.27]

The development of employment law affording protection against sex discrimination to temporary workers has not been nearly so extensive as the development of the law appertaining to part-time workers. Nevertheless, it can be argued that temporary workers suffer discrimination in relation to access to certain statutory employment protection rights where these rights are dependent on a minimum period of qualifying service. Given that temporary working is prevalent in professions such as nursing, teaching and catering which in general employ more women than men, there may be an argument that any contractual benefits in these sectors that are made dependent on a minimum period of service would be indirectly discriminatory against female employees. The key question then would be whether the length of service requirement could be objectively justified.

A major challenge to the rights of employees with short service was taken to the ECJ during the 1990's by the Equal Opportunities Commission

(EOC). In *R v Secretary of State for Employment ex parte Seymour Smith and Perez [1995] IRLR 464*, the EOC argued that the then two-year qualifying period of service (now one year) required for unfair dismissal claims indirectly discriminated against women. Statistics were produced covering the period from 1985 to 1991 which showed a distinct gap between the number of men and the number of women in Britain who had actually worked for their employer for two years of more. The case ultimately failed following the House of Lords judgement that at the time the two-year qualifying period was implemented by the UK Government, it was justified as a measure reasonably applied for the legitimate purpose of encouraging recruitment by employers and maximising employment opportunities.

Future legislation will give further rights to temporary workers who work through employment agencies. In the spring of 2002, the European Commission published a draft Directive under which temporary agency workers would be granted the right not to suffer less favourable treatment than comparable employees engaged directly by the organisation in which they were placed, unless such treatment could be objectively justified (see **CHAPTER 5** for fuller information about temporary agency workers).

Examples of Indirectly Discriminatory Provisions [9.28]

Some examples of indirect sex discrimination that could relate to part-time or temporary workers are as follows:

- Where the provision of a company benefit, for example an annual bonus or an extra day's holiday, was offered to full-time but not to part-time employees. Assuming the majority of part-time employees in the organisation in question were female (as is usually the case), this provision would have a disproportionate adverse impact on the part-timers. In any event, less favourable treatment of part-time workers in terms of pay and benefits is also unlawful under the *Part-Time Workers (Prevention of Less Favourable Treatment) Regulations 2000 (SI 2000 No 1551)* (see **CHAPTER 3** at **3.5**).

- Where an employer insisted that employees must be willing to work full-time in order to qualify for a promotion. Such a requirement could discriminate against women, since more women than men have family commitments which might prevent them from being available to work full-time. Unless the requirement to perform the promoted post on a full-time basis could be justified on objective grounds, it would be unlawful.

- Where an employer imposed an arbitrary length of service requirement on employees before they could qualify for enhanced maternity or parental leave beyond the minimum provided for in statute. If the majority of temporary workers in the organisation were female, and if the length of service requirement meant that more women than men were excluded from the benefit, this would indirectly discriminatory on grounds of sex. Once again, it would be open to the employer to justify the length of service barrier on objective grounds related to the needs of the business.

Checklist [9.29]

- Review the terms, conditions and benefits of part-time and temporary workers on a regular basis to ensure these are not less favourable (whether collectively or individually) than the terms of comparable full-time, permanent workers.

- If a disparate impact between the conditions of part-timers and full-timers, or between temporary and permanent workers, is identified, check whether there is an objective reason that justifies the difference in treatment other than the part-time or temporary status of the worker(s) in question.

- Adopt a policy of giving serious consideration to all requests to work part-time, whether these come from an existing employee or a job applicant.

- Realise that part-time and temporary employees may be as committed to giving effective and efficient job performance as full-time, permanent employees.

- Do not impose arbitrary length-of-service requirements on access to company benefits unless there is an objective reason why the service requirement is necessary.

- Do not view part-time workers or temporary workers as second-class citizens – their contribution to the productivity of the organisation may be as important and substantial as that of any full-time or permanent worker.

Redundancy Selection [9.30]

Traditionally, many employers have adopted policies to deal with redundancies that operate to the disadvantage of certain groups, for example those with short service. If an employee's dismissal for redundancy is to be fair under unfair dismissal law, the criteria used for selecting employees for redundancy will have to be fair and objective and be applied objectively and consistently. However, even if selection criteria are fair and objective, care should be taken to ensure that a particular criterion does not inadvertently place a particular group at a disadvantage if that group consists predominantly of women (or men). Otherwise, the criterion could be indirectly discriminatory on grounds of sex.

The Guidance Notes that accompany the *Part-Time Workers (Prevention of Less Favourable Treatment) Regulations 2000*, provide that in the event of a redundancy programme, part-timers should not be treated less favourably than their full-time equivalents, unless different treatment can be justified on objective grounds. Thus, redundancy selection criteria must not discriminate against part-time employees, and any policy that has the effect of favouring the retention of full-time employees as compared to part-time employees is likely to be unlawful. Such a policy would, in addition, be indirectly discriminatory against women since the majority of part-timers in the UK are women.

Key Case   **[9.31]**

In respect of temporary employees, a redundancy selection policy that discriminates in favour of those on long-term, permanent contracts may also be indirectly discriminatory against women, as was the case in *Whiffen v Milham Ford Girls' School & anor Court of Appeal 21.03.01* in which the employer adopted a policy of automatically selecting fixed-term employees for redundancy first:

Whiffen v Milham Ford Girls' School & anor Court of Appeal 21.03.01

Facts

Ms Whiffen, a language teacher, had worked at a girls' school on a series of fixed-term contracts for a period of more than five years. When the employer decided that they needed to make redundancies, they applied a well-established policy under which teachers engaged on fixed-term contracts would be selected for redundancy first before any teachers on permanent contracts were considered. In respect of Ms Whiffen, this meant that her fixed-term contract was not renewed on account of redundancy. The policy of selecting those working on fixed-term contracts first before any teachers engaged on permanent contracts were considered was applied automatically irrespective of employees' length of service or any other factor. If, after that process was complete, further redundancies were necessary, teachers who worked on

---

permanent contracts would be subject to a structured redundancy selection process based on a number of factors.

Having been made redundant, Ms Whiffen brought a claim to an employment tribunal for indirect sex discrimination, arguing that her ex-employer's redundancy policy had a disproportionately adverse impact on female teachers. This was based on evidence that all the teachers who worked on fixed-term contracts were women.

Findings

The tribunal upheld Ms Whiffen's argument, accepting that the employer had applied a condition that a teacher had to be engaged on a permanent contract in order to be included in the redundancy selection process. They went on to rule that this requirement was indirectly discriminatory against female staff, but that the redundancy policy could be objectively justified in relation to the aims of the school.

On appeal to the Court of Appeal, however, the tribunal's decision that the redundancy selection policy was objectively justified was overturned. The Court of Appeal held that the policy of automatically selecting employees on fixed-term contracts for redundancy first without giving them an opportunity to be included in the redundancy selection process along with permanent staff was not a necessary requirement in relation to the effective running of the school.

The Equal Opportunities Commission [9.32]

The Equal Opportunities Commission (EOC) has published a document on the management of part-time workers titled '*Part-time workers, not second-class citizens*'. The following is an extract:

'Part-time working or job-sharing may make it easier for women to return to work after maternity leave, and for both men and women to provide childcare and elder-care for their dependants. Refusing to allow an employee to work part-time can, in some circumstances, amount to unlawful discrimination. Such arrangements can also have advantages for employers, including increased efficiency and improved staff morale. While returning from maternity leave is something which only women do, alternative working arrangements should not be restricted to women, for by so doing an employer discriminates directly against men. Whatever arrangements are made for working non-standard hours, these should be available to male and female employees.'

Part–Time and Temporary Employees' Pay and Contractual Terms [9.33]

Employers must not discriminate against part-timers in terms of their basic hourly rate of pay, commission payments, any bonus entitlement, entitlement to overtime payments, pay rises or pension benefits. Part-timers who suffer such unfavourable treatment can bring a claim to tribunal under the *Part-Time Workers (Prevention of Less Favourable Treatment) Regulations 2000* (see **CHAPTER 3** at **3.5**), or under sex discrimination legislation if the majority of part-time workers within the particular workforce are women.

Pay [9.34]

It is discriminatory and unlawful to afford a part-time worker a lower rate of pay than a full-time worker performing similar work purely because the person works part-time. A part-timer so affected could bring a claim for unlawful treatment under the *Part-Time Workers (Prevention of Less Favourable Treatment) Regulations 2000* (see **CHAPTER 3** at **3.26**) and, for female part-timers, a claim for indirect sex discrimination would also succeed unless the difference in pay could be objectively justified.

Bonuses [9.35]

The ECJ has ruled in *Krüger v Kreiskrankenhaus Ebersberg [1999] IRLR 808*, that the denial of a Christmas bonus to part-time staff in an organisation that usually paid an end-of-year bonus to full-timers was indirectly discriminatory against women and could not be justified on account of broad social policy considerations. It follows that employers should make any bonus that is paid to full-time employees payable (on a pro-rata basis) to part-timers performing a similar role.

Overtime [9.36]

In relation to overtime payments, the ECJ has ruled (in *Stadt Lengerich v Helmig [1995] IRLR 216* and five other cases), that any premium rate of overtime offered to full-time employees who work beyond their normal hours need not be paid to part-time employees who work overtime until the part-time employee has worked the equivalent of full-time hours. The ECJ took the view that there is no unequal treatment where part-timers are paid for overtime hours at single time whilst full-timers earn a premium rate for overtime hours, simply because part-time employees in these circumstances receive the same overall pay as full-time employees for the same number of hours worked.

In the German case of *Arbeiterwohlfahrt der Stadt Berlin e V v Bötel [1992] IRLR 423*, the ECJ held that it was contrary to Article 141 and the *Equal Pay Directive* for an employer whose part-time workforce consisted predominantly of women to refuse to pay a female part-time worker who attended a full-time training course additional pay for the hours spent on the course that exceeded her normal working hours. This decision, like the *Stadt Lengerich* decision above, is consistent with the general principle of equality of treatment as between full-time and part-time employees.

Seniority and Service-related Increments [9.37]

It will be discriminatory to differentiate between full-time and part-time employees with regard to seniority, service-related increments or criteria for promotion. This principle was upheld by the European Court of Justice in the case of *Nimz v Freie und Hansestadt Hamburg [1991] IRLR 222*. The case concerned an employee in Germany who worked 20 hours per week. A collective agreement was in force under the terms of which employees working at least 75 per cent of full-time hours could move up the salary scale after six years continuous service. By contrast, employees working fewer than 75 per cent of normal hours had to be employed for at least twelve years to qualify for an increase. It was argued before the ECJ that this distinction constituted indirect sex discrimination against women since more than 90 pr cent of the employees working under 75 per cent of full-time hours were female.

The ECJ ruled that the rules on service-related increments contained in the collective agreement were discriminatory on grounds of sex and could not be justified unless the employer could show objective reasons why the distinction between the requirements of full-time and part-time employees was necessary. Such justification would have to involve evidence that the skills and experience necessary for an increment were related to the number of hours worked. The ECJ held that although experience doing the job is inevitably linked to the number of hours worked, this does not mean that a disparity in the length of service requirements between full-time and part-time employees is objectively justified.

Key Case [9.38]

Another more recent case was that of *Hill and Stapleton v Revenue Commissioners and Department of Finance [1998] IRLR 466*.

> ## Hill and Stapleton v Revenue Commissioners and Department of Finance [1998] IRLR 466
>
> Ms Hill and Ms Stapleton had worked on a job-share basis for the Revenue for two years, each working half the hours of a full-time employee. Whilst working on the job-share arrangement, the two employees had moved one point up the incremental pay scale at the end of each of their two years of service. Both employees then transferred to full-time working. At that point, however, their position on the incremental pay scale was adjusted down by one point because the employer adopted the view that a year's part-time service equated to six months full-time service. This meant that an employee working on a job-share basis for two years should be entitled, when being placed on the incremental pay scale, to be credited with only one year's full-time service.
>
> This course of action was challenged by the two employees in the Irish courts who referred the matter to the ECJ. It was clear to the ECJ that the two employees had been put at a disadvantage as a direct result of their having worked on a part-time job-sharing basis, when compared to equivalent full-time workers in the organisation. They ruled that, because 98 per cent of those employed on a job-share basis were women, the service criterion applied by the employer was indirectly discriminatory on grounds of sex. Unless the difference in treatment could be objectively justified therefore, it would be unlawful. The ECJ also ruled that such justification could not be based on considerations such as staff motivation, commitment and morale, nor on the grounds of cost.

It follows that any policy under which part-time employees have to work for a longer period than full-time employees to qualify for a promotion or pay increment will be discriminatory unless the differing requirements can be objectively justified.

Occupational Pension Schemes   [9.39]

In the past, many employers' occupational pension schemes were open only to full-time employees, and part-time employees who were refused access had no remedy because death and retirement benefits were originally excluded from the both the *Sex Discrimination Act* and the *Equal Pay Act*.

All that changed, however, following the case of *Bilka-Kaufhaus GmbH v Weber von Hartz [1986] IRLR 317*, in which the ECJ held that occupational pensions constituted 'pay' within the meaning of Article 141. The ECJ went on to state that if the rules of an employer's occupational pension scheme excluded part-time workers from joining the scheme, this would be indirectly discriminatory against women if the majority of the part-time workforce were women, unless the exclusion of the part-timers could be objectively justified by the employer.

Some time later both the *Sex Discrimination Act* and the *Equal Pay Act* were amended by the *Pensions Act 1995* which introduced an 'equal treatment rule' into all occupational pension schemes where no such rule was expressly stated. This meant that men and women had to be given equal rights to join a pension scheme and were entitled to receive equal benefits under the scheme.

In the meantime, the ECJ had made another important ruling in the case of *Barber v Guardian Royal Exchange Assurance Group [1990] IRLR 240.* This case concerned the level of benefits under an occupational pension scheme rather than access to the scheme. The ECJ held that benefits under pension schemes must be equal for men and women and must not, for example, be available to men and women at different ages as had been the case for Mr Barber.

The combined effect of these and other rulings is that where an employer operates an occupational pension scheme:

- The employer must make access to the scheme available equally to men and women, and since in most organisations where part-timers are employed the majority of the part-time workforce are women, access must be made available equally to part-timers.

- The employer must ensure that all benefits under their occupational pension scheme are equal for men and women. Part-timers will be entitled to equal benefits under the scheme as compared to full-timers, subject to the pro-rata principle.

It is, however, lawful for occupational pension schemes to have a length of service requirement in relation to eligibility to join the scheme. This can act to exclude employees engaged on short-term contracts. Even it could be argued that such a requirement was indirectly discriminatory against female staff, it would be likely to be objectively justifiable on the grounds that providing access to a company pension scheme to employees engaged on very short-term contracts would be disproportionately expensive in comparison to the provision of pension benefits to longer term employees.

Equal Opportunities Policies [9.40]

It is advisable for every employer, whatever their size, to devise and implement an equal opportunities policy.

Model Equal Opportunities Policy Statement [9.41]

XYZ Company is committed to ensuring equal opportunities in the workplace for all its workers, including part-time and temporary staff. The Company wishes to draw upon the widest possible pool of talent and ensure that the diversity of its workers' backgrounds, experiences and abilities is fully recognised and developed.

The aims of this policy are:

- To ensure the Company provides a working environment in which all workers feel comfortable and confident that they will be treated with respect and dignity.

- To ensure there is no discrimination whatsoever against any worker or job applicant for any reason that is not directly relevant to the effective performance of their job.

- To promote diversity and ensure that all workers are valued for their individual qualities, skills, experience, abilities and contribution to the organisation, rather than being judged on personal factors such as gender or race.

It is therefore the Company's policy to treat all employees equally and fairly irrespective of their sex, marital status, race, colour, nationality, ethnic origin, national origin, religion, age, sexual orientation, disability. The Company is also committed to ensuring that no policy, rule, requirement, condition, provision, criterion or practice that could put individuals at a disadvantage on any of the above grounds will be applied unless it is necessary and appropriate to meet a genuine business objective and proportionate to the achievement of that objective.

This equal opportunities policy applies to every aspect of the Company's business. It therefore applies throughout the process of recruitment, during employment and during the process of termination of employment. Application of the policy should ensure that employees are treated fairly and equally as regards their terms and conditions of employment (including pay), opportunities for promotion, transfer and training and company procedures such as the disciplinary and grievance procedures.

All judgements and decisions about job applicants, employees and other workers (including temporary and part-time workers) for the purposes of recruitment, development and termination will be made solely on the basis of the individual's experience, ability and potential in relation to the needs of the job and the Company.

The overall responsibility for the policy lies with [named senior person]. All staff are, however, expected to act in accordance with the policy's aims and to behave in a way that reflects the policy.

Any breach of the policy, or any type of discriminatory behaviour towards another employee, will be viewed very seriously and any employee who breaches the principles of equal opportunity enshrined in this policy will be liable to disciplinary action up to and including dismissal.

This equal opportunities policy represents a statement of the Company's general approach and attitude to equal opportunities. It is not intended to form a contractually binding statement.

Conclusion [9.42]

Any less favourable treatment of part-time or temporary workers in relation to their terms of employment or general treatment at work could potentially give rise to claims of indirect sex discrimination, since larger numbers of women than men work part-time and in temporary jobs. It is therefore advisable for employers to review the detail of the remuneration packages and other benefits offered to part-time and temporary employees to check that there are no instances of less favourable treatment when compared to full-time, permanent employees. If any such differences are identified, the employer should take steps to review the reasons for the differences and whether they are necessary to achieve a legitimate business aim. If there is any evidence that differences in treatment are related to the part-time or temporary status of the employees rather than being required for an objective business reason, then the differences should be removed. Otherwise, the organisation may face claims for indirect sex discrimination from those whose treatment is less favourable.

Questions and Answers [9.43]

Question

Do the laws on sex discrimination result in women being entitled to advantageous treatment in the workplace as compared to men?

Answer

Protection against sex discrimination in the workplace applies equally to men and women, although in practice more women than men bring claims since they are more often the victims of sex discrimination. Women are not entitled in law to any advantageous treatment.

Question

What is the inter-relationship between employees' rights under the *Equal Pay Act* and their rights under the *Sex Discrimination Act*?

Answer

The distinction is that the *Equal Pay Act* covers inequality of pay and other terms and conditions of employees' contracts of employment, whilst the *Sex Discrimination Act* protects employees from discrimination in areas that are not governed by the terms of the employment contract, for example application of policies and procedures, access to promotion, transfer and training and general treatment at work.

Question

Does sex discrimination legislation protect part-time and temporary workers?

Answer

Yes, all workers including part-timers are eligible to protection against sex discrimination. Because there is no minimum service qualification to bring a claim for unlawful sex discrimination to an employment tribunal, temporary and fixed-term workers are protected from the first day of their employment.

Question

If a part-time worker believes their pay has been set at an unfair level, can they take a complaint to an employment tribunal under the *Equal Pay Act*?

Answer

Not necessarily, because the *Equal Pay Act* does not address the issue of fair wages in a general sense. Employees have no general statutory right to equal pay with other employees where any differences in pay rates are not due to the gender of the individuals. However, part-time workers do have a statutory right to the same rate of pay (on a pro-rata basis) as comparable full-time workers under the *Part-Time Workers (Prevention of Less Favourable Treatment) Regulations 2000*.

Question

What are the criteria for a claim for equal pay to succeed?

Answer

To bring a claim under the *Equal Pay Act*, an employee has to compare their treatment with a colleague of the opposite sex who works in the same employment and who is performing like work, work rated as equivalent or work of equal value. If the employee can succeed in showing one of these three elements, an equality clause implied into their contract will operate to entitle them to be placed in the same position as their comparator in relation to each of the terms of their contract of employment. This will be the case unless the employer can show that the difference between the woman's and the man's contract was caused by a 'genuine material factor' unrelated to sex.

Question

If a part-time or fixed-term worker is the victim of sex discrimination at work, who carries the liability for their unlawful treatment?

Answer

Any act of sex discrimination perpetrated by a manager against any worker, including fixed-term and part-time workers, or by one colleague against another, will create liability for the employer whether or not the company's management were aware that a discriminatory act had taken place. In certain circumstances, the individual who perpetrated the act of discrimination can also be held liable.

Question

In terms of winning a claim for sex discrimination at an employment tribunal, to what extent is it necessary for an employee to prove that their treatment amounted to sex discrimination?

Answer

When a complaint of sex discrimination is brought to tribunal, the burden of proof lies with the employer rather than with the employee. This means that once the employee has established facts from which a court or tribunal could conclude that sex discrimination occurred, the tribunal is bound to rule that the employee's treatment was discriminatory unless the employer can provide concrete evidence that there was an alternative credible reason for the unfavourable treatment of the employee that was unrelated to their sex. If no alternative reason for the employee's treatment can be put forward, or if the tribunal considers the employer's explanation to be inadequate or untrue, they will uphold the employee's claim.

Question

What is indirect sex discrimination?

Answer

Indirect sex discrimination occurs when the employer applies a provision, criterion or practice which, although applied equally to all employees, places a considerably larger proportion of women than men at a disadvantage (or vice versa). If the provision, criterion or practice operates to the detriment of an individual woman (or man) and the employer cannot show objective justification for its application, the woman will be the victim of unlawful indirect sex discrimination.

Question

If a policy or procedure within the organisation could in practice place women at a disadvantage, does this mean that the employer must discontinue it?

Answer

The law on indirect sex discrimination does not mean that employers can never apply policies, procedures, rules, requirements or practices that may adversely affect female (or male) employees. However, if the policy or procedure that is potentially disadvantageous to women (or men) is to be lawful, the employer would have to show that its application was necessary in order to achieve a legitimate business aim and was appropriate to the achievement of that aim. It will not be enough to show that the measure was based on administrative convenience or management preference.

Question

Is it unlawful for an employer to operate provisions that indirectly cause a disadvantage to part-time workers?

Answer

Any provision that places part-timers at a disadvantage when compared to full-time staff may be indirectly discriminatory against female staff on grounds of sex if it has a disproportionate adverse effect on female employees. This principle has come about simply because the vast majority of part-timers are, in practice, women. Thus, if in a particular organisation more women than men are employed on a part-time basis, the provision of inferior terms, conditions, benefits, policies, procedures or practices to part-timer workers will have a greater adverse effect on women than on men and will be discriminatory.

Question

Why is it potentially discriminatory on grounds of sex to refuse to permit a woman to work part-time?

Answer

Insisting without justification that a job must be done full-time can amount to indirect sex discrimination against a woman because fewer women than men are able to work full-time as a result of family responsibilities. In other words, a requirement that a particular job must be performed on a full-time basis places a considerably larger proportion of women than men at a disadvantage. Unless the employer can objectively justify the requirement for the employee to work full-time on objective business grounds, the result will be indirect sex discrimination.

Question

Is it potentially discriminatory on grounds of sex to impose length of service requirements on company benefits?

Answer

If an employer imposes an arbitrary length of service requirement on employees before they can qualify for certain benefits, this could be indirectly discriminatory against women if the majority of temporary workers in the organisation are female, and if the length of service requirement has the practical effect that more women than men are excluded from the benefit. If, however, the employer can justify the length of service rule on objective grounds related to the needs of the business, it would not be unlawful.

Question

In the event of a redundancy programme, is it legitimate for the employer to select part-time or fixed-term workers for redundancy first before full-time or permanent staff are selected?

Answer

No. Under the *Part-Time Workers Regulations*, part-timers must not be treated less favourably than their full-time equivalents, unless different treatment can be justified on objective grounds and redundancy selection criteria that discriminate against part-time employees will therefore be unlawful. As regards fixed-term employees, the Court of Appeal has held that a policy of automatically selecting employees on fixed-term contracts for redundancy first was discriminatory against female staff and could not be justified in the particular circumstances.

Question

What are part-timers statutory rights in relation to pay, bonuses, overtime and pension benefits?

Answer

Employers must not discriminate against part-timers in terms of their basic hourly rate of pay, commission payments, any bonus entitlement, entitlement to overtime payments, pay rises or pension benefits, otherwise there will be an infringement of the *Part-Time Workers Regulations*. In addition, such treatment is likely to amount to indirect sex discrimination against female staff, if the majority of part-timers in the organisation are women.

Question

What is the entitlement of part-time employees to premium overtime payments when they work additional hours beyond those specified in their contract?

Answer

Part-time employees who work additional hours are not automatically entitled to be paid for overtime at a premium rate even if premium rates are offered to full-time employees who work beyond their normal full-time hours. However, in the event that a part-timer's hours extend beyond the equivalent of full-time hours in a particular period, the part-timer would become entitled to receive the same premium overtime rate as full-time staff for the hours worked over and above normal full-time hours.

Question

When reviewing a part-time employee's length of service in relation to eligibility for a pay increase on an incremental scale, is it lawful to take the view that the part-time employee' service can be counted down in proportion to the number of hours they work for the purpose of placing them on the scale?

Answer

The European Court of Justice has ruled that it is discriminatory against female staff to differentiate between full-time and part-time employees with regard to service-related increments, unless such a differentiation can be objectively justified. Thus an employee who has worked on a part-time basis for four years (for example) would be entitled, when being considered for an incremental pay rise, to be credited with four years' service. Any policy under which part-time employees have to work for a longer period than full-time employees to qualify for a pay increment (or promotion) will be discriminatory unless the differing requirements can be objectively justified.

Question

Are part-time and temporary employees entitled in law to be offered membership of an occupational pension scheme if one is operated by the employer?

Answer

Because employers must in law make membership of an occupational pension scheme available equally to men and women, and because in most organisations where part-timers are employed the majority of the part-time workforce are women, membership must be made available equally to part-timers. It is, however, lawful for occupational pension schemes to have a length of service requirement in relation to eligibility to join the scheme. Although this can act to exclude employees engaged on temporary contracts and although such a requirement may be indirectly discriminatory against female staff, it would be likely to be objectively justifiable on the grounds that providing access to a company pension scheme to employees engaged on very short-term contracts would be disproportionately expensive.

10. Employees Moving to Part-Time Work

Introduction [10.1]

Many people nowadays would prefer to work part-time instead of committing themselves to the traditional full-time pattern of working hours. Many are in practical terms unable to work full-time, for example because of childcare or other family responsibilities. It is inevitable, therefore, that employers will from time to time encounter requests from existing employees to move from full-time to part-time working. This is particularly likely to occur when a woman who has taken maternity leave is ready to return to work and makes a request to return on a part-time or job-share basis.

The Implications of Refusing a Request to Work Part-Time [10.2]

Lack of Statutory Entitlement to Move to Part-Time Working [10.3]

The *Part-Time Workers (Prevention of Less Favourable Treatment) Regulations 2000 (SI 2000 No 1551)* do not grant any statutory right for workers (or job applicants) to demand part-time working hours, or indeed any set pattern of hours. The pattern and number of hours worked by any individual is a matter for joint agreement between the employer and the individual through the medium of the contract of employment. Any desire on an employee's part to reduce or otherwise change the number of hours worked is therefore subject to their obtaining their employer's agreement.

The contractual aspect of working hours is only one feature of this topic, however. Sex discrimination law has, over the years, made a considerable impact on the rights of women not to be required to work excessive hours, unsocial hours or even full-time hours (see **CHAPTER 9** for a full discussion on avoiding sex discrimination). Furthermore, employees returning to work following a period of maternity leave are in a particularly strong position in relation to any request to change or reduce their working hours or move to part-time working (see **10.14** below).

287

Despite the absence of legislative provisions entitling employees to move to part-time working, there is a DTI document titled '*The Law and Best Practice*' which contains guidelines that suggest ways in which employers can widen access to part-time work (see **10.5** below). Further information is available on the DTI's web-site at www.dti.gov.uk/er/ptime.htm. Full details of the *Part-Time Workers (Prevention of Less Favourable Treatment) Regulations 2000* are contained in **CHAPTER 3**.

Where an employer agrees to permit an employee to move to part-time working [10.4]

Despite the absence of any statutory requirement for an employer to agree to permit an employee to move from full-time to part-time working, certain protections are available to employees who do make the switch as a result of an agreement with their employer. These right are contained in the *Part-Time Workers (Prevention of Less Favourable Treatment) Regulations 2000, ss 3–4*. Specifically, the *Part-Time Workers Regulations* contain provisions that benefit full-time employees who, by agreement, move to part-time working in the same type of work within the same organisation, and also to those who return to work on a part-time basis after a period of absence from work.

Firstly, workers who move from full-time working to part-time working within the same organisation are entitled to compare the terms and conditions of their new part-time contract with their previous full-time terms and conditions. The worker has the right not to be afforded less favourable terms and conditions on a pro-rata basis than those that were applicable under their previous contract. This right applies irrespective of whether part-time working comes about as a result of a consensual variation to the terms of the contract or following a termination of the contract coupled with an offer to re-engage on revised part-time terms.

Secondly, workers who, by agreement with their employer, return to work on a part-time basis after a period of absence from work have a similar right, provided the period of absence has not been longer than twelve months. Thus, workers who have agreed with their employer that they will return on a part-time basis to the same job, or a job at the same level, after a period of maternity leave, parental leave, sickness absence, extended holiday or after a career break have the right to enjoy terms and conditions not less favourable (on a pro-rata basis) than those they would have enjoyed if they had returned full-time.

Full information about the *Part-Time Workers (Prevention of Less Favourable Treatment) Regulations 2000* is contained in **CHAPTER 3**.

The DTI's 'Law and Best Practice' Guidelines   **[10.5]**

There is also a DTI document titled *Law and Best Practice* that contains a number of recommendations on employers' handling of employees' requests to move to part-time working or job-sharing. The recommendations contained in this document are that employers should:

- Consider any request for part-time working or job-sharing seriously and explore the possibilities for accommodating an employee's request thoroughly.

- Consider seriously (before refusing a worker's request to move to part-time working) whether there is an objective business reason to refuse (in order to avoid the risk of indirect sex discrimination).

- Establish a procedure for discussing workers' requests to move from full-time to part-time working, irrespective of the reason for the request.

- Maintain a database of workers who are interested in moving to a job-shared post.

- Maximise the range of posts designated as suitable for part-time working or job-sharing.

- Adopt measures to ensure that information about full and part-time vacancies is effectively circulated throughout the organisation.

- Look for ways in which transfers from full-time to part-time work (and vice versa) can be facilitated.

- Take steps to arrange training in a way that is convenient for part-time workers.

- Monitor the organisation's use of part-time workers if possible.

It is advisable for employers to take these recommendations seriously and apply them wherever possible. Although the DTI document does not have legal status, a failure to follow its recommendations may lead an employment tribunal in certain circumstances to make a finding that an employer acted unfairly. This is particularly likely in a case where an employee has been dismissed on account of a refusal to continue to work full-time, or has claimed constructive dismissal on account of the employer's refusal without good reason to agree to permit them to move to part-time working. In such a case, a tribunal may find that the employer acted unreasonably, thus rendering the dismissal unfair and entitling the dismissed employee to compensation.

Model Policy and Procedure on Dealing with Requests to Move to Part-time Working [10.6]

This policy on part-time working is to be regarded as a set of guidelines for management and staff, and is not intended to confer any contractual rights on employees.

Policy

The company recognises the benefits that can be gained from part-time working and job-sharing arrangements, both from the perspective of the company's business needs and from the employee's point of view. It is the policy of this company to encourage part-time working whenever the workload/duties of a job can be undertaken in less than full-time hours or when the job is of such a nature that its duties and responsibilities can be divided into two part-time posts. It is recognised that part-time working does not adversely affect an employee's commitment to their job, nor their job performance.

The company recognises also that part-time working may allow employees flexibility and allow them to balance their working and family commitments more effectively, thus increasing their commitment and motivation in their job.

The company takes the view therefore, that where an employee requests a move from full-time to part-time working (or from part-time to full-time working), all reasonable efforts will be made to accommodate the request. It is recognised that it is better for the company to retain an existing employee on a part-time basis than create a situation in which the employee may choose to resign on account of being unwilling or unable to continue to work full-time.

It is also the company's policy that its part-time staff will be valued and respected in the same way as full-time staff, and no part-time worker will be treated unfavourably in any respect or placed at any disadvantage on account of their part-time status.

Procedure

When a full-time employee wishes to move to part-time work (irrespective of the reason for their request) the following procedure will be implemented:

1. An employee who wishes to move from full-time to part-time working for any reason should put their request in writing to their line manager who will consider the request on an individual basis subject to the needs of the company.

2. In making the request, the employee should specify the part-time hours that they would like to work, and any alternative working patterns that they would be willing to consider. The employee should endeavour not be too prescriptive in their request for reduced hours as a willingness to be flexible will increase the chances of the company being in a position to agree to a move to part-time working.

3. The manager will set up a meeting with the employee within two weeks of the employee's written request being received. The employee will be entitled (if they wish) to bring a colleague or trade union official of their choice to the meeting.

4. The purpose of the meeting will be to review and discuss how a part-time or job-share arrangement could be made to work satisfactorily in practice and to seek to reach agreement on the precise terms of any revised working arrangements.

5. The manager should carefully review, in conjunction with the employee, whether the job can be done satisfactorily on a part-time or job-share basis, taking into account factors such as continuity of service, job performance, safety, effect on colleagues, etc.

6. Whilst the employee has no contractual right to demand a change to the number of hours they work, the manager will take all reasonable steps to accommodate the employee's specific wishes in relation to a revised pattern and number of hours whilst also taking into account the needs of the company and the department. Realistically, however, some compromise may be necessary, and the employee should be willing to consider various options as regards a suitable pattern of part-time working.

7. If a job-share is being considered, the manager will review, in conjunction with the employee, the feasibility of splitting up the job in terms of hours or days worked and in terms of the responsibilities and duties of the job, and whether a revised job structure will fit in with the employee's request and the company's business requirements.

8. At the meeting, the manager will make sure the employee is fully aware of the implications of moving to part-time work, in particular the effect on the level of their pay.

9. If the manager is uncertain whether the employee's move to part-time working will allow the company to continue to meet its business needs, they may offer the employee part-time working for a trial period, with all parties being made aware that if the trial is unsuccessful, the employee will be required to revert to their previous full-time working hours. In deciding whether a trial can become a permanent arrangement, the focus of the manager's attention should be on the job and not on the job holder.

10. Where it is agreed that the employee may move to part-time working or a job-share arrangement, the manager will provide the employee with full details of all the terms of their contract that have been varied.

11. The final decision about part-time working will be made by the employee's line manager, who will communicate the decision in writing to the employee. Where the company is unable to agree to the employee's request to work part-time, the reasons will be stated in writing.

12. The employee will be entitled to appeal in writing against any decision to refuse a move to part-time working.

Factors Relevant in Considering a Request to Move to Part-time Working [10.7]

The DTI's *'Law and Best Practice'* Guidelines contain useful information for employers on the factors that they should consider when reviewing an individual's request to work part-time. The following list incorporates some of those recommendations. Employers should consider:

- Whether it is really necessary for someone to be present in the job during all the hours that the organisation is open for business (this should be objectively reviewed with a fresh eye).

- If part-time working is being considered, whether all the necessary work can be done within the hours requested.

- Whether the job can be re-defined or restructured in order to make it easier for it to be performed on a part-time basis.

- Whether some of the duties of the job can be separated and allocated to other employees.

- What the effects would be on other staff if the worker moved to part-time working and whether these effects would be acceptable.

- Whether it would be possible for the job to be performed on a job-share basis (again this should be reviewed objectively).

- Whether the worker who is requesting a move to part-time working could be moved to a different job at a similar level so as to accommodate their request to work part-time (if their existing job is found not to be suitable for part-time working).

- What the cost would be to recruit and train a new worker if the existing worker was to leave the organisation on account of a refusal to agree to part-time working.

- What benefits would accrue to the organisation if part-time working arrangements were agreed (see **CHAPTER 3** at **3.2**).

Implementing a Trial Period of Part-time Working   **[10.8]**

One sound approach towards dealing with requests to move to part-time work is to agree with the employee to permit a temporary period of part-time working, for example a three-month trial period (or longer if the issues involved are complex). This course of action would have several advantages:

- It gives the employee the opportunity to demonstrate in practice how part-time working can be made to work satisfactorily.

- It gives the employer the opportunity to review objectively and factually the degree of success of the part-time working arrangement.

- Any tangible problems that arise can be addressed in a practical way with a view to finding solutions that are acceptable to all.

- If part-time working does lead to significant problems that cannot be resolved, the employer will then have concrete evidence on which to base a decision not to make the arrangement a permanent one (in the event of a tribunal claim at a later date).

If a trial period of part-time working is instituted, the nature of the arrangement should be clearly set out in writing, so that it is clear that the change to the employee's hours is a temporary variation for a set period of time, and not a permanent change to the terms of the employee's contract. A sample document is given below in **10.9**. The letter or document should specify that if, at the end of the trial period, the part-time arrangement has been found to be unsatisfactory, the employer has the right to require the employee to resume normal full-time working, as per the terms of their contract of employment. The document should, of course be signed by both the employer and the employee.

Model Letter to a Full-time Employee Agreeing to a Trial Period of Part-time Working [10.9]

The following is a model letter that could be used to issue to an employee with whom it has been agreed to institute a trial period of part-time working. The letter could also be adapted for use in the event of a trial period of job-sharing, in which case both job-sharers should be issued with the letter and asked to sign their agreement to its terms.

'Dear (*employee's name*)

Following discussions between yourself and (*name of manager or other person who has been dealing with the employee's request to work part-time*) held on (*dates of meetings*), I would like to confirm that the following arrangements have been agreed:

As from (*date*), your hours of work will be temporarily amended to accommodate your request to work part-time. Under this temporary change to your contractual hours of work, you will work (*number of hours, e.g. 25*) hours per week, instead of your normal (*number of hours, e.g. 40*) hours. Specifically, your revised pattern of working will involve the following days and hours: (*state days of week and start/finish times for each day*).

As from the same date, your salary/wage will be reduced proportionately, with your revised salary/wage being £ (*state pro-rata weekly or monthly amount*). All other terms of your contract of employment will be pro-rated according to the reduced number of hours worked during this temporary period of part-time working.

The temporary trial period of part-time working will come to an end on (*date*). Approximately two weeks before that date, we will hold another meeting to review the extent to which the part-time trial period has been successful. You will be entitled (if you wish) to bring a colleague or trade union official with you to the meeting, the time and date of which will be arranged nearer the time. In the event that any problems have arisen as a result of your working part-time hours, we will discuss at the meeting how these problems might be satisfactorily resolved, whether alternative working hours (for example a compromise) might be appropriate or whether a return to full-time hours is necessary for operational reasons.

If the trial period of part-time working is deemed by management to have been successful, the company may agree to make a permanent change to your contractual working hours. It must be stressed, however, that the final decision on whether or not to implement a permanent variation to your hours of work is subject to the agreement of the company. However, agreement to a permanent move to part-time working will not be unreasonably refused.

It is a condition of this temporary agreement that you agree to revert to your normal full-time hours at the end of the trial period if asked to do so.

Would you please sign the attached copy of this letter to indicate your agreement to its terms, and return the copy to (name of manager).

Yours sincerely

(Name of manager)

I have read and understood this letter and agree to its terms.

Name of employee .... Date ....

Signature of employee ....

When Refusing to Agree to a Request to Work Part-time may Constitute Indirect Sex Discrimination [10.10]

As discussed in detail in **CHAPTER 9**, an employer may indirectly discriminate against a female employee by applying a provision, criterion or practice which places a considerably larger proportion of women (than men) at a disadvantage, which places the particular employee at a disadvantage, and which cannot be justified.

Thus, insisting without justification that a particular job must be done full-time, rather than on a part-time or job-share basis, would be indirectly discriminatory against a female employee because in practice a considerably larger number of women than men have the primary responsibility for childcare.

Key Case [10.11]

This principle has been accepted by courts and tribunals for many years since the landmark case of *Home Office v Holmes [1984] IRLR 299.*

Home Office v Holmes [1984] IRLR 299

Facts

The employee, an executive officer in the Home Office, asked after the birth of her second child to be allowed to return from maternity leave on a part-time basis. Ms Holmes was a single parent and had experienced practical difficulties in the past with the care of her first child. The Home Office, however, refused the request on the grounds that the employee's right was to return only on the basis of the same contractual terms (including hours of work) as before, and because it was departmental policy that employees in her grade should work full-time. Ms Holmes returned to work on a full-time basis, but subsequently brought a claim to tribunal on the grounds that the requirement placed on her to work full-time was indirectly discriminatory against her as a woman.

Findings

The tribunal accepted evidence that in practical terms, the responsibility for caring for young children falls more often to women than to men, despite the indisputable fact that the role of women in modern society has changed substantially over the years. Thus they accepted the principle that a considerably smaller proportion of women than men can in practice comply with a requirement to work full-time, and further held that Ms Holmes had been subjected to a detriment when her request to return to work on a part-time basis had been refused. This left only the question of whether the employer could justify its policy of insisting on full-time working for employees in the executive officer grade. The tribunal went on to hold that the employer had provided no objective justification for the stated policy that full-time working was necessary. The findings were upheld by the EAT thus setting a precedent that has been followed countless times since then by courts and tribunals throughout Britain.

Analysis   **[10.12]**

On further analysis, a refusal to agree to an employee's request to work part-time could constitute indirect sex discrimination in the following circumstances:

- The employer imposes a requirement that a particular job must be done on a full-time basis (irrespective of who is performing the job).

- Because it has been accepted (see the *Holmes* case in **10.11** above) that fewer women than men are able in practice to work full-time (due to family responsibilities), the requirement to perform a job on a full-time basis places a considerably larger proportion of women than men at a disadvantage.

- If the job in question is held by a woman, if the woman has requested and been refused a move to part-time working, and if she can show that the requirement for her to work full-time places her at a disadvantage, a potential case for indirect sex discrimination could be established.

- If the employer is unable to show that the requirement for the job to be done on a full-time basis by one person (rather than on a part-time or job-share basis) is justifiable on objective grounds and irrespective of the job-holder's gender, the employee's case will succeed.

Contractually, employees do not have any intrinsic right to change their hours of work. This is because the terms of a contract of employment can be varied only with the agreement of both sides, and the employer is not in any way obliged to agree to an alteration to an employee's hours of work or pattern of working just because it might suit the employee's personal purposes. A model letter refusing an employee's request to move to part-time working (or job-sharing) is provided in **10.13** below.

Despite the contractual position, it may, as discussed above, be discriminatory and hence unlawful to refuse a female employee's request to move to part-time working or to job-share, especially following her return from maternity leave (see **10.14** below).

Tribunals today are generally prepared to accept the argument (without detailed statistical analysis) that a requirement to work full-time hours disproportionately affects women because it is generally known and accepted that the primary responsibility for child-care falls in most cases to women. Indirect sex discrimination on account of a refusal to permit a female employee to work part-time is most likely to arise (as in the *Holmes* case detailed in **10.11** above) when a woman who has been on maternity leave makes a request to return to work on a part-time basis, and is refused without justification (see **10.14** below).

Model Letter to a Full-time Employee Refusing a Request to Move to Part-time Working or Job-sharing [10.13]

The following is a model letter that could be used to issue to an employee who has requested a move to part-time working or job-sharing, where management has decided to refuse the request.

'Dear (*employee's name*)

I refer to the discussions between yourself and (*name of manager or other person who has been dealing with the employee's request to work part-time*) held on (*dates of meetings*) in relation to your request to move to part-time working (or *job-sharing*).

Having reviewed your request carefully, and given thorough consideration to how part-time hours in your job could be made to work successfully, it is with regret that the company has concluded that your request must be refused.

The reason(s) for refusing your request to move to part-time working (*or job-sharing*) are:

(*State reasons – examples below*):

- The company believes that part-time working in your job would cause substantial practical difficulties to the business (*or to damage to relationships with the company's clients or difficulties for other employees*).

- Your job is highly specialised, and despite substantial efforts to recruit a job-share partner, we have been unable to identify anyone with a suitable background for this role.

- The company believes that levels of production (or quality of service, productivity, safety standards etc) would be impaired if you were to move to part-time working.

- It is the company's belief based on our experience that part-time working in your job or a job-share arrangement would create an unacceptable risk of mistakes (or omissions, damage to customer continuity, etc).

Your hours of work will therefore remain as per your contract of employment. If you wish to discuss the company's reasons for refusing your request in more detail, please contact the undersigned.

Alternatively, you have the right to appeal against this decision by writing to (*name of a different manager*) within seven days of the date of this letter, stating the specific grounds for your appeal.

Yours sincerely

(*Name of manager*)'

Employees Returning Part–time after Maternity Leave
[10.14]

It is becoming increasingly common for women who are returning to work following maternity leave to ask their employer to allow them to move to part–time working in order to enable them to spend quality time with their new baby. Many women may in practice find it impossible or highly impracticable to reconcile full-time working hours with their new child–care responsibilities. Thus employers may face requests for a switch to part–time work, a request for a job-share or a reduction in overtime working or shift-working.

As explained above in **10.10**, insisting without justification that a job must be done full-time rather than on a part-time or job-share basis can constitute indirect sex discrimination against a female employee unless the refusal to agree to part-time working can be justified on objective job-based grounds. This is because fewer women than men can in practice work full-time due to childcare and other family responsibilities, a principle that is particularly likely to apply when a woman has a young baby.

It follows that if an employee makes a request to move to part-time working following maternity leave, and this request is refused, the employee may bring a claim for indirect sex discrimination to an employment tribunal. In assessing whether or not the employer was justified in refusing the employee's request to move to part-time work, the tribunal will weigh up the balance between the discriminatory effect of the requirement on the employee on the one hand, and the reasonable needs of the employer on the other.

There is a great deal of case law on this topic (see **10.23** below) and the key principle is that, if the employer is to succeed in their defence of such a case, they must be able to demonstrate to the tribunal that there was an objective, job-based reason for their refusal to agree to part-time working (rather than the decision being based, for example, on the personal views of the employee's manager). In the case of *Bilka-Kaufhaus GmbH v Weber von Hartz ECJ [1986] IRLR 317*, the ECJ held that the grounds for requiring a job to be performed full-time must relate to a real need on the part of the business, and must be appropriate and necessary with a view to achieving that need.

Practical Example [10.15]

Alice is a workshop supervisor with five years continuous service, employed by a fairly large organisation that manufactures and repairs computers. Alice supervises a team of 15 employees, and her team in turn is part of a larger department of about a hundred people. Other supervisors are in charge of other teams, and it is important that they all work together, as the company always has tight deadlines to meet.

Alice has been on maternity leave, and is due to return to work in two months time. Alice has approached Alistair, the department manager and indicated that she would like to return to work part-time, or on a job-share basis.

Alistair, however, holds the view that Alice's request must be refused because:

- Part-time working would not (in Alistair's opinion) be administratively convenient for the department.

- It would cause disruption to traditional ways of working (because none of the other supervisors work part-time).

- Employing two supervisors to supervise the same group of staff could cause problems in terms of ensuring the work was completed to agreed deadlines.

- To hire another part-timer or initiate job-share arrangements would cost the company (and Alistair's departmental budget) more money.

- Such an arrangement might set an undesirable precedent for others to follow.

If Alistair refuses Alice's request on these grounds, would she be likely to succeed in a claim for indirect sex discrimination at tribunal on the grounds that the reasons put forward by Alistair to justify the refusal of her request are insufficient?

Unfortunately for Alistair, none of the reasons that have been put forward constitute an objective justification for refusing Alice's request to return to work on a part-time (or job-share) basis.

The position in law is clear. A refusal to permit a woman returning to work from maternity leave to return on a part-time basis will constitute indirect sex discrimination unless the refusal can be objectively justified. Unless there is a solid, job-based reason why the job cannot in practice be done on a part-time basis, a refusal to consider part-time working or a job-share arrangement will be ruled discriminatory. If challenged in an employment tribunal, the onus is on the employer to prove that they had an objective business-based reason for their decision.

None of the reasons put forward by Alistair is capable of amounting to an objective reason for refusing Alice's request. By contrast, most of them are based on Alistair's personal views and opinions. For example, how does Alistair know that permitting Alice to work part-time would cause disruption to traditional ways of working? What concrete evidence is there to suggest that there would in reality be problems in terms of meeting deadlines if a job-share arrangement was instituted? As regards the cost of implementing a job-share, this is unlikely to be significant, particularly in light of the size of the department.

Equally none of the reasons for Alistair's refusal could be described as fulfilling the test set out in *Bilka-Kaufhaus GmbH v Weber von Hartz ECJ [1986] IRLR 317* (above), i.e. that the grounds for requiring full-time working must relate to a genuine business objective and be appropriate and necessary with a view to achieving that objective.

Checklists [10.16]

It is advisable for the employer to take a positive and open-minded approach to any request for a move to part-time working and consider carefully what (if any) grounds may legitimately justify a refusal to permit a woman returning from maternity leave to move to part-time working.

Factors to be Considered when Assessing a Request [10.17]

The following factors should be considered when assessing a request to move to part-time working:

- The type of job the employee is contracted to do, including the extent to which the work is specialised (if at all).

- Whether there is a genuine need for continuity in the type of work the employee performs, and the potential effect (if any) of part-time working or job-sharing on that continuity.

- The size of the business as a whole and its administrative resources.

- The number of other staff employed in similar work and whether cover would be available if one employee moved to part-time work.

- The level of genuine inconvenience to the business or to clients or customers that would result if the employee moved to part-time working.

- The likely effects (if any) on other staff if the worker moved to part-time working.

- Any existing systems of work organisation in place designed to provide cover during employees' periods of absence – and whether these systems could be adapted to apply to the situation in which an employee moves from full-time to part-time working.

- The extent to which the employer has made a genuine effort to accommodate the employee's request to move to part-time working (for example, whether the employer has advertised for a job-share partner and given full consideration to all the applications received as a result).

- Whether a trial period of part-time working can be arranged (see **10.8** above).

Unacceptable Reasons for Refusing a Request [10.18]

Factors that are unlikely to persuade an employment tribunal that the employer had an objective, job-based reason for a refusal to agree to part-time working include:

- Administrative inconvenience.

- The manager's personal view (without any evidence to substantiate it) that part-time working would be inappropriate, problematic or unworkable.

- A company 'policy' or stated principle not to employ part-time workers in particular jobs or in the company as whole.

- An argument that part-time working would disrupt traditional working practices or set an undesirable precedent.

- The seniority of the employee's job (unless there were additional factors based on which the employer could show that it would be extremely difficult to provide an adequate level of cover if the employee worked part-time).

Potential Justification **[10.19]**

Factors that could, potentially, be relevant to the justification of a refusal to agree to part-time working include:

- A tangible and demonstrable risk that the quality of the company's product or service would be adversely affected if part-time working or a job-share was implemented in a particular job.

- Concrete evidence that the organisation's continuity of production or service would be damaged, or that providing the same level of production or service would be extremely difficult.

- A clear indication that part-time working or a job-share arrangement would be likely to lead to a deterioration in job performance (for example an increase in the number of mistakes).

- Evidence that safety might be compromised as a result of part-time working or a job-share arrangement.

- Documentary evidence that the organisation has made all reasonable efforts to recruit a job-share partner, but has been unable to do so.

The above list is not exhaustive, but is intended to demonstrate that any reasons put forward by way of justification for a refusal to permit an employee to move to part-time working must be backed up by concrete evidence, rather than being based primarily on somebody's opinion. The employer would need to be able to show that the business was likely to experience genuine problems if the job in question was performed part-time or on a job-share basis. In *Lowe v Peter Bainbridge Optometrist [1999] Case No 5202334/99*, a case in which an employee had been refused a job-share following her return to work from maternity leave, an employment tribunal stated that the test for justifying a requirement to work full-time:

> 'really means that the job must be inherently unsuitable for job-sharing or that the efficiency of the employer's service would be significantly impaired by a job-sharing arrangement'.

In reality, it can be strongly argued that many jobs can be done perfectly well part-time or on a job-share basis provided management is prepared to support the concept of part-time working instead of sticking rigidly to traditional attitudes and assumptions about working patterns.

Recommended Actions for Managers **[10.20]**

Where a request for a move to part-time working is received, the manager responsible for making a decisions should:

- Consider the request objectively, carefully and thoroughly.

- Approach the issue with an open mind.

- Hold discussions with the employee as to how part-time working or a job-share arrangement could be made to work, and take all reasonable steps to accommodate the employee's request.

- Ensure that any refusal to grant an employee's request is based only on objective factors based on the needs of the business.

- Recognise that refusing a request out of hand is likely to lead to a successful claim of sex discrimination against the organisation.

Carrying out a Review of the Feasibility of Part-time Working [10.21]

One course of action that is particularly to be recommended is for employers to carry out an objective and comprehensive review of the feasibility of part-time working and job-share arrangements across the organisation. If such a review is carried out and its results implemented, the employer will be able to deal effectively with requests for part-time working when they arise. The employer will also be in a stronger position in the event that a case is taken against them to tribunal by an employee alleging indirect sex discrimination following a refusal to grant their request for part-time working. The organisation will able to prove to the tribunal that they took an objective and sensible approach to the employee's request and will be more likely to be able to demonstrate to the tribunal's satisfaction that their reasons for refusing the request in question were based on the genuine needs of the business, and hence justifiable.

Requests from Male Employees to Move to Part-time Working [10.22]

An important point to bear in mind is that, if an employer agrees to permit one or more female employees to work part-time, then a male employee whose circumstances are not materially different and who makes a similar request would have to be offered the same opportunity (unless the employer can show that circumstances are in fact different or that the position has changed since the female employee's request was granted).

For example if a male employee with children whose partner worked full-time was refused the opportunity of part-time working, he might have a legitimate claim for direct sex discrimination if he could show that he had been treated less favourably than a female employee who was performing similar work was or would have been treated. In a case supported by the Equal Opportunities Commission in 2001 (*Walkingshaw v John Martin Group*), a vehicle technician who had worked full-time for more than eight years (and whose wife also worked full-time) asked to be allowed to move to part-time working following the birth of his son. When the employer refused, the employee brought a claim for direct sex discrimination to tribunal, which he won. The tribunal held that the employer had given no meaningful consideration to the employee's request, and, observing that four female workers in the same company had been allowed to reduce their hours after having had children, concluded that, on the balance of probabilities, the request would have been granted if he had been a woman.

Examples of Tribunal Cases in Which the Lawfulness of a Refusal to Permit a Move to Part-time Working was Assessed
[10.23]

The following cases demonstrate how courts and tribunals tend to view claims for indirect sex discrimination from female employees who have been refused a move to part-time working upon their return from maternity leave. The key point for employers is that, if a request is to be refused, there must be a reason for the refusal that is capable of amounting to objective justification.

> *Lowe v Peter Bainbridge Optometrist [1999] Case No 5202334/99*
>
> *Facts*
>
> Ms Lowe, a qualified dispensing optician, had worked full-time for seven years when she became pregnant. She subsequently asked to be allowed to work part-time on her return from maternity leave. Some discussions took place, including a meeting about the possibility of job-sharing with another existing member of staff. Following on from the discussions, Ms Lowe was informed that the job-share arrangement would not be pursued further, and that a part-time position could not be offered. As a result, Ms Lowe did not return to work, and she brought a claim for indirect sex discrimination to tribunal.

Findings

The tribunal upheld Ms Lowe's complaint, having found that the employer could not objectively justify the requirement for the job to be done only on a full-time basis. Some of the factors leading the tribunal to this conclusion were that:

- Ms Lowe's job had been shared whilst she was on maternity leave.

- No clear reason was given why the job could not be shared in the future.

- The company had done nothing to bring Ms Lowe and the employee with whom the job might have been shared together to examine how the job could in fact be shared.

- There had been no consideration of options involving staff from the other five branches of the company.

- No job descriptions had been produced for consideration.

- No trial period had been considered.

Eley v Huntleigh Diagnostics Ltd [1997] EAT 1441/96

Facts

Ms Eley worked as receptionist for an ultrasound-instrument manufacturer, a company that relied heavily on the telephone to conduct its business. Following a period of maternity leave, Ms Eley asked her employer if she could return to work on a part-time basis on account of the fact that she was experiencing child-care problems. The employer, however, refused her request on the grounds that the company needed a full-time, experienced receptionist to ensure continuity and familiarity with customers.

Findings

The EAT accepted the company's argument that the need for one experienced and well-informed employee to fill the role of receptionist was essential for customer continuity, and was thus an objective justification for their stated requirement that the receptionist must work full-time. They noted that the company had evidence that they had experienced considerable disruption during the employee's absence on maternity leave and accepted that this would be likely to recur if part-time working was agreed to.

Bullen v HM Prison Service EAT 777/96

Facts

Ms Bullen, a prison officer employed in a prison in a remote location, had requested part-time working on her return from maternity leave. The Prison had attempted unsuccessfully to recruit a job-share partner, and the Prison Governor was concerned that if the job was converted to a part-time post, the staffing budget would be reduced the following year. Further attempts to accommodate the employee's request were made when the Governor proposed a restructuring package, but this was rejected by the Prison's staff following a ballot.

Findings

The EAT held that the Prison's refusal to agree to the employee's request for part-time working was objectively justified in the circumstances. Reasonable efforts had been made to accommodate the employee's request, but these had been thwarted due to factors outside the control of the Prison Governor. Because of the remote location of the prison, it was reasonable to view the matter in relation to the financial and administrative needs of the particular Prison, rather than considering the resources of the Prison Service as a whole.

Puttick v Eastbourne Borough Council [1995] Case No 3106/2

Facts

Ms Puttick was a clerical worker in the Council's tax department. When she was ready to return to work following maternity leave, she made a request to work part-time on a job-share basis This request was, however refused with three reasons being given. The Council maintained that:

- If the job was performed on a job-share basis, this would lead to inefficiency.

- Members of the public would find it confusing to have to deal with two people instead of one.

- Job-sharing would lead to increased training costs.

> ### Findings
>
> Having reviewed the Council's reasons for refusing Ms Puttick's request for a job-share, the employment tribunal held that none of the reasons put forward constituted an objective justification for their refusal. Their findings were that there was no concrete reason why job-sharing arrangements could not have been made. Ms Puttick's claim for indirect sex discrimination therefore succeeded.

Model Policy on Hours of Work for Employees Returning to Work after Maternity Leave [10.24]

This policy statement relates specifically to employees who are returning to work after a period of maternity leave. The policy is to be regarded as a set of guidelines for management and staff, and is not intended to confer any contractual rights on employees.

The company recognises that part-time working may allow an employee returning from maternity leave the flexibility she needs to balance her working and childcare commitments more effectively, thus increasing commitment to the job and to the company.

It is the company's policy that employees returning to work from maternity leave will, if they so request, be granted a move to part-time working whenever the company can reasonably accommodate the request. Any agreement to accommodate a request for a move to part-time working, will, however, depend on whether a review of the request shows that part-time working or job-sharing can be made to work satisfactorily in practice, in line with the business needs of the company. The company cannot guarantee that an employee's request to move to part-time working will be accepted, nor guarantee that any specific pattern of part-time working that the employee may request will be agreed to. Nevertheless, all reasonable steps will be taken to reach agreement on a part-time working pattern that will meet both the employee's personal needs and the needs of the business. This will be done through discussions with the employee (in the presence, if the employee so wishes, of a colleague or trade union official of the employee's choice).

Where an employee wishes to move to part-time working on return from maternity leave, she should make her wishes known to her line manager as soon as possible so that constructive discussions can take place at the earliest opportunity as to how the employee's request to move to part-time working can be reasonably accommodated.

Where a move to part-time working is subsequently agreed with the employee, the terms of the employee's contract will be altered. The employee's revised level of pay will be proportionate to the reduced number of hours agreed with her, and all other terms and conditions of employment will be pro-rated accordingly.

Once a move to part-time working has been agreed, the employee will not be entitled to demand a return to full-time hours at a future time, although the company will consider any request to return to full-time working on an individual basis depending on the availability of a suitable vacancy and the needs of the business at that time.

The Forthcoming Right for the Parents of Young Children to Request Flexible Working [10.25]

In November 2001, new proposals were announced in response to a study conducted by the *Work and Parents Taskforce* whose remit it was to identify the best way of encouraging and enabling employers to create more flexible working opportunities for their employees. These proposals have now been incorporated into the Government's Employment Bill and it is expected that they will be the subject of new legislation that will be brought into force during 2003. The underlying objective of the proposals is the Government's stated aim to '*make it easier for parents who choose to work to do so*'.

The key element of the proposals is to introduce a right for the parents of young children (both men and women) to request flexible working in order to care for a child under six years old, and a corresponding obligation on the part of their employer to give serious consideration to the request.

The proposals are that the right to request flexible working should be subject to a minimum period of qualifying service of 26 weeks, and should be available to all employees who have children under six years old. For the parents of disabled children, the right to request flexible working would continue until the child reached the age of eighteen. There are no proposed exemptions for small businesses.

Whilst there would be no obligation on employers to agree automatically to an employee's request for flexible working, they would be obliged to:

309

- consider the request seriously;

- follow through a procedure for discussion with the employee about the possibilities; *and*

- If the request was refused, provide a written explanation of the specific business grounds for the refusal.

The proposals suggest that, once an employee was granted a move to a different pattern of working, the arrangement would constitute a permanent variation to the terms of their contract of employment, i.e. the employer would not have the right to move the employee back to their original pattern of working once the employee's child had reached the cut-off age of six. Equally, there would be no right for an employee who had been granted flexible working to demand a move back to their original working pattern at a future date.

Different Patterns of Flexible Working [10.26]

The right to request flexible working could, of course, involve requests for many different types of working pattern: Proposals in the Employment Bill provide that eligible employees will be able to request changes to their terms of employment in relation to:

- The number of house they are required to work.

- The times (i.e. start and finish times) when they are required to work.

- The place they are required to work, e.g. put in a request to perform part or all of their work from their home.

Thus the proposal to grant employees the right to request flexible working is not only about employees who may wish to move to part-time working, i.e. reduce their working hours, but is intended to allow employees to request a different pattern of working based on their personal needs, provided they can demonstrate to their employer how that pattern of working could be made to work satisfactorily in practice.

There are, of course, many and variable patterns of flexible working that an employer and employee might review and consider. These include:

- Compressed hours, where the employee works full-time hours over a reduced period of time, for example over four days instead of five. Another example would be the application of the 'nine-day fortnight'.

310

- Staggered hours where different employees have different start and finish times based on the needs of the business and employees' individual preferences.

- Flexitime, giving individuals flexibility as regards their start and finish times each day within an overall framework that includes the establishment of core hours (during which every employee must be present in the workplace).

- Home working, in which employees perform part or all of their work from their home.

- Tele-working in which employees use a telephone and computer to work away from their employer's main business location.

- Shift working.

- Annualised hours in which the number of hours to be worked over a complete year is agreed allowing the employer flexibility to require employees to work longer or shorter hours during peaks and troughs in the workload.

- Part-time working where the employee regularly works a reduced number of hours.

- Job-sharing where two employees each work part-time in order to cover a single full-time post.

- Term-time working in which employees work only during the school term times and not during periods that coincide with school vacations.

The Proposed Procedure for Requesting Flexible Working and Dealing with Requests [10.27]

The proposed procedure for employees and employers in relation to requesting flexible working and dealing with requests involves the following elements:

- The employee would have to submit their request to their employer in writing.

- The employee would be required to set out the working pattern they wished to adopt, explain what effect, if any, they thought making the change would have on the employer and suggest how the effect could be dealt with in practice, taking into account the needs of the workplace.

311

- The employer would be obliged to consider the business case for accepting or rejecting the employee's request.

- The employer would have a duty to hold a meeting with the employee within four weeks of the request being received, at which the employee would be entitled, if they wished, to bring a representative. The purpose of the meeting would be to consider and discuss the employee's request, the issues it raised for the business, any compromises required and, if the request could not be met, any alternatives.

- The employer would have to write to the employee no later than two weeks after the meeting informing them of the outcome. This would be one of the following outcomes:

    — An acceptance of the employee's request for a different pattern of working and a confirmed start date for the new arrangements, accompanied by details of any action on which the agreement was dependent. The start date could be within a period of up to two months.

    — Confirmation of a compromise offered in the meeting and a timescale for the employee to respond to this offer or a suggested start date for the arrangement offered.

    — A rejection of the request accompanied by an explanation of the business reasons for the refusal and details of how the employee could appeal against the decision.

- The employer would have to allow a right of appeal against any decision to refuse an employee's request for flexible working. The proposals suggest that the procedure for dealing with the appeal could be part of an existing procedure such as a grievance procedure, and should allow the employee to be accompanied if the employee so wished. The employee would have to state the grounds for their appeal, examples of which are provided in the proposals as follows:

    — concern that the procedure for dealing with requests for flexible working had not been properly followed;

    — a belief that the business reason put forward for rejection of the request had not been sufficiently explained; *or*

    — the view that one of the facts contained in the explanation of the business reason for the refusal was incorrect.

- An employee who was refused a request for flexible working would ultimately have the right to complain to an employment tribunal. The tribunal would review whether the employer had properly operated the procedure and established a legitimate business reason for their refusal of the employee's request. The tribunal would not, however, have the power to question or examine the detail of the reason put forward by the employer for refusing the request unless the employee could show that the reason given was untrue or based on disputed facts. Where an employee's case succeeded, the tribunal would have the power to make an order requiring the employer to reconsider the employee's request, and to award compensation to the employee.

Business Reasons for Refusing a Request for Flexible Working [10.28]

The Employment Bill proposes that employers should be allowed to reject an employee's request for flexible working only if there are specific business grounds for doing so. The proposed list of legitimate business reasons that could provide objective justification for an employer's refusal of an employee's request for flexible working is limited and includes the following reasons:

- Agreeing to flexible working would impose additional costs that would be a burden to the business.

- Agreeing to flexible working would create a detrimental effect on the employer's ability to meet customer demand.

- Re-organising the work amongst existing staff would not be possible.

- There would be a detrimental impact on quality.

- There would be a detrimental impact on performance.

- The organisation was unable to recruit additional staff.

- There would be insufficient work during the periods the employee proposed to work.

- Planned structural changes.

- Any other reason that the Secretary of State might specify.

Conclusion [10.29]

Employers will inevitably encounter requests from employees to move from full-time to part-time working from time to time, particularly in circumstances where a female employee has taken maternity leave and wishes to resume working afterwards on a part-time or job-share basis.

Despite the absence of any statutory entitlement for employees to reduce their hours of work, an employer's refusal without good reason to agree to part-time working may give rise to a claim for sex discrimination.

When a request is received to move to part-time working therefore, the employer should consider it objectively, carefully and thoroughly, and be willing to discuss with the employee how part-time working or a job-share arrangement could be made to work satisfactorily in practice, and take all reasonable steps to accommodate the employee's request.

Questions and Answers [10.30]

Question

Do employees have any legal entitlement to demand a move to part-time working?

Answer

No, there is no statutory entitlement for employees or other workers to insist on a move to part-time working. The pattern and number of hours worked by any individual is a matter for joint agreement between the employer and the individual through the medium of the contract of employment. Any desire on an employee's part to reduce or otherwise change the number of hours worked is therefore subject to their obtaining their employer's agreement. If, however, an employee's request to move to part-time working is refused without good reason, there may still be problems under sex discrimination legislation.

Question

If an employer agrees that an employee may move from full-time to part-time working, what, if any, rights in law does the employee have following the move?

Answer

Certain protections are available to employees who make the switch from full-time to part-time working as a result of an agreement with their employer. Under the *Part-Time Workers (Protection of Less Favourable Treatment) Regulations 2000*, workers who move from full-time to part-time working in the same type of work within the same organisation have the right to enjoy terms and conditions not less favourable (on a pro-rata basis) than those they enjoyed under their previous full-time contract. Similar rights apply to workers who, by agreement with their employer, return to work on a part-time basis after a period of absence from work (for example maternity leave), provided the period of absence has not been longer than twelve months.

Question

Are there any guidelines for employers on handling requests from employees to move from full-time to part-time working?

Answer

There is a DTI document titled *Law and Best Practice* that contains a number of recommendations on employers' handling of employees' requests to move to part-time working or job-sharing, including a list of factors that should be considered when reviewing a request to work part-time. Although the DTI document does not have legal status, a failure to follow its recommendations may lead an employment tribunal in certain circumstances to make a finding that an employer acted unfairly. It is therefore in employers' interests to take the recommendations seriously and apply them wherever possible.

Question

What should an employer realistically do if there is uncertainty over whether or not a particular employee's move to part-time working would be successful from a business point of view?

Answer

One sound approach towards dealing with requests to move to part-time work is to agree to permit a temporary period of part-time working initially, for example a three-month trial period. This approach gives the employer the opportunity to review objectively and factually the degree of success of the part-time working arrangement. If a trial period is agreed, the nature of the arrangement should be set out in writing, so that it is clear that the change to the employee's hours is a temporary variation for a defined period of time, and not a permanent change to the terms of their contract. It should be made clear that the employer reserves the right to require the employee to resume normal full-time working if the trial period proves unsuccessful.

Question

What is the logic behind the principle that it is discriminatory and unlawful to refuse to permit a female employee to move from full-time to part-time working?

Answer

A refusal to agree to a female employee's request to work part-time could constitute indirect sex discrimination because a requirement that a particular job must be done on a full-time basis is one with which fewer women than men are able to comply in practice, due to the fact (accepted for many years by courts and tribunals) that a considerably larger number of women than men have the primary responsibility for childcare. If, therefore, a female employee has requested and been refused a move to part-time working, and if she can show that the requirement for her to work full-time places her at a disadvantage, a potential case for indirect sex discrimination can be established. However, if the employer is able to show that the requirement for the job in question to be done on a full-time basis is justifiable on objective grounds, a case for indirect sex discrimination will not succeed.

Question

How can an employer defend a claim for indirect sex discrimination taken against them following a refusal to permit a woman to return to work on a part-time basis after maternity leave?

Answer

In assessing whether or not an employer was justified in refusing an employee's request to move to part-time work, an employment tribunal will weigh up the balance between the discriminatory effect of the requirement on the employee on the one hand, and the reasonable needs of the employer on the other. If the employer is to succeed in their defence of such a case, they must be able to demonstrate to the tribunal that there was an objective, job-based reason for their refusal to agree to part-time working. Any reasons put forward by way of justification for a refusal must also be backed up by concrete evidence, rather than being based primarily on somebody's opinion. In the case of *Bilka-Kaufhaus GmbH v Weber von Hartz ECJ [1986] IRLR 317*, the ECJ held that the grounds for requiring a job to be performed full-time must relate to a real need on the part of the business, and must be appropriate and necessary with a view to achieving that need.

Question

What sorts of factors should an employer take into account in order to assess an employee's request to move to part-time working reasonably and objectively?

Answer

Factors that should be considered when assessing a request to move to part-time working include the type of job the employee is employed to do (including the extent to which the work is specialised), whether there is a genuine need for continuity in this type of work and the potential effect (if any) of part-time working or job-sharing on that continuity, the size and resources of the business, the number of other staff employed in similar work and whether cover would be available if one employee moved to part-time work, and the level of genuine inconvenience to the business, to clients or to other staff that would result if the employee moved to part-time working.

Question

What general steps should management take to deal effectively with requests to move to part-time work?

Answer

One course of action that is particularly to be recommended is for employers to carry out an objective and comprehensive review of the feasibility of part-time working and job-share arrangements across the organisation. This will enable the employer to deal effectively with requests for part-time working when they arise, and place them in a stronger position to defend any case taken to tribunal against them following a refusal to grant an employee's request for part-time working.

Question

What would be the position in law of a male employee who requested a move from full-time to part-time working?

Answer

If an employer has agreed to permit a female employee to work part-time, and if a male employee whose circumstances are not materially different makes a similar request, the male employee would have to be offered the same opportunity unless the employer could show that the position had changed since the female employee's request was granted. Otherwise the male employee might be able to succeed in a claim for direct sex discrimination, comparing his treatment to that of the female employee who had been permitted to move to part-time working.

Question

What new legislation is on the horizon in respect of employees' rights to move to part-time working?

Answer

Proposals contained in the Employment Bill and published in November 2001 are expected to be brought into force during 2003. The key element of the proposals is a new right for the parents of young children (both men and women) to request flexible working (which will include part-time working). There will be a corresponding obligation on the part of employers to give serious consideration to any request for flexible working, to hold discussions with the employee about the possibilities and, if a request is refused, to provide a written explanation to the employee stating the specific business grounds for the refusal. The proposals stipulate that the right to request flexible working would be available to employees who have children under six years old.

Index

Index

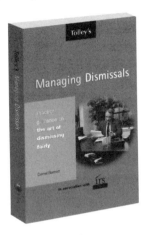

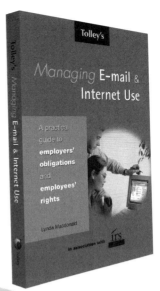